ROBERT B

THE LIFE

OF THE

RT. HON. GEORGE CANNING

Elibron Classics
www.elibron.com

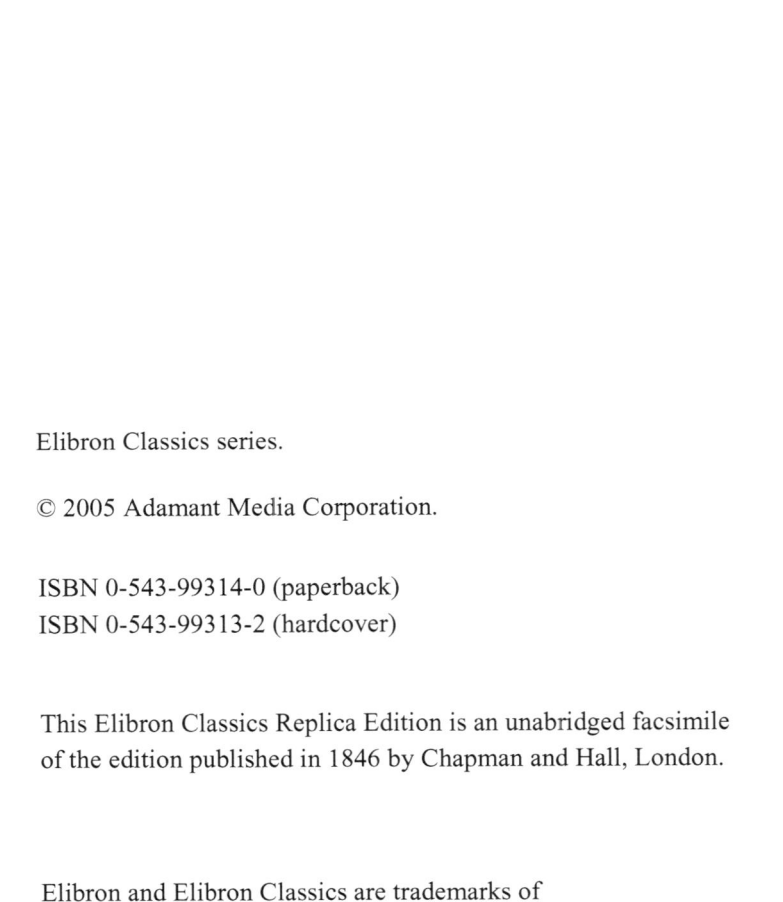

Elibron Classics series.

© 2005 Adamant Media Corporation.

ISBN 0-543-99314-0 (paperback)
ISBN 0-543-99313-2 (hardcover)

This Elibron Classics Replica Edition is an unabridged facsimile of the edition published in 1846 by Chapman and Hall, London.

Elibron and Elibron Classics are trademarks of Adamant Media Corporation. All rights reserved.

This book is an accurate reproduction of the original. Any marks, names, colophons, imprints, logos or other symbols or identifiers that appear on or in this book, except for those of Adamant Media Corporation and BookSurge, LLC, are used only for historical reference and accuracy and are not meant to designate origin or imply any sponsorship by or license from any third party.

THE LIFE

OF THE

RT. HON. GEORGE CANNING.

By ROBERT BELL,

AUTHOR OF "THE HISTORY OF RUSSIA," "LIVES OF ENGLISH POETS,"
&c. &c.

LONDON:
CHAPMAN AND HALL, 186, STRAND,

1846.

C. WHITING, BEAUFORT HOUSE, STRAND.

TO

THE RIGHT HON.

HENRY-ROBERT, LORD ROSSMORE,

LORD-LIEUTENANT OF THE COUNTY OF MONAGHAN,

&c. &c. &c.

IN MEMORY OF SOME HAPPY HOURS IN THE SOLITUDES OF GLEN EERZA;

AND, AS A

SLIGHT TRIBUTE TO QUALITIES OF HEAD AND HEART WHICH

MAKE THE PUBLIC MAN RESPECTED, AND THE PRIVATE BELOVED,

THIS BIOGRAPHY

IS INSCRIBED BY

THE AUTHOR.

THE LIFE

OF THE

RIGHT HONOURABLE GEORGE CANNING.

I.

GENEALOGY. FAMILY HISTORY. BIRTH OF GEORGE CANNING. MRS. HUNN.

THE name of Canning is derived from the original seat of the family at Bishop's Canninges, in Wiltshire, where the line continued until the reign of Henry VII., when it expired in co-heiresses. One of the cadets of the family had, long before, in the reign of Edward II., settled at Bristol, and founded that branch which afterwards became so famous in the annals of the city, and from which the illustrious subject of this memoir was descended.

William Canynge represented Bristol in several successive Parliaments, and was mayor no less than six times in the reigns of Edward III. and Richard II. He died in 1396, and his eldest son, John, succeeded to his honours, both in Parliament and the corporation. Of three sons he left at his death, in 1406, Thomas, the second, was knighted and became Lord Mayor of London; and William, the youngest, was elected to the mayoralty of Bristol, which had become a sort of heir-loom in the family. William Canynge was a foremost man in his day, and stands out so prominently in the list of local worthies, that he was selected as the hero of the Rowley forgeries. He is supposed to have founded the beautiful church of St. Mary, Redcliffe, but his claim to that distinction is unfortunately set aside by the date of its erection—1294. It must be recorded, however, to his honour, that he repaired the edifice at his own private expense, on some occasion when it had been damaged by a thunder-storm—glory quite enough for the epitaph of a wealthy burgess. It was in the muniment room over the northern porch of this church, Chatterton pretended to have discovered his poetical reliques, and his list of painters; but, unluckily, the industrious Vertue had been there before him, and, finding nothing half so interesting, furnished Walpole with the cue which enabled him to show such sagacity in denouncing the delinquent genius.*

The monument of William Canynge is still to be seen in the interior of the church; and by a paper, discovered a few years since in the cabinet of Mr. Browning, of Barton, it appears that he was a liberal contributor of ghostly emblems for its embellishment, such as sundry figures of angels with wings; a holy sepulchre, well gilt; a heaven, made of wood and stained clothes, and other equally curious proofs of his munificent piety.† In the latter part

---

* There were six or seven old chests in the muniment-room, one of which was said to be *Mr. Canynge's cofre.* It was secured by six keys; but in process of time the six keys were lost, and the corporation resolved to break open the locks, under an impression that it contained writings of value. This was done in 1727, and all the documents relating to the church were removed, while the rest, which were of no importance, were left exposed. It was out of these dusty scrolls and parchments that Chatterton persisted in asserting he had collected the Rowlie poems.

† This singular document runs as follows:

"Item, that Maister Canynge has delivered, this 4th day of July, in the yeare of our Lord, 1470, to Maister Nicholas Petters, vicar of St. Mary Radcliffe, Moses Conterin, Philip Barthelmew, procurators of St. Mary Radcliffe aforesaid, a new sepulchre, well gilt with gold, and a civer thereto.—Item, an image of —— rising out of the same sepulchre, with all the ordinance that 'longeth thereto (that is to say) a lathe made

of his life he entered into holy orders, and founded the Priory of Westbury, where he died in 1476.

John, the eldest of the three brothers, was the father of Thomas Canning, who married the heiress of the Le Marshalls, of Foxcote, in Warwickshire, a family which had enjoyed that possession from the time of the Conquest. The eldest branch of the Canning family removed upon this marriage to Foxcote, where its lineal representatives are still seated.*

George, a younger son of Richard Canning, of Foxcote,† received a grant of the manor of Garvagh, in Londonderry, from James I, in 1618;‡ and, proceeding to Ireland, established a junior branch of the family on that property. This grant must be regarded as one of those violent appropriations of land in that country, which, under the pretext of defective titles, or other legal quibbles industriously supplied by the attorney-general of the day, formed so conspicuous a feature in the management of Irish affairs throughout that memorable reign.§ The new proprietors

of timber and the iron work thereto.—Item, thereto 'longeth h-v-n, made of timber and stained clothes.—Item, h-ll, made of timber and iron work thereto, with devils to the number of 13.—Item, 4 knights armed, keeping the sepulchre, with their weapons in their hands (that is to say) two axes and two spears, with two pares.—Item, 4 payrs of angels' wings for 4 angels, made of timber, and well painted.—Item, the fadre, the crown and visage, the well, with a cross upon it, well gilt with fine gould.—Item, the H—— G—— coming out of h-v-n into the sepulchre.—Item, 'longeth to the 4 angels, 4 chevaliers."

* See Genealogical Table.

† A Correspondent of the " Gentleman's Magazine" (Vol. xcviii.) says, that there is a pedigree at Foxcote, attested by Sir William Segar in 1622, in which George Canning of Barton-on-the-Heath (then, or afterwards, Garvagh), is stated to be the eighth, and not the fourth son, as set forth in the Peerages.

‡ In nearly all the notices extant of the Canning family, this grant is said to have been made by Queen Elizabeth; but it is dated 1618, and Queen Elizabeth died in 1603.

§ A transparent form of judicial inquiry was occasionally instituted into defective titles, of which many were known to exist; and wherever the slightest flaw could be detected, the property was forfeited to the crown. To such a proceeding, however hard in particular instances, no

of Garvagh could hardly hope to escape the common penalties of a position so odious in the eyes of the people; and the Cannings, accordingly, had their share of the wild justice which made reprisals upon the settlers for the misdeeds of the government. One of them was killed by the populace, and another attainted by the parliament of James II. But, notwithstanding these disasters the family managed to keep possession of their property. George Canning, the grandson of the first settler, married a daughter of Robert Stratford, Esq., of Baltinglass (aunt of the first Earl of Aldborough), by whom he had two sons, Stratford and George. The line was continued through Stratford Canning, who had three sons: George, the father of the statesman; Paul, whose son was created Baron Garvagh;* and Stratford, afterwards a London merchant, and father of Sir Stratford Canning, the diplomatist.

The descent of the Right Hon. George Canning from the mayor of Bristol, through the Cannings of Foxcote and Garvagh, is thus clearly traced. The following table exhibits the pedigree of the family:

legal objection could be offered; but the true character of the appropriation is unveiled by the notorious fact, that when the juries refused to find for the king, they were censured or imprisoned. The result was, that convictions were obtained in almost every case. Leland says that "there are not wanting proofs of the most iniquitous practices, of hardened cruelty, of vile perjury, and scandalous subornation employed to despoil the fair and unoffending proprietor of his inheritance." It is needless to say that such forfeitures, although apparently accomplished through a process of law, were, in reality, acts of naked spoliation.

* Paul, the second son, died in November, 1784. He married Jane, second daughter of Conway Spencer, of Tremany, county of Down, sister of Sir Brent Spencer, and of the Marchioness of Donegal. This lady died in Dublin in October, 1825. There were four children by this marriage, but only one, George, lived to maturity, and he was created Baron Garvagh in 1818. He was twice married, first to Lady Georgiana Stewart, fourth daughter of the first Marquis of Londonderry; and second to Rosabelle-Charlotte-Isabella, eldest daughter of the late Henry Bonham, Esq., and now Lady Dowager. By this marriage there was issue two sons and a daughter. Charles Henry Spencer George Canning, the present Baron Garvagh, was born in 1826, and succeeded to the title in 1840.

THE LIFE OF CANNING.

WILLIAM CANNING,

Representative of Bristol in several successive Parliaments, and six times Mayor of the City, between 1360 and 1390. He left three Sons and three Daughters.

JOHN CANNING,

Representative of Bristol in Parliament, and Mayor of the City in 1392 and 1398.

- Sir Thomas Canning, Knt.,
  Lord Mayor of London in 1150.

- William Canning,
  The Restorer of St. Mary Redcliffe, and Hero of the Rowley Poems; Mayor of Bristol, and Dean of the Priory of Westbury, which he founded. Died in 1476.

- Several other Children not enumerated.

  - John Canning.

    - Thomas Canning,
      by intermarriage with Agnes, the co-heiress of the Le Marshalls, became possessed of Foxcote, in Warwickshire.

      - Richard Canning.

        - Thomas Canning.

          - Richard Canning.

            - Richard Canning,
              from whom the Foxcote estate proceeded in a right line through six generations to

              - Francis Canning.

                - Robert Canning,
                  the present possessor, who succeeded his brother in 1831. This gentleman is a Magistrate, and Deputy-Lieutenant of the County, and served the office of High-Sheriff in 1832.*

  - Paul Canning.

    - Paul Canning,
      Father of Lord Garvagh.

    - George Canning.

      - William Canning, killed by the Papists in Ireland, A.D. 1641.

        - George Canning, attainted in the Parliament held by King James II. at Dublin, A.D. 1690.

          - George Canning.

            - Stratford Canning.

              - George Canning.

                - Stratford Canning,
                  Father of Sir Stratford Canning.

              - Paul Canning,
                Father of Lord Garvagh.

              - George Canning,
                Father of the Rt. Hon. George Canning.

* The particulars concerning the elder (Foxcote) branch of the Canning family, in the above table, are derived chiefly from Mr. Burke's "Dictionary of the Landed Gentry"—a work of extraordinary research and incalculable utility.

George Canning, the eldest son and heir of Garvagh, had the misfortune to incur the parental displeasure by falling in love without his father's consent. Of this incident, which exercised a material influence over subsequent events, no particulars have transpired. Nothing is known of the lady or the *liaison*, further than that the father disinherited the son, and dismissed him from his house with a scanty allowance of 150*l*. a year, accompanied by a stern announcement that the offender was to look for no more from his bounty for the rest of his life. It is impossible to believe that so venial an offence could have been visited by so vindictive a punishment, unless the family dissensions had been aggravated by other circumstances. Strong political differences existed between father and son. The son had taken the liberty of choosing for himself in politics, as he had done in love; and the one was no more to be forgiven than the other. The father thought he had a right to select opinions as well as wives for his children; and being a gentleman of implacable temper and violent prejudices, he seized upon the first tangible excuse that offered to drive forth upon the world a son who had so much sense and liberality as to embrace principles the very reverse of his own.

In 1757, we find George Canning in London, banished from his native country, which he was doomed never to see again. In that year he entered the Middle Temple, and in due time was called to the English bar. But he never practised his profession. Politics and literature, either from choice or necessity, drew him off from the study of law, and it was natural enough that the conversation of poets and quidnuncs should possess greater attractions for a young barrister without connexions than the uncertain prospects of Westminster Hall. The favourable reception given to sundry fugitive verses, which he contributed to the miscellanies of the day, confirmed his alienation; while the freedom of his principles procured him the intimate friendship of Wilkes, in whose affairs he seems to have taken a zealous interest. Churchill, Lloyd, and Whitbread, the elder Colman, the good-natured Mr. Cambridge, and, doubtless, many other wits and poetasters of Dodsley's set, were amongst his associates and acquaintances; and although he never obtained much distinction as a writer, his claims to admission into the literary circles were cheerfully conceded on all hands.*

The first publication by which he attracted notice, was an ardent defence of civil and religious liberty, in a poem, entitled " An Epistle from William Lord Russell to William Lord Cavendish," supposed to have been written by the former on the night before his execution.† This piece was published in 1763, and met with such success as to reach a second edition in a few months. Its reception must be attributed solely to the boldness of its political doctrines, for its literary claims are very slender. But the author makes some compensation for the feeble monotony of his lines, by his vigorous horror of priestly intolerance and kingly tyranny. He was fortunate also in appearing at a moment when such sentiments were certain to cover a multitude of worse sins than indifferent verse. The "North Briton" had only recently opened its

* It is not improbable that Mr. Canning may have contributed to the latter part of the collection of poems made by Dodsley, who published nearly all his works; but, after a diligent inquiry on the subject, I cannot trace any evidence of the fact. A writer in the "Gentleman's Magazine" (Vol. xcvii) says that the Epistle from Lord William Russell to Lord Cavendish is preserved in Dodsley's collection. This is a mistake. No such poem is to be found in the six volumes. Perhaps the writer was led into this error by discovering that Dodsley was the publisher of the epistle.

† Noticed, with high commendation, in the "Monthly Review" for 1763.

fire upon Lord Bute and the "Auditor," and in the state of the public mind at that period, such passages as the following, enunciating the popular doctrine, that all power emanates from the people, and is only held in trust for the people, must have been sure of admiring audiences:

> " What! shall a tyrant trample on the laws,
> And stop the source whence all his power he draws?
> His country's rights to foreign foes betray,
> Lavish her wealth, yet stipulate for pay?
> * * * *
> In luxury's lap lie screen'd from cares and pains,
> And only toil to forge his subjects' chains?
> And shall he hope the public voice to drown,
> *The voice which gave, and can resume his crown?*"

It would be scarcely just to say that this is a fair sample of the poem. There are better lines in it—and worse. But Mr. Canning evidently laid more stress on his political opinions than on the vehicle through which they were conveyed. Verse was the fashion of the day, and with enough of taste and education to make a correct use of so nice an instrument, he selected it as the most popular medium for the expression of popular opinions. The success of the attempt was probably as great as he anticipated. Some passages were praised for their tenderness and pathos: such as the parting address to Lady Rachel Russel, beginning—

> " Oh! my loved Rachel! all-accomplished fair,
> Source of my joy, and soother of my care!
> Whose heavenly virtues and unfading charms
> Have blessed, through happy years, my peaceful arms!"*

But notwithstanding occasional touches of this sort of

---

* It has been supposed, that in this passage Mr. Canning gave vent to his own conjugal feelings; but, unfortunately for this ingenious conjecture, he was not married until five years after the publication of the poem.

conventional refinement, the main purpose and surviving interest of the piece must be finally traced to its open and manly advocacy of opinions, which could not at that time be avowed, without a certain risk of odium and persecution.

Perhaps to that very circumstance may be attributed a fierce attack, which appeared in the "Critical Review" on his next work—" A Translation of Anti-Lucretius : by George Canning, of the Middle Temple;" published by Dodsley, in 1766. This volume contained an English version of the first three books of Cardinal Polignac's well-known poem, in which the doctrines of various schools of philosophers, but especially that of Lucretius, were dissected with masterly power, and in a style at once compact and graceful.* Upon the whole, the translation was diffuse, and occasionally careless and inelegant; but the writer in the Review exceeded all reasonable bounds of animadversion, and ran into such outrageous abuse of the book, as to draw an indignant rejoinder from Mr. Canning.† The "Critical Review" was notorious for the scurrilous malignity of its articles, which frequently descended to the lowest personalities; and Smollet, who appears to have done his best, or his worst, to deserve the distinction, generally got credit for all papers of an offensive character which appeared in its pages. On this occasion, Mr. Canning attacked him unsparingly with his own weapons, and got the best of the argument, as well

* A translation of the first book had been previously made (1757) by Mr. Dobson (the translator into Latin of the " Paradise Lost") and reviewed by Oliver Goldsmith in the " Monthly Review," Vol. xvii., p. 44. See "Prior's Life of Goldsmith," *passim.*

† "An Appeal to the Public from the malicious Representations, impudent Falsifications, and unjust Decisions of the anonymous Fabricators of the ' Critical Review.' By George Canning, of the Middle Temple. *Provoco ad populum.* Dodsley. 1767."

as of the abuse. But Smollet had no character to lose, and suffered such things with the impunity which attaches to people who cannot be much further damaged by exposure. He belonged to the class of literary undertakers, a numerous body at that time, who were ready to grub at any sort of work for hire, and who were trying new speculations every day, at the manifest cost of decent reputation, in the desperate struggle to keep soul and body together. Smollet—various and shuffling, the harlequin of book-makers—trafficked in this description of ware, as publicly as sordid, cheese-paring Griffiths and his wife, who boarded and lodged their ill-paid critics, by way of starving them both ways into their drudgery.* They all belonged to the same herd; but Mr. Canning, with keen and discriminating scent, singled out the basest of them all—the man who, with some real right to take rank as a genius, or something very near it, degraded himself into a mercenary jobber, who put Garrick into history to propitiate his influence in the greenroom, and stuck the royal arms on the front of his book, to lure high patronage, just as pastrycooks hang out the regal sign over their shop-doors.† Mr. Canning knew how to deal with such shabby venality as it deserved, and not merely scourged it, but treated it with loathing and contumely.

* Griffiths boarded Goldsmith in part payment of his articles in the "Monthly Review," and Mrs. Griffiths cut and scored them to measure. But this worthy couple, although they seem to have carried the system to perfection, had not the honour of originating it. The booksellers' hack existed in all his nakedness as far back as the Augustan age of Curll, so admirably satirised by Swift. Davenant boarded his women-actresses in Lincoln's-inn Fields; but they were better off than the authors, for he fed them exquisitely, and honoured their caprices with rosa-solis and usquebagh.

† The dedication, addressed to Smollet himself, will show the spirit in which this uncompromising *brochure* is written. "To Tobias Smollett, M. D. Uniformly tenacious of the principles he was nursed in—famous

The "Appeal" was followed, in 1767, by a collected edition of his poems, including, amongst other additions, the fourth and fifth books of the "Anti-Lucretius." The introductory address to his early friend and preceptor, Shem Thomson, D.D., opens with a confession of the straits to which he had become reduced by his imprudence, and a resolution to forsake his unprofitable dalliance with the muses, and devote himself to the law; a resolution, unfortunately, which was taken too late. He was at this period only thirty-one years of age.

for his stories, histories, and his continual continuations of complete histories, as the single personage with whom the unnamed putters-together of the 'Critical Review' utterly disclaim all manner of connexion (graceless rogues to disown their father)—the ensuing Tractate is, with singular propriety, inscribed by its author." And, as a specimen of the crushing contempt with which the writer treated his hireling critics, the following passage is strikingly characteristic : "I would conclude with a piece of friendly and Christian admonition to these public plunderers, who have too long subsisted by literary rapine upon the spoils of many reputations. It is briefly this, *to go back to the place from whence they came*, and there to follow the lawful occupations for which they were instituted by art or designed by nature. Their offence, in my opinion, comes within the express letter of the statute of 9th Geo., cap. 22, being 'An Act for the more effectually punishing wicked and evil-disposed persons going armed in disguise, and doing injury and violence to the persons and properties of his Majesty's subjects,' vulgarly called the *Black Act.* Away then, ye Banditti, while your necks are yet unbroken; but be cautious wherever ye shall handle the honest implements of industry, lest your employer should discover the vile practices ye have been guilty of; for he who knows you would not trust one of you with the cobbling of a shoe, lest he should be pricked by a hobnail, left wilfully sticking up on the inside of the heel-piece." That the writers in the "Critical Review" deserved all this abuse, seems to have been acknowledged by every body. The fugitive publications of the day teem with allusions to their scurrility and injustice, and Churchill charges them with forging deliberate falsehoods :

"To Hamilton's the ready lies repair—
Ne'er was lye made which was not welcome there."
"The Apology."

The worst of it was, that the innocent were hunted down on bare suspicion, as well as the guilty; and poor Murphy, who never wrote a line in the obnoxious periodical in his life, was gibbeted by Churchill, under the belief that he was one of the gang.

> " Formed by thy care to hopes of simplest praise,
> Taught to pursue the best and safest ways,
> The paths of honour, riches, and renown,
> How have I fall'n beneath fell fortune's frown!
> How seen my vessel founder in the deep,
> Her ablest pilot, *Prudence*, lull'd to sleep!
> But hence *Despondence!* Hell-born hag, away!
> Oft lours the morn, when radiance gilds the day:
> Hard if all hope were dead, all spirit gone,
> And every prospect closed at thirty-one.
>   Then welcome *Law!* Poor Poesy, farewell!
> Though in thy cave the loves and graces dwell,
> One Chancery cause in solid worth outweighs
> *Dryden's* strong sense, and *Pope's* harmonious lays."

The bold avowal of his principles under circumstances so discouraging, at a time when they operated as a complete bar to advancement in his profession, was martyrdom to a man so situated; yet he exults in his creed, and boasts of the sacrifices made by his family in the cause of liberty. It is a pity that the historical illustration is not more satisfactory, for the sanguinary attempts to transplant Protestantism into Ireland, in which his ancestors " fought, bled, and died," may appear, to some comprehensions, as acts of the most unwarrantable tyranny.

> " When Popery high her bloody standard bore,
> And drenched *Ierne's* blushing plains with gore,
> While, for a time, pale Liberty, in vain,
> Th' o'erwhelming deluge labour'd to restrain,
> We boast of ancestors, with mutual pride,
> Who fought, who bled, and (let me add) who died.
>   Ne'er be thy charms, fair Liberty, resign'd,
> Birthright bestow'd by Heaven on all mankind!
> Every delight is tasteless but with thee!
> *No man's completely wretched who is free!*"

Throughout all the writings of this gentleman, the same generous and manly spirit predominates; and if his lines were not so frequently flat and prosaic, their honest patriotism might have secured them durable applause. But permanent reputations are not made out of good intentions.

Mr. Canning's next publication was in 1768. Although he had taken leave of Helicon, he had not yet got out of the troubled waters of politics. The American revolution had just broken out, and Franklin had arrived in England, in a sort of semi-ministerial capacity. The subject engrossed universal attention. Mr. Canning took it up with his usual warmth and enthusiasm, in "A Letter to Lord Hillsborough,* on the Connexion between Great Britain and her American Colonies,"† contending for the urgent necessity, as well as the right, of the supreme legislature to frame money bills and other laws for America.‡

There is nothing very remarkable in this pamphlet, except that the general manner bears a curious resemblance to some peculiarities in the style of George Canning, the son. Certain artifices of treatment might easily be mistaken—such as the explosion of a train of reasoning, by an unexpected flash of pleasantry, or the suddenly breaking off into a fervid apostrophe in the midst of a close argument. Thus, speaking of the supineness of Britain, in reference to American affairs, he says, that if her rights are not speedily and efficiently asserted, her

* Lord Hillsborough had just been appointed to a new office for managing the business of the plantations.
† Published by Beckett.
‡ Looking back at this distance of time upon the agitation produced by this question—a question which now appears so clear and simple!—it is instructive to observe how widely men of the same political leaning were divided upon it. Thus Junius protested against the American claims, and, like Mr. Canning, asserted the right of the mother country to control popular sentiment in the colony—for that was what it amounted to; while Lord Chatham—who was Junius's idol—maintained exactly an opposite opinion.

empty declarations " will soon sound as ridiculous as the Cham of Tartary's gracious permission to the potentates of the earth to sit down to their dinner:"—and again, in an access of enthusiasm, he exclaims: "Would to God that all mankind enjoyed freedom and happiness in the highest, most perfect, and permanent degree: would to God there were no pain, or other evil, in the world. But how vain are such wishes! How futile are the dreams of the philosopher in his study, when he creates worlds by his fancy, and models systems by his caprice; for reasoning, abstracted from fact and experience, will always degenerate into fancy and caprice." The reader who is thoroughly familiar with the orator's periods, and those impulsive and passionate flights with which he used to electrify the senate, will easily recognise a family likeness in these scraps; but it is, of course, more obvious in the general manner, than in detached passages.

Mr. Canning had now been eleven years in London, mixing largely in society, and endeavouring to sustain his precarious position by various literary efforts. His expenses were unavoidably greater than his small income justified; nor could he diminish them without risking the only prospect of advancement he enjoyed through his intercourse with the popular men of his party. His profession brought him nothing but disappointment; his publications nothing but empty compliments; his connexion with Wilkes and the opposition destroyed all chance of patronage at the bar. The consequence was, that he became more and more embarrassed every day, and had no resource at last, but to seek assistance through the members of his family. The way in which this assistance was rendered, shows that the domestic disunion had acquired increased bitterness during the long interval of separation, the political prejudices of the father having been no doubt grievously outraged by the audacious independence with which the son continued to maintain his opinions. A proposal was made to pay off his debts, but accompanied by a condition so galling and oppressive, that sheer extremity alone could have compelled him to accept it. The condition was, that he should join his father in cutting off the entail of the estate, thus renouncing for ever his own legal rights as heir-at-law. To this cruel alternative he was forced to submit by the immediate pressure of circumstances; and the sacrifice was no sooner made, than he had the mortification of seeing the estate settled upon his younger brother Paul. It is a curious sequel to this transaction, that the son of the very George Canning, who was thus disinherited, should have afterwards acquired such personal distinction as to be considered, politically at least, the head of the family; reasserting, in his person, the ascendancy of the elder branch.

The relief which Mr. Canning purchased at so heavy a cost of prospective advantages, afforded him but a temporary escape from his difficulties after all. He soon got into debt again as deeply as ever; and, as if there were a fatality in his embarrassments by which he was predestined to incur the heaviest responsibilities at the times when he was least qualified to discharge them, this was the moment he thought fit to become a husband. The excess of the imprudence seems to have fascinated his imagination. In this year, 1768, without any resources on either side, but his own poor allowance, or any prospect of increase, except the increase of expense, he married Miss Costello, an Irish lady of considerable personal attractions, and good family.* Miss Costello, at that time residing

* The marriage is thus recorded in the " Gentleman's Magazine" for

with her maternal grandfather, Colonel Guydickens, was only eighteen years of age, extremely beautiful and captivating, but portionless.* We hear nothing more of Mr. Canning's early attachment. It had either passed away, or been broken off, or it had faded in the light of the new and brighter enchantment. An alliance formed under such inauspicious circumstances, so far as fortune was concerned, could not fail to exasperate the resentment

May, 1768 : " George Canning, of the Middle Temple, Esq., to Miss Mary Ann Costello, of Wigmore-street." They were married at Marylebone church.

* Colonel Guydickens had formerly held diplomatic appointments at some of the courts of Europe, and his son, Gustavus Guydickens, Esq., was gentleman usher of the privy chamber in the queen's household. Miss Costello's family, on her father's side, was no less respectable; and I avail myself of this opportunity to show that the assertion, so frequently repeated in print, that she was a person of " low birth," has not a shadow of foundation in fact. The branch of the Costellos from which she was descended is of considerable antiquity, as may be seen from the following genealogical particulars with which I have been obligingly furnished from an authentic quarter. The family of the Costellos, originally called McCostello, were settled long before the Conquest, in the Barony of Costello, parish of Aughamore, county of Mayo, from which possession they were styled Lords or Barons of Costello. Of this stock there were three sons, amongst whom the barony was divided. The eldest son, who lived in Lismeganson, married into the noble family of the Jordans, who were Barons of Gallon and Island. The second son, Edmond, settled at Talahan, now called Edmondstown, was married to a sister of Lord Lowth's; and the third son connected himself by marriage with Lord Dillon of Clonbrock and the Castle Kelly family. This last branch emigrated, and are now settled in opulence at Cadiz.

Miss Costello was descended from the eldest branch. Her great grandfather, Edmond, the son of Jordan Costello, was married to Miss Dowell of Brickliff Castle, near Boyle, county of Sligo, by whom he had issue six sons and two daughters. The greater part of his property was confiscated by Oliver Cromwell, in consequence of his attachment to the cause of the Stuarts; and three of the younger sons, Charles, Thomas, and Gasper, being thus deprived of their inheritance, and unable to find employment in the army or navy, on account of their profession of the Roman Catholic faith, went into business in Dublin. Charles Costello married Miss French of Frenchlawn, county of Roscommon, by whom he had a son, Jordan, who married Miss Guydickens, and had issue Mary Ann Costello, afterwards married to Mr. Canning, and mother of the Right Honourable George Canning. Colonel Guydickens appears to have been twice married ; first to Miss Hancock of Athlone (mother of Miss Guydickens), and afterwards, in 1762, to Miss Tracey.

of his family to the utmost; it effectually crushed all hope of reconciliation. Mr. Canning never returned to Ireland, and never saw his father again. The only members of his family with whom he held any intercourse after his marriage, were his two brothers, and his eldest sister.

His union with Miss Costello awoke him to the necessity of more energetic exertions than he had hitherto made in his flirtations with literature and politics, but they resulted only in a succession of failures. The situation of this young couple, in the great conflict upon which they were cast, was painfully embittered by constitutional inaptitude for the worldly strife. Highly gifted, sensitive, and ambitious, they were dragged down into sordid cares which wounded their pride, and forced them to attempt means of extrication for which few people could have been so ill fitted. The close retirement in which they found it necessary to live was cheered by the birth of a daughter; but the child died early, and their pecuniary distresses now growing more urgent than ever, Mr. Canning, eager to embrace every hopeful opportunity that presented itself, tried several experiments in business. He set up as a wine-merchant, and failed, as might have been expected. Other speculations were entered upon with no better success; and in the midst of these overwhelming troubles, on the 11th of April, 1770, George Canning was born. He must have been a brave prophet who should have predicted that the child of such afflictions would one day be Prime Minister of England.*

According to some authorities, this event took place

---

* Yet this prophecy was actually made a few years later, as we shall see.

in Paddington; others, with greater likelihood, assign the honour to the parish of Marylebone, where George Canning was baptized on the 9th of the following May.* The register of St. Clement, East Cheap, contains entries of the baptisms of several members of the Canning family; but these were the children of Mr. Stratford Canning, the merchant, including Sir Stratford Canning, Mr. Charles James Fox Canning (for the merchant was a thorough Foxite), and others.

Upon this happy occasion Mr. Canning forgot his renunciation of the muses, and published anonymously a little poem addressed to his wife, entitled " A Birthday Offering to a Young Lady from her Lover," full of the tenderest images and most refined gallantry.† The reader of to-day must not be surprised at this mode of address, which, according to our usages, would lead him to suspect any thing rather than that the person so apostrophised was a married woman. But it was the custom of that age, and

---

* Mr. Canning was generally supposed to be an Irishman: and, unlike the supercilious Congreve, he had no objection to be thought so. In a biographical work called "Literary Memoirs of Living Authors," published in 1798, he is described as " a native of Ireland;" and Moore, in the " Life of Sheridan," and Sydney Smith, in the " Edinburgh Review," speak of him as an Irishman. But, to take his own humorous version of it, he was only an Irishman born in London. When Sir Walter Scott was in Ireland, in 1825, enjoying the proverbial hospitality of that country, Canning writes to him: " I rejoice to see that my countrymen (for though I was accidentally born in London, *I consider myself an Irishman*) have so well known the honour you are paying them."—"Life," viii. p. 129.

† The authorship was not avowed, but there appears to be no doubt that it was his production. It was published by Dodsley, and the " Monthly Review" (May, 1770), speaks of having seen it advertised in his name. The verses have something of the point and polish, and not a little of the conceit of Waller; as when he says that his mistress's beauty, defying the destroying influence of Time, shall outlast the heavens themselves:

" Long e'er thy menac'd ills can harm,
Though every hour should steal a charm:
Long e'er, by twenty stars a day,
The spangled heaven would wear away !"

was frequently carried to a still greater height of absurdity.*

The birth of his son created a new source of anxiety, and made a fresh demand upon the energies of Mr. Canning; but his spirit was broken by disappointments, and after another year of increasing embarrassment and frustrated efforts, he finally sunk under his misfortunes. The remorse he felt, at having deprived his child of his rightful inheritance, preyed incessantly on his spirits, and hurried him to his grave. He died on the 11th of April, 1771, the anniversary of his son's birthday, and was buried in the churchyard at Marylebone.†

These close details concerning the family and birth of Mr. Canning acquire an extraneous interest, from the charge of illegitimacy which was once flung upon him, and industriously propagated by his political enemies, in the old days of rotten-borough deliquency and electioneering corruption, when nothing was too base or monstrous for the foul malignity of faction. The absurd calumny would now be scarcely worth notice, were it not for this curious coincidence, that a similar libel was cast upon his early and life-long friend, Mr. Huskisson, who was stigmatised as " an illegitimate alien," and who found it necessary to refute the infamous slander from the hustings at Liverpool. Such foul aspersions must be regarded as

* No extremity of matronly experience disqualified a lady from retaining the style of girlhood. One instance may sufficiently illustrate the custom : " Monody to a Young Lady who died in Child-bed. By an afflicted Husband." This piece was published in quarto in 1768; and if the reader desire any further satisfaction, he may have his curiosity gratified by inspecting the archives of the Museum.

† His tomb bears the following inscription from the hand of his widow:
" Thy virtue and my woe no words can tell,
Therefore, a little while, my George, farewell;
For faith and love like ours Heaven has in store
Its last best gift—to meet and part no more."

the wild retaliation of the mob, worked up to frenzy by acts of oppression and injustice. When the people found a man rising to a position of weight and influence, by the mere force of his talents, they committed the great error of reproaching him with the lowliness of his origin, as if it were an indelible disgrace; as if he had no right to ascend to station or authority; or, as if power should be held only by those who were born to it—the very principle against which they themselves were contending all the time. Mr. Canning eloquently rebuked them for this perfidy to their own cause; a rebuke which illustrates an anomaly we have latterly become familiar with—the defence of democratical principles against the assaults of the people themselves. " Are they so little read," he exclaimed, " in the British constitution as not to know that it is one of the peculiar boasts of this country, and one main security for its freedom, that men as humble as myself, with no pretensions to wealth, or title, or high family, or wide-spreading connexions, may yet find their way to the cabinet of their sovereign, through the fair road of public service, *and stand there upon a footing of equality with the proudest aristocracy of the land?* Is it from courtiers of the people, from admirers of republican virtue and republican energy, that we hear doctrines which would tend to exclude from the management of public affairs, all who are not illustrious by birth, or powerful from hereditary opulence?"* But the true solution of this popular perplexity was the uneasy distrust that lay at the bottom. The people felt, with a natural sense of justice, that men who sprang from their own ranks, ought to be found fighting in them. They resented as a wrong their union with the dominant party,

* Speech at Liverpool, 17th of October, 1812.

not because it was dominant, but because it was antagonistic. They were so eager to show their impatience of the individual desertion, that they overlooked the larger right, which was so perversely, but conspicuously vindicated through its operation.*

Upon the death of Mr. Canning, the allowance of 150*l.* a-year reverted to the Garvagh family, and his widow was

* Mr. Canning was constantly called an "adventurer" in newspapers, and squibs, and political meetings. He was persecuted with the term to the end of his life. The only intelligible reproach which could be extracted from it was, that he was not born a lord; for he certainly sprang from the ranks of the gentry, was descended from families of some centuries' standing, and was as well entitled, on the score of birth, to the elevated position he ultimately occupied as any gentleman in the country. But still he was an "adventurer," because he acquired personal distinction by merit, and not by inheritance. Nobody questions the honours accorded to lofty birth, but every body has a fling at the honours bestowed upon lofty minds, probably lest they might eclipse all the rest in the long run. Buonaparte was obliged to put up with similar treatment, while he was dictating to the crowned heads of Europe; and all that need be said about it is, to express one's unfeigned regret that there are not many more such "adventurers" in the world. Mr. Canning frequently alluded to this imputed ignominy, and in one of his speeches, after having been elected at Liverpool, he used these memorable words: "Gentlemen, there is yet a heavier charge than either of those which I have stated to you. It is, gentlemen, that I am an adventurer. To this charge, as I understand it, I am willing to plead guilty. A representative of the people, I am one of the people; and I present myself to those who choose me only with the claims of character (be they what they may), unaccredited by patrician patronage or party recommendation. Nor is it in this free country, where, in every walk of life, the road of honourable success is open to every individual—I am sure it is not in this place that I shall be expected to apologise for so presenting myself to your choice. *I know there is a political creed which assigns to a certain combination of great families a right to dictate to the sovereign and to influence the people*; and that this doctrine of hereditary aptitude for administration is, singularly enough, most prevalent amongst those who find nothing more laughable than the principle of legitimacy in the crown. To this theory I have never subscribed. If to depend directly upon the people, as their representative in Parliament; if, *as a servant of the crown, to lean on no other support than that of public confidence*—if that be to be an adventurer, I plead guilty to the charge, and I would not exchange that situation, to whatever taunts it may expose me, for all the advantages which might be derived from an ancestry of an hundred generations."—Speech after the chairing at Liverpool, 12th of June, 1816. The "*combination of great families*" never forgave him who uttered this bold and honest declaration.

left destitute. In this extremity she was tempted by the recommendation of friends, to seek an independence on the stage, for which she appeared qualified by talents and personal qualifications.

The biographical notices which have hitherto appeared of her distinguished son treat this circumstance with an air of prudery and reserve, as if there were something in it to be ashamed of. It is time that we were done with this miserable affectation.* The shame, if there be any in the matter, is at the side that would try to evade the frank recognition of an art which has conferred such permanent grace upon our literature; and which has transmitted its civilising influence too often through the aristocracy itself, to be set aside by the genteel finesse of a biographer. Indeed, there have been so many intermarriages between art and aristocracy, and their issues have become so diffused through the upper classes, that one might have thought it hardly safe to offer such a sinister indignity to the players. At all events it is quite certain that nobility has mingled its blood often enough with the stage to give it a legitimate right to gentle usage and fair report.

Whether Mrs. Canning had any previous connexions amongst the actors there are no means of ascertaining;

* Imitated, too, by actors themselves, who, often sprung from honest handicraft, sometimes (out of family pride) change their names when they go upon the stage, as if any calling were more creditable than that! This is the true tinfoil of false pretences. So Garrick would have been a more respectable member of society, "living in Durham-yard, with three quarts of vinegar, and calling himself a wine-merchant," than Garrick interpreting the humanities of Shakspeare. Foote shows the absurd side of this wretched cant, when he makes *Papillon* in the "Lyar" say: "As to players—whatever might happen to me, I was determined not to bring a disgrace on my family, and *so I resolved to turn footman.*" This is almost as good, with its epigrammatic nose turned up, as the old story: "Mother, mother, the players be coming." "Lord a mercy, child, run and take in the clothes!"

but some such probability is suggested by the discovery of the name of Costello in the Drury Lane company in 1740. This Mr. Costello was in a subordinate grade, filling insignificant parts ; and we afterwards trace him to Covent Garden, where he is mentioned in the bills as playing the second grave-digger in " Hamlet," and where he died on the 9th of August, 1766. The coincidence of names gives a colouring of likelihood to the conjecture ; but leaves it only a conjecture still.

Through the intercession of some friends at court, probably Colonel Guydickens's son, Mrs. Canning's situation was brought under the notice of Queen Charlotte, who desired to know how she might serve her; upon which Mrs. Canning requested that her majesty would be good enough to become the medium of making her known to Mr. Garrick, with a view to her appearance on the stage. Her majesty graciously acceded to this request, and the desired arrangement was effected through the agency of Lord Harcourt.

Mrs. Canning made her first appearance on the stage at Drury Lane, on the 6th of November, 1773, in the character of *Jane Shore*. Her peculiar circumstances excited so much interest, that Garrick, stimulated a little by the expectation of court patronage, resumed the part of *Hastings*, which he had long before relinquished. The play was repeated on the following evening, and was acted altogether six times, after which Mrs. Canning's name is found only rarely, and at intervals, in the bills of the theatre. Her next appearance was on the 12th of April, 1774, as *Perdita* in " Florizel and Perdita " (the " Winter's Tale " reduced to a farce) for the benefit of Gentleman Palmer, as the favourite actor of that name was familiarly called. On the 26th, she took her benefit, playing *Mrs. Beverly* in the "Gamester;"* and on the 28th, she appeared for the first and only time in *Octavia*, in "All for Love." From that time, she dropped into inferior parts,† and all the leading characters she had hitherto performed were transferred to other persons. On the 7th of May, *Perdita* was played by Mrs. Smith, a singer; and on the 27th, when the "Gamester" was repeated, the character of *Mrs. Beverly* was acted by Miss Younge.‡ The truth was, that the attraction anticipated from her beauty had failed through her inexperience, and Garrick, who never stood on much ceremony in such matters, finding her forsaken by the court, made no scruple in reducing her at once to a lower position in the theatre. But this result might have been anticipated from the first. A mere novice could not have reasonably hoped to contest the honours of popularity in a metropolitan theatre with such actresses as Mrs. Abingdon and Mrs. Barry.§

Thus discouraged in London, Mrs. Canning went into

---

* From the play-bill, which is still preserved, it appears that the performances were " by particular desire," and that the " Gamester" was revived for the occasion, Reddish playing *Beverley*, and Palmer *Stukely*. The play was followed by a dance—the Mountaineers—and a comic opera—" The Wedding Ring." The doors opened at five and the play began at six. Mrs. Canning resided at that time in Great Queen-street, Lincoln's-inn Fields.

† Such as *Isabella* in the " Revenge," *Anna* in " Douglas."

‡ Afterwards Mrs. Pope, a popular and fashionable actress, who long held possession of the stage. She retired in 1797.

§ Although Mrs. Canning did not succeed in London, her failure was by no means discreditable. Bernard, who was present at her first appearance, says that " she put forth claims to the approbation of the critical: one thing, however," he adds, " must be admitted, that she was wonderfully well supported—Garrick was the *Hastings*, and Reddish (her future husband) the *Dumont*."—" Retrospections." A critic of the day (in a work called " Theatrical Portraits epigrammatically delineated"—1774) compliments her highly on her performance of *Jane Shore*, in a couplet which is unfortunately not fit, on other grounds, to be presented to the reader. He contrives, with considerable ingenuity in so short a compass, to eulogise at once her beauty, her talents, and her virtue.

the provinces. In 1775, we find her at Bristol,* playing *Julia* in the "Rivals" with some *éclat*, under the management of Reddish, of Drury Lane.† Her subsequent career cannot be traced with much certainty, in consequence of her marriage with Mr. Reddish, whose name it seems, was borne by several actresses, with some of whom she has doubtless, in many instances, been confounded.‡ It is unlikely that she ever returned to the London stage, although she has been conjecturally identified with a Mrs. Reddish, who was severely treated at Drury Lane, in 1776.§ The greater probability is, that she continued in the country, making the usual tour of the provincial theatres with the usual fluctuating fortune; being at one time engaged with Whitelock's company, a travelling corps in Staffordshire and the midland counties;

* Not Southampton, as misquoted in Genest's "History of the Stage." The fact is mentioned in a letter from Miss Linley, in Moore's "Life of Sheridan."

† Reddish, plunged over head and ears in debts and disgraces of all sorts, purchased on credit a share in the Bristol Theatre (then unconnected with Bath) from the elder Lacy. In September, 1775, he apologises to Garrick for giving him only a small portion of a sum he owed him, excusing himself on account of the necessity he was under of paying off the arrears to Lacy.

‡ There were several actresses who appeared at Bristol under the name of Reddish. Speaking of one of them, Miss Hannah More says in a letter to Garrick: "This is the second or third wife he has produced at Bristol; in a short time we have had a whole bundle of Reddishes, and all remarkably unpungent."—"Garrick Correspondence." The Bristol audience resented these outrages, and used to hiss him violently whenever he made his appearance. They once "pelted him," says Miss More, "for a quarter of an hour before they would let him speak."

§ The play was "Semiramis," a tragedy by Captain Ayscough, nephew of Lord Lyttleton, produced on the 14th of December, 1776. Some opposition was made to the play, and to the actress, perhaps on that account. "Mrs. Reddish was very cruelly treated," says Oulton, in his "History of the London Theatres;" "from her very first entrance on the stage to the last scene, she was violently hissed by the galleries. It was a regular attack, uniform in its sound and direction, where she filled her part tolerably, as well as where she failed." Upon which Mr. Genest suggests that "this actress was *perhaps* Mrs. Canning, who *sometimes* played as Mrs. Reddish." Whoever it was, this was the only time she appeared; and in the printed copy of the piec , the character she performed is stated to have been played by Miss Hopkins, which throws a new suspicion over the whole.

at another time making a sensation with Reddish in Dublin;* afterwards failing at Hull under Tate Wilkinson, and then leading the tragic business under Mr. Bernard, at Plymouth.†

Mrs. Canning's marriage with Mr. Reddish, into which she suffered herself to be drawn against the advice and remonstrances of her friends, was the source of many bitterer trials than any she had yet endured.‡ This Reddish was a person of intemperate habits and bad character, disguised under the most fascinating manners. He acquired some notoriety for acting the villain on the stage, and no less for acting the profligate in real life. He was the son of a tradesman at Frome; made his first appearance at Drury Lane in 1767; and was one of the principal actors there during Mrs. Canning's first season, playing *Dumont* to her *Jane Shore*, *Beverly* in "The Gamester," *Antony* in "All for Love."§ When he

* Some of the Canning family were in Dublin at the time, and taking offence at her appearance, avoided the theatre. On the night of her benefit the boxes were empty, although every other part of the house was crowded.

† In 1791. "As an actress," says Bernard, "her efforts were more characterised by judgment than genius; but nature had gifted her in many respects to sustain the matrons."—"Retrospections." It must be remembered that this was written nearly twenty years after she had made her *début* at Drury Lane. Bernard tells a curious story of her having taken lodgings in a haunted house, and braving the supernatural terrors alone at night with extraordinary courage. He pledges himself to the truth of the story, and adds that the fact was known to many other persons. It was exactly the sort of exploit she was very likely to have undertaken.

‡ Mr. Genest says that "Mrs. Canning had, at one time, such a friendship for Mr. Reddish, that she assumed his name," from which it might be inferred that she adopted it merely as a *nom de guerre*. The statement, however, which I have given above, of her marriage with Mr. Reddish, rests on an authority which properly closes all discussion on the subject. It is defective only in the date when the circumstance took place, and this I have not been able to ascertain. Mrs. Canning's acquaintance with Mr. Reddish began in 1774, during her first season at Drury Lane; and she certainly played under his management at Bristol, in 1775, in her own name, as mentioned by Miss Linley.

§ Although Reddish contrived, somehow, but chiefly by subserviency to Garrick, to monopolise a class of characters, which com-made his *début* at Drury Lane, there was a Miss Hart in the theatre, who enjoyed an income derived from a degrading source, and Reddish, tempted by her money, and utterly indifferent as to how it was acquired, wooed and married her in less than ten weeks. Afterwards prevailing upon her to sell her annuity, he dissipated the proceeds, and then abandoned her.* But the end of his infamous

pelled Henderson to go to Covent Garden, and acquired such influence as to drive Macklin from the theatre, he was an indifferent actor after all, without a spark of genius. Stevens, in a letter to Garrick, groups him with three or four others, whom he describes as a pack of contemptible strollers.—"Garrick Correspondence," vol. ii., p. 35. In a contemporary work, called "The Theatres; a Theatrical Dissection, by Nicholas Nipclose" (1772), he is said to have had neither "expression, dignity, nor ease:"

"A figure clumsy, and a vulgar face,
Devoid of spirit as of pleasing grace;
Action unmeaning, often misapplied,
Blessed with no perfect attribute but pride."

It seems that one of the peculiarities of Reddish was a certain vulgar insolence of deportment, which gave great offence to the public. Another critic, in a publication entitled "Theatrical Portraits epigrammatically Delineated" (1774), thinks rather better of him as an actor, but gently dismisses him to the contempt of posterity on account of his private life:

"Reddish while living plays *Posthumus* well—
But his posthumous character no one can tell."

* Miss Hart, announced as a "gentlewoman," appeared for the first time at Drury Lane, in October, 1760, as *Lady Townly* in the "Provoked Husband," Sheridan playing *Lord Townly*. If Churchill may be believed, she possessed other attractions as well as the wretched 200*l.* a year. He specially applauds the elegance of her carriage:

"Happy in this, behold, amidst the throng,
With transient gleam of grace, Hart sweeps along."
"The Rosciad."

But this description could have applied to her only very early in her career, for she afterwards grew so gross and coarse, that the author of the "Theatrical Biography" in 1772, thinks that Churchill must have strained his poetical licence for this compliment. Thus, too, the author of "The Theatres," speaking of her after her marriage:

"Reddish without a relish we produce,
As profitless for pleasure as for use;
Worse than a cypher—why? because we find
She moves a FIGURE of obnoxious kind."

Her figure was large and masculine, and produced such an aversion in Garrick, that he used to call her the "horse-reddish." She was married to Reddish in 1767, appears to have left the stage about 1772 or 1773, and afterwards died in abject distress.

course was retributive. After passing through a variety of disgraceful escapades,* he became diseased in his brain, appeared for the last time, in 1779, as *Posthumus*,† was thrown upon the Fund for support, and lingered out the remnant of his miserable life as a maniac in the York Asylum, where he died in 1785.

During the term of this miserable union, Mrs. Reddish's personal exertions were rendered more than ever imperative by the state of her husband's health, and by fresh claims upon her maternal solicitude. Reddish, prostrated both mentally and physically, was early disabled

---

* He once appeared drunk upon the stage, for which he was compelled to make a public apology. On another occasion he was absent from the theatre, and, by way of excuse, made an affidavit that he thought it was an oratorio night. He was fond of making affidavits, the refuge of base and vulgar minds, as if he felt that his word was not to be believed. He tried to clear himself in the same way in Macklin's business. At another time, being overwhelmed by debts in Dublin, he called his creditors together, apologised for past disappointments, and affecting great penitence, prevailed upon them to take a certain number of tickets for his benefit in part payment, solemnly promising that the money received at the doors should be applied to the liquidation of the remainder. When the tickets were presented at the doors, however, they were refused admittance, and money was demanded; and when an explanation was required the next morning, it was found that Reddish had decamped with the cash, and was already on his way to England. In the midst of these shameless practices, the only instance in which he extracted a good joke out of his total want of principle, was in reply to one Robinson, a member of his Bristol Company, who challenged him to fight a duel, in consequence of some flagrant breach of articles; upon which Reddish wrote to him to beg that he would put it off till after his benefit, for that he was so poor he could not afford to die just then.

† Ireland, in his "Life of Henderson," says, that Reddish, on his way to the theatre, had the step of an idiot, his eye wandering, and whole countenance vacant. Ireland congratulated him on his being able to play, and he said, "Yes, sir, and in the garden scene I shall astonish you!" He could not be persuaded but that he was going to play *Romeo*, and he continued reciting it the whole way. At last they pushed him on the stage, expecting that he would begin with a speech of *Romeo*; but the moment he came in sight of the audience, his recollection seemed to return, and he went through the scene "much better," says Ireland, "than I had ever seen him." The most curious part of this strange mechanical process was, that on his return to the green-room the image of *Romeo* came back into his mind, and so the same delusion went on till he was again recalled to the business of the scene.

from the pursuit of his profession;* but his death, after many years of suffering, at last released her from the responsibility she had so rashly incurred.

She still continued in the provinces, playing at Birmingham, Hull, and other places, but especially at Plymouth, where she was a great favourite with the audience, and where her stage triumphs happily terminated in a conquest of a still more gratifying kind—her marriage with Mr. Hunn, a respectable silk mercer of that town. Mr. Hunn was a constant frequenter of the theatre, and a great lover of plays, with some pretensions to the character of a critic, which he occasionally displayed in the newspapers, to the infinite mortification of the actors. But they had their revenge upon him. Some time after his marriage, he failed in business; and his wife was once more compelled to resume the profession, Mr. Hunn resolving at the same time to attempt the stage himself. He made his *début* at Exeter. The players, however, set the town against him, and, notwithstanding the interference of Mrs. Hunn, who enjoyed much popularity there, his reception was so discouraging, that he wisely relinquished the experiment. He subsequently ob-

* There is no doubt that even in the June of 1775, Reddish was rapidly declining into that state of mind, which, in three years afterwards, terminated in imbecility. "With respect to the service he can do the theatre next season," says Parsons, writing to Garrick, in June, 1775, from Bristol, "I am sorry to tell you I have great doubts; and he himself has very dreadful apprehensions. He fell down and continued very long in a fit eight days ago, and has not been able to perform since his arrival here. His countenance undergoes the most sudden alterations. His memory fails him, and he has all the alarming symptoms of a disorder *hastening to insanity.*"—"Garrick Correspondence," ii. p. 61. He struggled on, however, notwithstanding these fearful warnings—and played throughout the season of 1775-76, at Drury Lane, under Garrick, and 1776-77, under Sheridan. He now became incapable, does not appear to have acted in 1777-78, and staggered on for the last time at Covent Garden, under the coalition in 1778-79.

tained a mercantile situation, in which he died, leaving his widow with two daughters and a son.

Throughout all these vicissitudes, Mrs. Hunn was cheered by constant proofs of the devotion of her son George, who, passing through school and college, and gathering valuable friendships by the way, was never seduced into forgetfulness of her claims upon his duty and affection. He made it a sacred rule to write to her every week, no matter what might be the pressure of private anxiety or public business.* His letters were the charm and solace of her life ; she cherished them with proud and tender solicitude, and always carried them about her person to show them exultingly to her friends.† In his boyhood, his correspondence treated upon every subject of interest on which his mind was engaged—his studies, his associates, his prospects, his dream of future distinction, nourished in the hope that its realisation might enable him, at last, to place his mother in a position of independence. And when he finally reached the height of that dream, he continued to manifest the same earnest and faithful feelings. No engagements of any kind were ever suffered to interrupt his regular weekly

* It has been generally stated that these letters were written every Sunday. This is an error. They were written so that they should reach his mother's hands every Sunday.

† " I remember," says a private correspondent, now living, who was personally acquainted with Mrs. Hunn, " I remember that one evening she called me aside in the Bath-room, and read to me two long letters of her son's, from Lisbon—extremely well written (as may be supposed) explaining and vindicating his diplomatic conduct, and abounding in declarations of his attachment to her." This was in 1815 or 1816. On another occasion she showed an immense pile of these letters to a friend, and, after dwelling affectionately upon their contents, she added— " Yet, they must be all burned. I have not the heart to destroy one of them myself, but they must be burned when I die." This precious correspondence, however, was not destroyed, but returned to the writer at his own request, after the death of his mother.

letter. At Lisbon, during his embassy there, although the intercourse with this country was frequently suspended for several weeks together, he still wrote his periodical letter; and it happened on such occasions that the same post came freighted with an arrear of his correspondence. In the midst of the toils of the Foreign Office, harassed by fatigue, and often preyed upon by acute illness, he always found, or made, opportunities for visiting his mother. He writes to Sir William Knighton, in 1826, like one released for a holiday, " I am just setting off for Bath, with a good conscience, having so cleared off the arrears accruing during parliament time, that I believe I do not owe a despatch to any part of the world."* When Mrs. Hunn was performing at Plymouth, he would sometimes leave his studies at Lincoln's Inn, to comfort her with his presence ; and whenever he came it was a Saturnalia! Shortly before her final settlement at Bath, in 1807, she resided at Winchester, where she had some cousins in an inferior walk of life ; and when her son—at that time the centre of popular admiration wherever he moved—used to visit her there, it was his delight to walk out in company with these humble friends, and with them to receive his " salutations and greetings in the market-place." One recognizes a great man in such behaviour.

It had always been an object of paramount anxiety with him to take his mother off the stage; and the first use he made of the first opportunity that presented itself, was to carry that object into effect.† This occurred in

* " Memoirs of Sir William Knighton." Mr. Canning frequently went to Bath to see his mother. In January, 1825, he visited the theatre there with Lord Liverpool, who had desired the performance of Morton's " Town and Country."

† There was a strange story circulated in the newspapers upwards of fifty years ago, giving a romantic account of the way in which this

c 2

1801, when, retiring from the office of Under Secretary of State, he was entitled to a pension of 500*l.* a-year,* which, instead of appropriating it to his own use, he requested to have it settled as a provision on his mother.†

result was brought about. According to this statement, Mrs. Hunn was then playing somewhere in Scotland, and Mr. Canning happening accidentally to go into the theatre, to his utter astonishment recognised his mother on the stage. The story ends dramatically enough, by her immediate removal from the profession, and her independent settlement for life. It is unnecessary to say that the whole affair is pure invention.

* Mr. Canning did not retire until 1801; but I am informed on unquestionable authority, that the date of the first warrant, made payable to his mother, was May, 1799.

† For this act, one of the noblest of his life, Mr. Canning suffered almost daily martyrdom at the hands of his less scrupulous political adversaries, from Peter Pindar down to Hunt and Cobbett. The circumstances of his mother's history—her connexion with the stage and the pension list—were perpetually recalled in a spirit of coarse and unmanly ridicule. But the only effect these lampoons produced, was to make Mr. Canning more than ever desirous of testifying his regard for her. Peter Pindar was so indiscriminate in his abuse, that his doggrel has long since rotted into oblivion. It had not enough of the salt of wit to preserve the corrupt mass from decomposition. He assailed every body—Dundas, Pitt, Rose, Jenkinson; spurned Canning's Latin, and affected to despise the learning of Gifford and Mathias. He makes Pitt pick the nation's pocket to pension fools and knaves—

" Gifford, that crooked babe of grace,
And Canning, too, shall be in place,
And get a pension for his mother."

All this would have passed off well enough for mere party ribaldry, but that he sometimes overshot the mark with naked lies. *Ex. gr.*

" I must have something, Canning cries,
And fastens on some rich mince pies;
As dexterous as the rest to rifle;
Ecod! and he must something do
For *mother* and for *sisters* too,
So steals some syllabubs and trifle."

Mr. Canning had no sisters; and Mrs. Hunn's children, by her third marriage, were rather too young at that time (1801) to quarter on the public. Few men, possessed of such opportunities, ever made such little use of them for family aggrandisement. Peter, going on in the same strain, says, that "with sinecures to a large amount, squeezed from the vitals of the nation, this modest and generous youth could not afford to yield his poor mother, Mistress Hunn, *alias* Mistress Reddish, *alias* Mistress Canning, a pittance. No! the kingdom must be saddled with five hundred pounds a year for her support." The sinecures had no more existence than the sisters; and the kingdom was not saddled with the support of Mrs. Hunn, for, at her time of life, being then fifty-five, the transfer of the pension from a " youth" of thirty-one was

It has been observed by a great authority, that the mothers of distinguished men have generally been women of more than ordinary intellectual power; and the remark will lose none of its force in reference to the mother of Mr. Canning. Indeed, were we not otherwise assured of the fact from direct sources, it would be impossible to contemplate his profound and touching devotion to her, without being led to conclude that the object of such unchanging attachment must have been possessed of rare and commanding qualities.

Mrs. Hunn was esteemed by the circle in whose society the latter part of her life was passed, as a woman of great mental energy. This strength of character communicated itself to her aspect and even to her utterance. Her conversation was animated and vigorous, and marked by a distinct originality of manner and a choice of topics fresh and striking, and out of the common-place routine. Like most persons who derive their social advantages from a practical intercourse with the world, Mrs. Hunn was more distinguished by natural talents than mere accomplishments—by nervous individuality and good sense, rather than superficial refinement. To persons who were but slightly acquainted with her, the energy of her manner had something of an air of eccentricity. She retained traces of the beauty of her youth to the last.

The closing years of her life were spent in retirement at her house in Henrietta Street, Bath; where she died, after a lingering illness, in her eighty-first year, on the 27th of March, 1827. Her son paid his last visit to her

---

clearly in favour of the public. It is a curious commentary on the Billingsgate patriotism of Dr. Walcot, that, after a life spent in casting obloquy upon public men for alleged venality, he is said to have been bought up in the end! " He dropped his pen," says the author of " All the Talents," " while snatching at a pension."

sick room on the 7th of the preceding January, the day after the Duke of York's funeral, where he caught the cold, which, acting on a frame shattered by anxiety, laid the foundation of his last fatal illness; and he, who was so attached to her while living, in five months followed her to the grave.

II.

BOYHOOD. WINCHESTER. ETON. THE MICROCOSM. OXFORD.

THE childhood of George Canning was passed under the inauspicious guardianship of Mr. Reddish, whose disorderly habits excluded the possibility of moral or intellectual training. The profligacy of his life communicated its reckless tone to his household, and even the material wants of his family were frequently neglected to feed his excesses elsewhere. Yet amidst these unpropitious circumstances, the talents of the child attracted notice ; and Moody, the actor, who had constant opportunities of seeing him, became strongly interested in his behalf. Moody was a blunt, honest man, of rough bearing, but of the kindliest disposition ; and foreseeing that the boy's ruin would be the inevitable consequence of the associations by which he was surrounded, he resolved to bring the matter at once under the notice of his uncle, Mr. Stratford Canning. The step was a bold one;—for there had been no previous intercourse between the families, although the boy was then seven or eight years old. But it succeeded. Moody drew an indignant picture of the boy's situation ; declared that he was on the high-road to the " gallows" (that was the word); dwelt upon the extraordinary promise he displayed; and warmly predicted, that if proper means were taken for bringing him forward in the world, he would one day become a great man. Mr. Stratford Canning was at first extremely unwilling to interfere; and it was not until the negotiation was taken up by other branches of the family, owing to honest Moody's perseverance, that he ultimately consented to take charge of his nephew, upon condition that the intercourse with his mother's connexions should be strictly abridged.

Having undertaken this responsibility, Mr. Stratford Canning discharged it faithfully. He was a member of the banking and mercantile firm of French, Burroughs, and Canning, at that time largely concerned in the Irish loans, and a strong Liberal in politics. At his house George Canning was introduced to Burke, Fox, General Fitzpatrick, and other leaders of the Whig party. Here, too, he first met Sheridan, but it was reserved for later years and other opportunities, to ripen into intimacy the acquaintance which was thus begun; for Mr. Stratford Canning died before his nephew was old enough to enter upon public life.* He had the satisfaction, however, of witnessing the dawn of his talents, and of placing him in the most favourable circumstances for the completion of his education. A small estate in Ireland had been set aside for that exclusive purpose, at the urgent solicitations of Mr. George Canning's grandmother — so small, that it yielded nothing more than was barely sufficient to defray unavoidable expenses.† But this settlement, penurious

---

* He died a short time before Mr. Canning left Eton.
† This trifling annuity, producing about £200 a year, was drawn from Kilbrahan, County of Kilkenny, which forms part of the style of the Canning viscounty. A writer in the "Gentleman's Magazine," tells us that there are two accounts of the way in which this small estate came into Mr.

as it was in amount, showed that the family recognised the claims of the son, although they refused to extend the same consideration to his mother.

Mr. Canning received the rudiments of his education under the Reverend Mr. Richards, at Hyde Abbey School, in the neighbourhood of Winchester; and entertained throughout his life so grateful a sense of the advantages he derived from that excellent establishment, that when he came into power, towards the close of his career, he presented his old tutor to a prebendal stall in Winchester Cathedral.*

Canning's possession. According to one version, his grandfather, when he cut off the entail, forgot to include this little property in levying the fine, so that on his decease it devolved upon his grandson, as heir-at-law. According to the other account the omission was intentional, the grandfather settling Kilbrahan in fee on his disinherited son for the purpose of more effectually barring him from any further claims. ("Gent. Mag." vol. xcviii.) It is scarcely necessary to say that these statements, which so flatly contradict each other, are equally irreconcileable with facts.

* Mr. Richards did not enjoy his preferment long. He died in 1833, at the age of seventy-nine, and was buried in the nave of the cathedral. He appears to have been held in universal respect for the strictness of his moral character; and to have inspired at the same time no less terror amongst his refractory pupils, by the excessive severity of his punishments. In some instances, these cruelties of the old school were never forgotten or forgiven. One of his scholars, many years afterwards, retained so vivid a recollection of the chastisements he had received at the hands of this rigid disciplinarian, that, writing home from India, he said, "I am amongst savages, it is true, but none so savage as old Richards!" It may be presumed that Mr. Canning's studious and regular habits preserved him from experiencing any of the evil effects of a system which, it is only justice to observe, prevailed at that time in most of the public schools. Mr. Richards' establishment enjoyed great popularity until he retired from its personal superintendence, when it suddenly fell off, and was soon afterwards given up altogether. The school-house has subsequently undergone some strange reverses, being used at different periods as a Mechanics' Institute, and a Dissenting Chapel. The building stands apart from the rest of the premises, and is said to have been the first house in Winchester that was covered with slates. It is now lying empty and idle; yet, *malgré* desertion and antiquity, it has somewhat of a new and jaunty air. The pilgrim who takes an interest in visiting such scenes must not confound it with Hyde Abbey, from which it derives its name; which stood on the opposite side of the street, and of which nothing now remains but a massive archway and broken gable. The garden and play-ground of

Even at this early period he procured some applause for his skill in verse-making, and when he was removed to Eton, where that talent is the surest qualification for eminence, he was at once placed as an oppidan, between the age of twelve and thirteen. He was sent to Eton by the advice of Mr. Fox, who took a personal interest in his progress.

There he soon acquired distinction for the easy elegance of his Latin and English poetry, and the suavity of his prose; discovering also in his character the germ of those traits for which he was afterwards so much admired in public life—great generosity of temper, quickness of apprehension, and firmness of purpose. By the happy constitution of his powers, and unswerving steadiness in their cultivation, the boy was in this instance the perfect father of the man. He appears to have commenced his studies with a sort of prescience of the course which lay before him, and to have trained his intellectual faculties carefully for that end. His progress, undisturbed in the outset by any of the retarding incidents of youth, maintained one uniform direction, acquiring increased strength as he advanced. His youth, serious without austerity, elastic and persevering, disclosed a faithful prophecy of his maturer life. There are no boyish delinquencies to record in his Eton days, no rebellion of the

the school are still to be seen just as they were sixty or seventy years ago; only a little dishevelled and overgrown. Even the little grating in the low door, through which the apple and cake venders used to extract the pocket-money of the boys, is still extant; and the countless names of many an idle aspirant after mural distinction, scrawled with nails and penknives, may yet be traced on the surrounding walls. Mr. Canning's is not to be found amongst them; an evidence, perhaps, of the staidness of his youth, which looked to be remembered through inscriptions of another kind. We have a glimpse of his boyish sobriety in the following passage in Mr. Wilberforce's diary. " C. knew Canning well at Eton. He never played at any games with the other boys; quite a man, fond of acting; decent and moral."—" Life of Wilberforce," v. 139.

animal spirits; the calm of scholarship appears to have settled down at once upon his blood. With a brilliant wit, and a taste scrupulously refined, he possessed a capacity of application which enabled him to give the utmost practical effect to his talents. The assiduity he displayed, showed how little he relied upon the mere inspirations of genius. He felt the necessity, and knew the full value of laborious habits; and from the very start applied himself with unremitting industry to his studies.

His reputation rose rapidly at Eton, and drew about him the chief spirits amongst his young contemporaries. A society existed there for the practice of discussion, and used to meet periodically in one of the halls of the college. This little assembly was conducted with a strict eye to parliamentary usages; the chair was taken by a speaker duly elected to the office; the ministerial and opposition benches were regularly occupied; and the subject for consideration was entered upon with the most sincere and ludicrous formality. Noble lords, and honourable and learned gentlemen, were here to be found in miniature, as they were in full maturity in another place; the contest for victory was as eager; and, when it is added that amongst the earlier debaters were the late Marquis Wellesley and Earl Grey, it will readily be believed that the eloquence was frequently as ardent and original. In this society Mr. Canning soon won distinction by the vigour and clearness of his speeches, anticipating upon the themes of the hour the larger views of the future statesman. And here, too, in these happy conflicts, he formed some solid friendships, that lasted through his life.

The purity of sentiment, and congeniality of pursuits in which these personal attachments had their origin, flowered out into a little literary enterprise, which has conferred celebrity upon the spot from whence it issued—the famous boy-periodical called the "Microcosm," projected by a few of the more accomplished Etonians, with Canning, then advancing towards the seventeenth year of his age, at their head.

The first number of the "Microcosm" appeared on the 6th of November, 1786. It was a small weekly paper, published at Windsor, price twopence; on the plan of the "Spectators," "Ramblers," &c., which at that time, and even to a still later date, were the favourite models with all literary tyros. The original design of the work was to treat the characteristics of juvenile Eton, in the same style of didactic humour which had been applied to general society by Addison and his followers; but the writers found it impossible to keep strictly within such circumscribed limits; and, gradually breaking bounds, extended their observation, touching, mimetically, upon men and manners at large, with a degree of freedom, and an occasional felicity of illustration, not unworthy of the experienced moralists in whose train they moved.

The plan was not hit upon by chance. It was laid down with abundant seriousness of intention, by the literary conclave, who ventured to predict, out of the materials around them, the future glories of their country. "I consider the scene before me as a microcosm," says the editor, Mr. Gregory Griffin, in the opening paper; "a world in miniature, where all the passions which agitate the great original are faithfully pourtrayed on a smaller scale; in which the endless variety of character, the different lights and shades which the appetites or peculiar situations throw us into, begin to discriminate, and expand themselves. The curious observer may here remark in the bud, the different casts and turns of genius, which will in future, strongly characterise the leading features of the mind. *We may see the embryo statesman, who hereafter may wield and direct at pleasure the mighty and complex system of European politics, now employing the whole extent of his abilities to circumvent his companions at their plays, or adjusting the important differences which may arise between the contending heroes of his little circle; or a general, the future terror of France and Spain, now the dread only of his equals, and the undisputed lord and president of the boxing-ring. The Grays and Wallers of the rising generation here tune their little lyres; and he, who hereafter may sing the glories of Britain, must first celebrate at Eton, the smaller glories of his college."** Of this grand destiny that was to crown the ambition of the Etonians, it is curious to note how accurately the embryo statesman at least (to whatever twilight nooks of fame his associates may be assigned) realised the aspirations of his wise and witty boyhood.

The principal writers in the "Microcosm," were the Messrs. J. and R. Smith, Frere, and Canning. Lord Henry Spencer contributed a couple of trifles; Mr. Mellish, a whole number; Mr. Littlehales and Mr. Way, a letter each; and the respectable Mr. Capel Lofft volunteered a defence of Addison, which the young essayists received with the deference due to his years. One can readily understand how the knot of school-boys must have incontinently rejoiced over the middle-aged gentleman they had caught so unexpectedly in their net.

Mr. Canning supplied the largest individual share of the forty numbers; but Mr. J. Smith appears to have performed the functions of editor, for the work dropped

* The paper from which this extract is taken was written by Mr. J. Smith.

when that gentleman went to Cambridge. The "Microcosm" gave up the ghost when Mr. J. Smith felt, to use his own phrase, "that he was no longer a man of this (Eton) world." The care and propriety with which his papers are composed afford a hint of the judicial qualifications which may have entitled him to the post of moderator.*

The sobriety of the "Microcosm," as a whole, and the surprising air of ease which pervades it, helped largely, no doubt, by the celebrity of its principal writer, have attracted more curiosity than was ever before bestowed upon a production of its class.† And certainly none ever deserved it so well.‡ It would be difficult to detect in any of the articles, the "'prentice hand" of youth. The only exceptions, perhaps, are the contributions of Mr. Frere,

* In July, 1787, Miss Burney went " to hear the speeches" at Eton. The Royal Family were present. "The speeches," she tells us, "were chiefly in Greek and Latin, but concluded with three or four in English; some were pronounced extremely well, especially those spoken by the chief composers of the 'Microcosm,' Canning and Smith."—"Diary of Madame D'Arblay," iii., 413. This was on the 29th of July. The work was discontinued on the 30th, so that the "chief composers" (Miss Burney may be acquitted of the phrase) must have been tolerably well known in spite of their playing at masks with their readers. But when was such a secret ever kept in such a community as that of Eton?

† The "Microcosm" has passed through several editions: the fifth edition was published in 1825. A curious document is still in existence bearing Mr. Canning's signature, and dated 31st of July, 1787 (the day after the work was discontinued) by which, for the sum of fifty guineas the copyright was assigned to Mr. Charles Knight, of Windsor, the father of the accomplished editor of Shakspeare.

‡ Several imitations of the "Microcosm" have been attempted at different schools, the "Kensingtonian" for example; but none of them survived their birth. The great success of the "Microcosm" induced the Harrow boys to get up a rival periodical, which was ostentatiously published with a foolish frontispiece representing the two publications in a balance, the "Microcosm" being made to kick the beam. Upon seeing this print, Mr. Canning is said to have made the following epigram:

"What mean ye by this print so rare,
  Ye wits of Harrow jealous?
Behold! your rivals soar in air,
  And ye are *heavy fellows!*"

the intimate friend of Mr. Canning, whose papers betray a tone of effort and inexperience, with bright glimpses, however, of that playful sagacity which afterwards shone so so brilliantly in the " Anti-Jacobin." But Mr. Canning's are incomparably the most compact and *aged* essays ever produced by a boy of little more than sixteen.* There are no such specimens elsewhere of English prose written at that age, so weighty of purpose, so chaste and finished in expression. The influence of the sententious modes which were in vogue at the close of the last century, may be constantly felt tempting him into glaring imitations ;† but, putting aside the question of originality, these fugitive papers exhibit striking evidences of the early

---

* Mr. Canning's essays were specially praised by the critics of the day for that quality of subtle humour which he afterwards employed with such effect in the House of Commons.

† The most direct imitations for which he is responsible are a letter from "Nobody," deploring his ill-treatment in the world, and Gregory Griffin's account of the various opinions he hears in society regarding himself and his works. On sitting down to these essays his imagination was evidently heated by a recent perusal of the famous petition of "Who and Which" (the prolific parent of a whole race of discontented nonentities), and the " Spectator's" account of the contradictory criticisms of his club. But he, nevertheless, vindicates his originality by some new and witty touches. Particularly happy is the lurking irony of that passage, where Gregory Griffin, himself personally unknown, says that he has sometimes been ready to sink with shame and gratitude when he chanced to meet gentlemen who cleared him of all his faults, by kindly taking them on themselves, candidly confessing that they were the real authors of such and such papers. " To these gentlemen," he adds, " I am proud of an opportunity to return my thanks for the honour they confer on me, and to assure them that all my papers are very much at their service; provided only, that they will be so kind as just to send me previous notice which they may think fit to own ; that my bookseller may have proper directions, if called upon, to confirm their respective claims ; and for the prevention of any errror which might otherwise arise, should two persons unfortunately make the same choice." In this sort of sarcasm he was unequalled. He applied it with marvellous effect in the House of Commons. It was even more dreaded by his opponents than that fierce ridicule rising into invective, which, says Scott, fetched away both skin and bone, and was the special terror of the " Yelpers."

severity and daintiness of his taste. A gentlemanly contempt for the false and affected in real life and in literature, suggests such themes for his ridicule as the mincing effeminacy of fops, the foolish custom of garnishing conversation with oaths, the vices of bombastic criticism, and pointless witticisms. This choice of a class of subjects, taken from the traditions of English manners, and already exhausted by previous essayists, discloses the source at which the writers of the "Microcosm" drank their first draughts of inspiration. They regarded the school of Addison (aerated however, by the sparkling gaiety of Steele—a step in advance of most followers of the "Spectator," who see nothing in it but its trim morality) as the perfection of English prose ;* and they imitated it with scholastic precision, not merely in the texture of its diction, but in that prudential pleasantry which gives it such a colouring of constitutional goodness. The work abounds in touches of well-bred humour, and quaint irony of amiable foibles, and sedulously displays a proper sense of the genteeler virtues, and an amusing sympathy for all sorts of oddities, especially that superannuated order of correspondents who represent abstract ideas and exploded eccentricities. As in the "Spectator," so in the "Microcosm," social weaknesses are laid bare—social vices never; or only in a way to give the greater importance to the externals of decorum, insisting with overwhelming sententiousness upon the doctrine of appearances, while great offences,

* The Duke of Sussex, whose miscellaneous intercourse with books gives weight to his judgment in such matters, thought Addison's style the best adapted to all subjects: he said that it never tired. Sir James Macintosh seems to have held the same opinion. He told Mr. Rush, that the "Spectator" had lost its value as a book of instruction, but that it would always last as a standard of style—an assertion which may be reasonably doubted. Rush says, that he described Franklin as a better Addison, with more grace and playfulness.

too mighty for ridicule, are suffered to stalk abroad with impunity. The ethics of the "Spectator" are diligently slipped and transplanted into this lighter soil, and blossom, as all such transplantations do, in diminished force and fainter hues. Every thing is tested by a judgment too cautious and exceptional to throw out much vigour or freshness; the ear is lulled by the flowing repose of undulating periods; and we have the satisfaction of retracing, in smooth and agreeable cadences, a whole anthology of truisms.

The modes and customs ridiculed by the "Microcosm" are the modes and customs of the "Spectator," and had passed away long before. The "scowrers" had vanished from the purlieus of Covent Garden, country-gentlemen no longer held it a special mark of good breeding to "kiss all round," and fine ladies had renounced snuff, although they might still, here and there, affect the coquetry of patching. The manners depicted in the "Microcosm" survived only in print. The "Lounging Club" was but a reflection of the "Ugly Clubs," and "Everlasting Clubs" (themselves little more than shadows of the "No-Nose-and-Surly Clubs" of a previous day); and the youngsters who took these things from books, believing all the time that they were describing an actually existing state of society, might as well have reanimated Duke Humphrey and the tenpenny ordinaries. The critics felt this, and with all their admiration of the extraordinary merit of the juvenile "Spectator," especially in its serious papers, they could not help hinting that it was sometimes "out of nature;" by which they really meant that it was sometimes out of convention.

The notion of setting up any author as an universal standard of style, is false in principle; since style, to be of any instrumental value, ought to be flexible and adaptive. Yet the prose of Addison, so delicately embellished with what Gibbon calls " the female graces of elegance and mildness,"* enjoyed this distinction for a long period, by the indolent acquiescence of the reading public, who seemed waiting for some convulsion to rouse them into more active perceptions. It is curious that Johnson should have given such an impulse to this opinion, by an emphatic dictum, which he notoriously violated in his own writings.† It was as if he thought it discreet, for the sake of the public, to defer to forms of which he felt the hollowness; just as a certain sort of people, who are not over-particular themselves, keep up a pretence of prudery about words and behaviour before children, of the absolute futility of which, as a practical means of virtue, they are all the time thoroughly conscious. The style of Addison was a refinement upon the rugged elliptical styles of his greater predecessors; but it wanted their breadth, manliness, and sincerity, and will not bear comparison with the healthy vigour of De Foe, the muscular energy of Dryden, and the prodigal magnificence of

---

* "Memoirs," 4to. p. 86.

† In Johnson's character of Addison, he applauds his style for being voluble and easy (which was, perhaps, what Boswell meant when he said that he wrote like a gentleman), and adds that, whoever wishes to attain an *English* style, ought to give his days and nights to the volumes of Addison. Burney furnishes us with an amusing key to what was intended by the expression " English style." Being once in conversation with Johnson on this subject, he ventured to observe, that, although Johnson praised Addison, he had not adopted him as his model, no two styles being more different; suggesting that the difference consisted, probably, in this—that Addison's prose was full of idioms, colloquial phrases, and proverbs, which, although so easy to an Englishman as to give his intellect no trouble, was extremely difficult, if not impossible of translation; while Johnson's prose, being strictly grammatical and free from any peculiarity of phraseology, would fall into any other language as easily as if it had been originally conceived in it. Johnson assented to the accuracy of the distinction—leaving us to conclude that he esteemed that to be the best English style which was least capable of being rendered intelligibly into any other language.

Milton.* Addison had the merit of reducing the art of prose to an attainable level, laid out with gracious fields and pleasant walks, but still a flat. It was wonderfully accessible, and popular in proportion; for the grand and the elevated, which are not so easily reached, can never be so generally admired. But no outlay of skill upon the surface can prevent flats from becoming tedious; one longs for a break, or irregularity of some kind, to relieve the monotony. Where the whole landscape lies mapped out on the plain, we see too far in advance to care much about getting to the end of the journey. And this is now felt with Addison. His writings, always attractive at first by their ease and propriety, disappoint us at last by their uniformity. The sameness of the charm wears out its interest; for the most agreeable mannerism must ultimately produce indifference, by ceasing to excite expectation.

On the other hand, this mannerism, when it becomes elevated by popular admiration into an authority, sometimes gets credit for more than it is worth, and enables vague generalities to pass for new truths. Commonplaces are frequently carried into general circulation, as current coin of great value, merely because they happen to be minted off with the stamp of a well-established style. Pope is a conspicuous example of this. And it may be said of Addison that he is not always as profound as he looks.

The morality of Addison, be it observed, also, is very

* Even in his own day the effeminacy of Addison's style did not escape criticism. The political paper called the "Freeholder," which he wrote in defence of the government, was specially ridiculed by Steele, who thought the humour too nice and gentle for such noisy times. Johnson tells us that Steele is reported to have said of the "Freeholder," that the ministry made use of a lute, when they ought to have called for a trumpet.

much of the old conventional fashion—solemn gravity of feature, with a liquorish tooth beneath. The contrasts between the demure axioms and sinister humours of the " Spectator," are things, also, to " give us pause." And yet, with all this hovering on the verge of dangerous indulgencies, there is no imagination in it—no luxuriance of fancy—not a breath of odours from the ideal world— nothing to spiritualise its suggestive pruriency. This want of aerial truth is felt chiefly in a long train of skeleton figures that move through the essays. Delightful Will Honeycomb, and immortal Sir Roger, and the rest of the club (all called into life by Steele), are living people, as familiar to us as fire-side faces; but the rest, who, for distinction, may be called episodical, including most of the correspondents, are representatives of mental characteristics, rather than of real life; not men and women, but specimens of dried reason.*

The " Spectator" must always be honoured for its wit and good sense, and may long continue to live on the reputation of its purity, which had no inconsiderable merit in its own day, although it descends to our somewhat more decent times with abated influence. But who now recurs to Addison for a mastery of English, for an example of the power of the language, for the study of its capabilities, its strength, or its beauty? He is gone with his age. The French and American revolutions have utterly swept away the literary influences of that middle age of attenuated

---

* The difference between the real man of common life, and the abstraction of the essayist, is forcibly illustrated in the Croaker of Goldsmith, and the Suspirius of the " Rambler," from which the former is said to have taken the idea. Every body knows Croaker—but who has ever realised Suspirius to his imagination? The mere difference between the dramatic and the didactic forms is not enough to account for the difference in the impression made by two characters identical in their elements.

delicacy and Augustan polish. Bolder and more picturesque styles have superseded them—styles that address themselves to the wants of the time, expanding with its conquests, and giving open utterance to its emancipated spirit. Men who seek distinction in this age must throw their hearts and brains into the matter, and leave forms to adjust themselves. The lagging mannerist who stops to pick his steps and trim his phrases in the sun will speedily find himself outstripped and forgotten.*

If Mr. Canning adopted Addison to some extent as a model of style (for emulation rather than imitation), there is apparently conclusive evidence in the "Microcosm" that he did not think very highly of him as a critic—the single feature in the estimate of his literary character which Johnson has ingeniously contrived to shirk, by insinuating an indefinite defence without venturing a decisive opinion. Two of Canning's essays are occupied with a mock examination of an epic poem called "The Knave of Hearts," a bit of boyish doggrel which has found its way into every nursery in the kingdom.† From the structure of this cri-

* The "British Essayists" must for ever be indispensable to an English library—a sort of traditionary Penates. But their future functions seem to be clearly marked out, as supplying the best easy moral reading for the young—the happiest combination of amusement and instruction; for, let grown-up people say what they please, they seldom turn back to these books except for an occasional pleasure. Hazlitt, who really admired and relished them, admits that he outlived his taste for them. "'The Periodical Essayists,' he tells us, "I read long ago. The 'Spectator' I liked extremely—but the 'Tatler' took my fancy most. I read the others soon after, the 'Rambler,' the 'Adventurer,' the 'World,' the 'Connoisseur.' I was not sorry to get to the end of them, and have no desire to go regularly through them again."—"The Plain Speaker," ii. p. 77. If people would confess it, this is the case with a large majority of readers.

† "The Queen of Hearts
She made some tarts,
All on a summer's day,
The Knave of Hearts
He stole those tarts,
And—took them—quite away! &c."

The criticism on this pleasant absurdity produced a curious com-

tique, its humorous formality, and its application of ponderous canons to a ludicrously insignificant subject, it seems to have been intended as a parody on Addison's critique on "Chevy Chase," which Johnson himself abandoned to the contempt of Dennis, when he admitted the poem to be a piece of chill and lifeless imbecility. But it is equally clear that the young essayist meditated another stroke of ridicule in this critique, as the following passage will testify:

"The author has not branched his poem into excrescences of episode, or prolixities of digression; it is neither variegated with diversity of unmeaniug similitudes, nor glaring with the varnish of unnatural metaphor. The whole is plain and uniform: so much so indeed, that I should hardly be surprised if some morose readers were to conjecture, that the poet had been thus simple rather from necessity than choice ; that he had been restrained not so much by chastity of judgment as sterility of imagination."

The poised and turgid pomp cannot be mistaken. His pure taste, which took delight in the perspicuity of Addison, revolted from the three-piled grandeur of Johnson. He was never reconciled to writers of that class, and to the last disliked the glitter of Junius. Fox also held the style of Junius in aversion, as might be expected from

mentary some years afterwards, (1796), from a correspondent of the "Monthly Magazine," who tells his readers that he had found the prototype of Mr. Canning's jest in a French composition called "*Le chef-d'œuvre d'un inconnu, poeme*, &c." "Its object," says the writer, "is to expose the jargon of criticism. The poem has an affected silliness (*niaiserie*) of thought and style." So far, the resemblance is close enough, and the opening of both criticisms, extolling the simplicity of the poems, and the absence of invocations, are much alike. But there is nothing surprising in this. The form of such travesties existed long before, and had been frequently employed by other writers. The merit consisted not in applying this mode of ridicule, but in applying it effectively. And this merit may be freely accorded to the essay in the "Microcosm;" since it is still remembered for its point, which outlives the occasion, while all similar specimens of that sort of satire are forgotten. This is the final test. Besides, it may be reasonably doubted whether Mr. Canning, then a school-boy at Eton, had ever heard of his French predecessor; who it seems published a fourth edition of his "*chef-d'œuvre*," in 1758, in two volumes:—a fact, as to bulk, which goes a great way to account for the rapidity with which it sunk into oblivion.

the largeness of his intellect and the copiousness of his eloquence.

The strong English temper of Mr. Canning's mind, his earnest nationality, paramount even in its prejudices, constantly breaks out in these essays. Wherever opportunity offers (and sometimes he went out of his way to make it) he stands up for the English character, and throws himself on the defensive at the first approach of art or fashion to tamper with its sturdy simplicity. England was his party from the beginning, and continued so to the end.

At Eton, he first discovered a political bias. The boy was an ardent Whig. His noble poem on "The Slavery of Greece," in one of the early numbers of the "Microcosm," shows that he inherited his father's principles, which he knew how to set off with a higher grace. But he gave a more practical proof of his opinions on the occasion of a contested election for Windsor—when he threw himself boldly into the popular tumult in opposition to the court nominee. There was no mistake here. Students who are visited in their dreams by visions of Marathon and Thermopylæ, must not be held too strictly responsible for their classical enthusiasm, if it lean (as it always does!) towards the side of public liberty; but here was a question of the day, between might and right—into which forms such struggles, at that time, but too plainly resolved themselves. And the young politician, with the whole collected force of his mind, was found battling on the side of the people; speaking, huzzaing, swelling the shout and chorus of the weaker party, which, being the weaker, is generally the first chosen of generous and heroic natures. But how could it be otherwise? His education had been all along superintended by his uncle, one of the most zealous liberals of the day. His Eton, and afterwards his

Oxford vacations, were passed either at his uncle's, or at Mr. Crewe's, or at Mr. Legh's, of Cheshire,* or amongst the Sheridans—all of the same colour. What politics was he likely to hear in such circles?—or where could they have been so temptingly presented to his imagination? His progress, too, was watched with daily interest by Fox, who calculated upon attaching him to the Whigs; and he was already looked upon with such confidence as their legitimate property, that Sheridan absolutely announced his coming in the House of Commons.†

The death of his uncle just before he went to Oxford, removed at once the example and the authority under which his youthful convictions were formed; and further endangered their permanency by separating him from his early associations, and casting him, at the impressionable age of seventeen, into a university, hostile, by tradition, to the cultivation of popular sentiments. In going to Oxford, he had passed out of the atmosphere of Whiggery, and there was little left, at least no urgent or direct influence, to draw him back again. But it was not so easy to shake off his Eton impressions. The sudden antagonism to which they were exposed, only confirmed them the more. He was a stronger liberal, with more thoughtful and deliberate purpose, in his scholastic retirement at Christ Church than amidst the riot of a Windsor election. There was a touch of chivalry in this, and an evidence of that clinging affection for old ties, which many years afterwards made him revert to the scenes and sports of his

---

* A connexion of the Rev. Mr. Legh, of Ashbourne, in Derbyshire, who was an uncle of Mr. Canning's.
† This was on the occasion of Mr. Jenkinson's first speech in Parliament, which excited much applause on the ministerial side. Sheridan personally alluded to Mr. Canning; and declared that when he appeared he would far eclipse the talents of his friend.

boyhood, the play-ground and the Montem, with feelings of unaltered delight.*

In 1788, Mr. Canning entered Christ Church College, Oxford. His Eton companions were nearly all scattered; the only relative who took an interest in his education was gone, and he was committed, in this critical juncture, to the sole guidance of his own discretion. But his habits were already formed, and he was safe. Good taste, no less than prudence, led him to shun the frivolous waste and life consumption of the majority of his contemporaries. He "consorted" with none of these, restraining himself for higher aims.

New friendships sprung up at Christ Church, of a class materially calculated to influence, if not to decide, the subsequent direction of his life. Amongst his more immediate associates, were the Hon. Mr. Jenkinson, afterwards Earl of Liverpool, Mr. Sturges Bourne, Lord Holland, Lord Carlisle, Lord Seaford, Lord Granville, and Lord Boringdon. Most of these gentlemen, especially Mr. Jenkinson, were educated with a specific view to a participation in the government of the country;

* He was attached to the old haunts to the last, and scarcely ever omitted a Montem. His own enjoyment on such occasions, was to the full as real as that of the boys; and he entered with such unflinching zest into the hilarious humour of the scene, that the statesman was soon forgotten in the Etonian. It was at the Montem of 1823, that he met Mr. Brougham, for the first time after that fierce contention in the House of Commons, about Mr. Canning's conduct on the Catholic claims, for which they were both nearly committed to the custody of the serjeant-at-arms. Their political enmity, if either of them entertained such a feeling, vanished on the instant; and Mr. Canning stretched out his hand to his adversary, to the infinite delight of the spectators. The action was a trifle in itself, but at such a moment, and on a spot sacred to happier associations than those of the House of Commons, it touched a chord of the human heart, which never fails in its response to generous impulses. At the Eton regatta of the following summer, Mr. Canning was the sitter in the "ten-oar," the post of distinction to which the most illustrious visiter is promoted. We are told that he huzzaed with the loudest of them as the boats shot past the crowded shores.

and Mr. Canning, although he could reckon upon none of the advantages of patronage or hereditary position, was soon admitted to the freedom of their intercourse by virtue of claims more powerful and commanding. His wit, eloquence, and scholarship established an ascendancy amongst them, never wholly free, to be sure, from the jealousies of rank, but always superior to its naked accidents. He was here, for the first time, placed upon a familiar footing with lords and statesmen in training; here he took his first lesson in aristocracy; and he used its admonitions wisely. And it is something no less to the purpose to add, that although political differences frequently separated him in after life from some of these intimate companions of his college days, he retained their personal attachment to the close. The friendships of his boyhood never suffered check or interruption. He was no less happy in the fidelity of his friends, than in the choice of them.

The closest intimacy existed between Mr. Canning and Mr. Jenkinson. The latter had entered Christ Church in the preceding spring or summer. They were constantly together, and their most frequent companion was Lord Henry Spencer, third son of the Duke of Marlborough. This young nobleman was a few months younger than Mr. Canning, had been his inseparable associate at Eton, and accompanied him to Oxford. Of all the writers in the "Microcosm," he approached the nearest to his friend in the delicacy and polish of the slight compositions he contributed to its pages. His "Ars Mentiendi" affords a very remarkable specimen of his cultivated talents, so early developed, and so soon cut off. The death of Lord Henry, in the very flower of youth, was a source of inexpressible sorrow to his friends, and to none more than to the chosen companion of his boyhood. Before he had reached the age of twenty, he was called to the diplomatic service. In the following year, the grave responsibilities of the embassy at the Hague devolved wholly upon him, in consequence of the absence of Lord Auckland, and he discharged his trust with so much ability, that he was soon afterwards appointed envoy extraordinary to the court of Stockholm. Here, worn out by the premature activity of his mind, he died in his twenty-fifth year. No man ever gave fairer earnest of capacity to serve his country, or left behind him a purer reputation.

While these three congenial spirits remained at the university, they maintained the strictest friendship. Mr. Canning was the centre of attraction; the soul of their mock debates, their trials of wit, and classical controversies ; and his genius rendered for ever memorable the *noctes cœnæque* of Christ Church.*

The vacations were generally passed in some country house, where the accomplishments of the student were exercised upon lighter themes. It was the age of scrapbooks and *vers de société;* every boudoir had its volume ready to receive the offerings of the visiter, who, if he had the slightest reputation or celebrity of any kind, was put under contribution by collectors, whose levy it was vain to resist. Mr. Canning's penalties in this way were in-

* Mr. Canning always looked back with affectionate interest to this period of his life, and was a frequent visiter at Christ Church after he took his degrees. On a subsequent occasion he wrote two copies of verses for the installation of the Duke of Portland, as Chancellor of the University, which were spoken in the theatre—Mr. Burke and Mr. Windham being amongst the audience—by Mr. Dawkins and Lord John Beresford, afterwards Archbishop of Dublin. I have sought in vain for these poems, nor is there any repository in which the *Encænia* of that installation are preserved.

numerable; things thrown off on the impulse of the moment, intended only for the moment, and so exquisitely trivial, that, even if we had the power, it would be scarcely fair to submit them to the ordeal of publication. Most of these gay trifles are, no doubt, swept away in the common ruin of all old-fashioned memorials, trinkets, autographs, and the like; and many a dusty page, full of antiquated gallantry and tea-table wit, has shared the fate of the hereditary receipt-books, and gone the way of all lumber. Any attempt to trace Mr. Canning's sportive effusions on the sundry occasions that provoked and entrapped his youth into scrap-books, hermitages, mazes, grottos, showers of rain, and similar suggestions, incidents, and places, would now be quite hopeless. The loose leaves scribbled over with precious impromptus are scattered—perhaps to the winds or the flames; and, except here and there in some revered nook in a far-off country mansion, where things are husbanded up in the alphabeted niches of old secretaires, and ticketed like choice specimens in a museum, it would be idle to hunt after such relics.

But I am fortunately enabled, through private channels, and by the aid of a valued friendship, unwearied in discharging offices of kindness, to gratify the reader's curiosity with a sample or two of these early verses, the interest of which arises chiefly from the period of life they illustrate; for their intrinsic merit, stripped of personal associations, is not very remarkable. This is generally true of all juvenile poems; yet the popular appetite for devouring the first fruits of men of genius, is not the less keen on that account.

Amongst the recollections of Crewe Hall is a little *jeu d'esprit*, which has as good a right to be preserved as most quips. Mr. Canning, then about eighteen or nineteen years of age, was walking in the grounds with Mrs. Crewe, who had just lost her favourite dog, Quon, and wanted an epitaph for him. The dog was buried close at hand, near the dairy-house. Mr. Canning protested he could not make epitaphs ; but the lady was not to be denied, and so he revenged himself with the following:—

EPITAPH ON MRS. CREWE'S DOG.
Poor Quon lies buried near this dairy,
And is not this a sad quondary?*

On another occasion he inscribed the following verses in the scrap-book, on leaving Crewe Hall :—

LINES OCCASIONED BY MRS. CREWE HAVING MAINTAINED IN A CONVERSATION AT HER FARM, " THAT ALL NERVOUS AFFECTIONS PRODUCE A CRAVING APPETITE."

"Happy the fair, who, here retired,
"By sober contemplation fired,
"Delight from Nature's works can draw."
('Twas thus I spoke, when first I saw
That cottage, which, with chastest hand,
Simplicity and taste have planned.)
"Happy, who, grosser cares resign'd,
"Content with books to feed her mind,
"Can leave life's luxuries behind;
"Content within this humble cell,
"With peace and temperance to dwell,
"Her food, the fruits,—her drink, the well.
"'Twas thus of old—" But as I spoke,
Before my eyes what dainties smoke!
Not such as Eremites of old,—
In many a holy tale enroll'd,—

* This will recall Sheridan's well-known epigram on Lady Payne's monkey—the pretty and ill-used Lady Payne.
"Alas! poor Ned,
My monkey's dead,
I had rather by half
It had been Sir Ralph."

Drawing from but their frugal hoard,
With nuts and apples spread the board;
But such, as fit for paunch divine,
Might tempt a modern saint to dine.
Then thus, perceiving my surprise,
Which star'd confest thro' both my eyes,
To vindicate her wiser plan,
The fair philosopher began—
" Young gentleman, no doubt you think"
(And here she paus'd awhile to drink)
" All that you've said is mighty fine—
" But won't you taste a glass of wine?
" You think these cates are somewhat curious,
" And for a hermit, too luxurious;
" But such old fograms (Lord preserve us)
" Knew no such thing as being nervous.
" Else had they found, what now I tell ye,
" How much the mind affects the *belly*;
" Had found that when the mind's opprest,
" Confused, elated, warmed, distrest,
" The body keeps an equal measure
" In sympathy of pain or pleasure;
" And, whether moved with joy or sorrow,
" From food alone, relief can borrow.
" Sorrow's, indeed, beyond all question,
" The best specific for digestion;
" Which, when with moderate force it rages,
" A chicken or a chop assuages.
" But, to support some weightier grief,
" Grant me, ye gods, a round of beef!
" Thus then, since *abstract* speculation
" Must set the *nerves* in agitation,
" Absurd the plan, with books and study
" To feed the mind—yet starve the body.
" These are my tenets, and in me
" Practice and principle agree.
" See then beneath this roof combined
" Food for the body and the mind.
" A couplet here, and there a custard,
" While sentiment by turns, and mustard,
" Bedew with tears the glistening eye.
" Behold me now with Otway sigh,
" Now revelling in pigeon pie;

"And now, in apt transition, taken
"From Bacon's Works—to eggs and bacon."

Dear Mrs. Crewe, this wondrous knowledge
I own, I ne'er had gained at college.
You are my tut'ress; would you quite
Confirm your wavering proselyte?
I ask but this, to show your sorrow
At my departure hence, to-morrow,
Add to your dinner, for my sake,
One supernumerary steak!

At Mrs. Legh's, in Cheshire, he left behind him many similar tokens of whim and pleasantry. The Leghs were an old county family and divided with the Davenports the dominion of Cheshire, where it was a common saying, that "the Leghs were as plenty as fleas, and the Davenports as dogs' tails." The following amusing lines were addressed to Mrs. Legh on her wedding-day, in reference to a present of a pair of shooting breeches she had made to Canning, and were probably written during the early part of his Oxford course:

TO MRS. LEGH.

While all to this auspicious day
Well pleased their heartfelt homage pay,
And sweetly smile and softly say
   A hundred civil speeches;
My muse shall strike her tuneful strings,
Nor scorn the gift her duty brings,
Tho' humble be the theme she sings,—
   A pair of shooting breeches.

Soon shall the tailor's subtle art
Have made them tight, and spruce, and smart,
And fastened well in every part
   With twenty thousand stitches;
Mark then the moral of my song,
Oh! may your loves but prove as strong,
And wear as well, and last as long,
   As these, my shooting breeches.

> And when to ease the load of life,
> Of private care, and public strife,
> My lot shall give to me a wife,
> > I ask not rank or riches;
> For worth like thine alone I pray,
> Temper like thine, serene and gay,
> And formed like thee to *give away*,
> > *Not wear herself*, the breeches.

Poetical epistles were still in vogue—that quaint old fashion of dressing up the sentiments of love and friendship in fine ceremonial suits. Odes and elegies were going out, or gone, and the epistles were following them; but the taste yet lingered here and there, just as we sometimes see scraps of antiquity scattered about a modern drawing-room. Of these epistles, the majority were very grand and solemn, having pretty much the tone of sombre Christmas pieces or historical tapestries, in which fat-ribbed ships, mounted in soft tranquillity on rows of waves, are made to represent storms, and huge-limbed women are thrown into the fiercest attitudes, to make them look as if their hearts were breaking. But there were also epistles which had a more direct bearing upon the lower world of reality—sportive communications, in which Lord William recounted an incident of indolent gallantry to Lady Ellen, or depicted the horrors of *ennui* in some country seat; all intended to be particularly gay and buoyant, the sprightliness being preserved against vulgarity by that natural dulness, which has always been considered, in such cases, a genteeler sort of attic salt.

What a lively influence such productions must have exercised on Mr. Canning's quick sense of the ridiculous, may be easily conceived; and no doubt the scrap-books contained many a jest of his upon them. The following apparently good-humoured satire upon these moping and ludicrous epistles, is the only MS. of Mr. Canning's, of this class, which I have been fortunate enough to obtain. Lord Boringdon (raised to the peerage in 1815, as Earl of Morley) and Lord Granville, were both amongst Mr. Canning's intimate college companions; and the Lady Elizabeth, alluded to in the poem, was one of the daughters of the Duke of Marlborough, and sister to Mr. Canning's friend, Lord Henry Spencer. Her ladyship married her first cousin (a quiet gentlemanly person, distinguished by nothing but a great love of music), the son of Lord Charles Spencer, and brother of William Spencer, the dandy and overpraised pet poet of the Devonshire House circle.

POETICAL EPISTLE FROM LORD BORINGDON TO LORD GRANVILLE (L. GOWER).

Oft you have asked me, Granville, why,
Of late I heave the frequent sigh?
Why, moping, melancholy, low,
From supper, commons, wine, I go?
Why lours my mind, by care opprest;
By day no peace, by night no rest?
Hear, then, my friend (and ne'er you knew
A tale so tender, and so true),
Hear what, tho' shame my tongue restrain,
My pen with freedom shall explain.
 Say, Granville, do you not remember,
About the middle of November,
When Blenheim's hospitable lord
Received us at his cheerful board;
How fair the Ladies Spencer smil'd,
Enchanting, witty, courteous, mild?
And mark'd you not, how many a glance
Across the table, shot by chance
From fair Eliza's graceful form,
Assailed and took my heart by storm?

And marked you not with earnest zeal
I asked her—if she'd have some veal?
And how, when conversation's charms
Fresh vigour gave to love's alarms,
My heart was scorch'd and burnt to tinder,
When talking to her at the *winder?*
   These facts premis'd, you can't but guess
The cause of my uneasiness,
For you have heard as well as I
That she'll be married speedily—
And then (my grief more plain to tell)
Soft cares, sweet fears, fond hopes, farewell!
But still, tho' false the fleeting dream,
Indulge awhile the tender theme,
And hear, had fortune yet been kind,
How bright the prospect of the mind.
Oh! had I had it in my power
To wed her—with a suited dower—
And proudly bear the beauteous maid
To Saltram's venerable shade.*
(Or if she lik'd not woods at Saltram,
Why, nothing's easier than to alter 'em).
Then had I tasted bliss sincere,
And happy been from year to year.
How changed this scene! for now, my Granville,
Another match is on the anvil.
And I, a widow'd dove, complain,
And find no refuge from my pain—
Save that of pitying Spencer's sister,
Who has lost a lord and gain'd a *Mister.*

Reputations acquired by such lively and ready talents are sometimes vague, and often magnified in proportion. But in this instance the power of making verses (such as they were) off-hand upon any subject, was associated with acquisitions so solid, that the pleasure faculty, instead of endangering Mr. Canning's scholastic character, only helped to confirm its right to the admiration it received

* The seat of the Earl of Morley—a beautiful residence within a few miles of Plymouth, near the Exeter-road.

on all sides. Great things were expected from him in the university, and he realised still greater. His orations, highly coloured by the liberal doctrines of the day, were universally applauded for their elegance and symmetry; and his Latin verses displayed not merely the resources, but the cultivated taste of the ripe scholar. He contested the prize for "The aboriginal Britons" with the Rev. Dr. Richards, and was beaten; but had the glory of transcending all competitors in the "Iter ad Meccam"—the best Latin prize poem Oxford has ever produced.* This work affords singular evidence of the value of a close study of Latin poetry—that is, of Virgil and Lucretius— with a view to the uses of specific and definite imagery. It is full of examples of this sort. The distinction will be obvious on comparison with his other serious poem (in English), "Ulm and Trafalgar," which deals in the most loose generalities and common-places. The fluency of this poem deserves special praise; and the description of the crescent standard of the Mahometans,

"vexillis fluitantibus intertexta,
Sanctum insigne micant crescentis cornua lunæ,"

may be cited as a wonderful instance of plastic Latinity in a modern.

His studies were pursued with unremitting diligence. There never was a collegiate career more distinguished by brilliant achievements and indefatigable industry. The character he built up at the university was in itself a prediction of the success that awaited him in the ambitious paths to which he aspired.

* This poem was recited by Mr. Canning, in the theatre, on the 26th of June, 1789, on the occasion of Lord Crewe's anniversary commemoration of benefactors to the university. The theatre was unusually full, and presented a distinguished display of fashion and beauty.

But great obstacles were in his way. He possessed none of the magic facilities of wealth, or patronage, or influential connexions. Every thing depended on his own genius—and poor genius had a hard battle to fight in those days when it chanced to be on the wrong side of power. The worst omen of all was that he was reared in a Whig nursery, and believed to be a disciple of Fox. This was fatal under the reign of Pitt, especially at a moment when the ministerial imagination was reeking with the horrors of the French Revolution. But omens, like dreams, must sometimes be read backwards. And so it happened with this student of Christ Church when he quitted the university and went up to London to study the law at Lincoln's Inn.

III.

LONDON AT THE CLOSE OF THE EIGHTEENTH CENTURY. THE CONVERT.

LONDON, towards the close of the last century, was a perilous place for a young man just come from the seclusion of the university, and settling himself down to read law in some dusky chambers in Lincoln's Inn, with the echoes of a living world of strange and suggestive excitement ringing in his ears. It was no longer the London to which the young imagination used to look forward as to a great moving panorama in the holidays. The panorama was there, but its jubilant aspect had given way to gloom and dismay. One predominant idea filled every man's mind; groups were to be seen in the streets exchanging hurried words, and hastily dispersing; the revels of the taverns had subsided into whispering coteries, arguing the signs of the times with "bated breath;"*

* The fear of spies was universal, and led to the abandonment of many an agreeable association which had nothing whatever to do with politics. An instance of this kind occurred in Liverpool. A few gentlemen had been in the habit of meeting once a fortnight at each others houses, and devoting the hour before supper to the reading of papers, or the discussion of literary questions. Amongst the members of this little party, which consisted of about a dozen persons, were Mr. Roscoe, Dr. Currie (the author of the "Life of Burns"), Professor Smyth, the Rev. W. Shepherd, and Dr. Rutter. "But even this peaceful and unoffending company," says Mr. Roscoe's biographer, "was not exempt from the violence of party feeling. Upon the appearance of Mr. Pitt's

even the playhouses were unsafe for audiences and actors, and opened their doors under surveillance.* Startling things were happening in the world: the American war —the French Revolution—the vibration of the distant earthquake agitating the length and breadth of England —open defiance in Scotland—Tooke and Hardy in the Old Bailey—Muir and Palmer in the hulks—and Pitt, to carry off the discontents, embarking in a war of principles with France. The whole country was in a state of terror, and London was the focus of the commotion.

The town was full of clubs, political juntas, and debating societies. The club was a special product of the age. With something of the easy gossiping characteristics of Will's and Button's, and something of the wit of the Mermaid, "so nimble and so full of subtle flame," the

proclamation against seditious meetings, and the consequent odium in which all who professed liberal principles were involved, the Literary Society found their meetings viewed with such jealousy and suspicion, that it was thought proper, for the time, to discontinue them, nor were they afterwards resumed. Mr. Roscoe, writing to Lord Lansdowne on the subject, says: "Under the present system every man is called on to be a spy upon his brother," and adds, "that the object of their meetings was purely literary, yet that he had good reason to believe that they were pointed out to government by the collector of the customs."— "Life of Roscoe," i., 128. Such was the prevailing frenzy that the liberal newspapers were overawed by threats, and compelled to disavow their principles; and although there were at that time four weekly papers published in the town of Liverpool, there was not one that would have dared to admit a contradiction of the gross calumnies which were daily circulated against the Reformers.

* One example will suffice to show the fright of the managers. A worthy gentleman who glorified himself upon an innocent devotion to the practice of archery, being struck with an ardent desire to exhibit the art worthily upon the stage, wrote an opera called "Helvetic Liberty; or, the Lass of the Lakes," founded on the dramatic story of William Tell. "I presented my opera to the theatre," says the honest Kentish bowman, "but in that paradise I found politics to be the forbidden fruit, lest the people's eyes should be opened, and they become as gods, knowing good and evil: in brief, my piece was politely returned, with an assurance *that it was too much in favour of the liberties of the people to obtain the Lord Chamberlain's licence for representation.*" A straw shows the course of the winds, and this straw was thrown up in 1792.

modern club had fiercer pleasures and a more practical bearing upon the transactions of the day. It was invented to meet certain social and political exigencies which were hourly expanding into broader development. Young men fresh from college; sprigs of aristocracy hunting up places or "sensations;" fashionable roués; and rich fools ready to be snared by the first springe, formed the chief material out of which these clubs were created. They were invaluable to the scouts of the great factions, whose activity in scouring the country for raw recruits was wonderfully assisted by having such capital head-quarters to billet them upon. When Pitt began his career, only a few years before (curiously enough, too, as a student at Lincoln's Inn), he saw the advantages to be derived from the clubs, and seized upon them with his unfailing sagacity. If he did not originate the system, he was one of the first to discover its political and parliamentary uses, and under his auspices it grew to maturity. There was scarcely a man of figure about town, who was not drawn into one or more of them: some for sheer publicity, and the *ton* of the thing; others, the mushrooms, to get brevet rank in general company; and not a few to be duped, cleaned out, and laughed at.*

* The choicest club in Pitt's younger days was Goosetree's, so called after the man who kept the house, since known as the Shakspeare Gallery. It was limited to twenty-five members, and included amongst them Pitt, Pratt, G. Cavendish, Bankes, Windham, and Wilberforce. White's, Brooke's, Boodle's, the Turk's Head, and Miles and Evans' were also leading clubs. Tickell, Sheridan's brother-in-law, put some of the celebrities, who made themselves conspicuous in these places, into sparkling couplets, which still survive amongst the *jeux-d'esprit* of the day. Gibbon rapping his box, " good-natured Devon," Beauclerc—
  " Oft shall Fitzpatrick's wit, and Stanhope's ease,
  And Burgoyne's manly sense, unite to please."
Lord Stanhope was the marked man of the Upper House, as president of the " Revolution Society"—the uncle of Pitt, the father of Lady Hester, the famous "Citizen" Stanhope, who carried his republicanism so far as to obliterate his arms from his plate and carriages; Fitzpatrick, no less prominent in the Commons, was still more distinguished in private by the laxity of his life and the versatility of his talents;

The apparent business of the clubs was to idle in the windows and yawn all day, sup at midnight, and drink and gamble late into the morning. Wilberforce, in spite of his conscience and his diary, was caught the moment he came to town, and whisked into the vortex, although he fought manfully against the cards and the champagne. The temptations were too subtle even for him, and he fell on the outside, just where they wanted him. The prodigal genius that flung about its enchantments so adroitly, lured him on insensibly, until at last he grew into such sworn brotherhood with Pitt, that he was never able to perform his public duty, when it took an adverse direction to the "heaven-born minister," without an apology from his private feelings. It was quite pitiable to see how this amiable struggle with an anti-political friendship, prostrated his powers and weakened his utility. He could not even move an amendment upon the war, against which his most solemn convictions revolted, without some sort of personal deprecation, which utterly deprived him and his appeal of all weight and influence.

It would be a great mistake to suppose that the clubs were simply places for libertine intrigues, where wits and debauchées did nothing but discuss dice, women, and horses, and get drunk over-night. There was an undercurrent which commanded the depths of these licentious

while accomplished Burgoyne enjoyed a quieter reputation from the flowing "gentility" of his writings. But these were not the only stars in Tickell's airy verses. Brookes himself came in for a snatch of the immortality, and appears to have deserved it as well as he could—the "liberal Brookes,"

"Who, nursed in clubs, disdains a vulgar trade,
Exults to trust, and blushes to be paid."

There was, unluckily, too much truth in this disreputable jest. A scurrilous work, called the "Jockey Club," says that Lord John Townshend (to whom it falsely attributes these verses) lived for a long time at Brookes's expense, and never paid him. However we may be disinclined to credit this assertion, there is no doubt that large balances were due to Brookes at his death.

orgies, and imperceptibly swayed their courses. While the surface presented all the dissolute attractions of fashionable dissipation, the real purpose beneath was to strengthen and extend the resources of party, to catch hesitating votes, to impound stray cattle like Wilberforce; to hatch cabals, and premeditate political *imbroglios*, to hold extra-cabinet councils, and to plan the incidents and cast the parts of the great parliamentary drama.

No means were left untried, in public or private, to accomplish the same purposes. The club was a brilliant decoy, and discharged its functions with admirable effect. But there were remoter ends to be served, and other " sweet voices" to be won, which required spells of a different kind.

The influence of the clubs upon private society was not equal to their power of mischief. Their disorderly habits placed them in an equivocal position, and nothing escaped from them into the circles, but occasional flashes of their symposia, transmitted through such conductors as Hare and Jekyll. It was necessary to employ more direct tactics in the management of the led lords and simpering toadies, who, picking up in London the latest political fashions, returned, at the close of the season, to announce them authoritatively in the country. These were the tactics in which the Whigs excelled.

The Prince of Wales was avowedly at the head of the opposition. He not only possessed the reputation of being the " first gentleman of the age," but was resolved to maintain it, in its princely sense at least, by the super-royal splendour of his expenditure. It was nothing to the purpose that the people were the munificent sufferers who paid for these luxuries. In 1787, parliament had discharged His Royal Highness's debts (nearly 200,000*l.*), on a full assurance from His Royal Highness, guaranteed in a royal message by His Majesty, that he would incur no more; but a very few years elapsed before the prince came down to the House again, and denied point-blank that he had ever promised to live within his income, giving at the same time the best possible proof of his determination not to do so, by requesting the Commons to pay off the liabilities he had incurred in the interim, amounting to no less than 600,000*l*. To do him bare justice, there never was a prince of the blood who entertained so large a contempt for the integrity of a promise of any sort, or who had so grand a way of over-running the constable. The festivities of Carlton House were famous all over Europe. The taste displayed at the prince's parties was worthy of their Oriental magnificence; for in the midst of the grossest depravities, he managed to surround himself with intellect and social talent of the highest order, and to secure for his table every foreigner of celebrity who visited the country. By such means, he sustained his political position, and communicated a tone to society that had an important influence upon those detached masses of floating opinion, which, although they never become resolved into a compact body, exercise a species of irregular power over the public mind. The prestige of the prince's name was formidable in the fashionable world. Even his vices were set off with such brilliancy and grace of style, as to render them attractive: moral repugnance was fascinated into admiration, and his showy and illusive popularity prospered upon his very delinquencies.

We suppose it is a providential dispensation in royal families, as it is sheer vulgar cunning in other families, which makes the son espouse contrary opinions to the father. Certain it is, that whenever England has been favoured with a Prince of Wales, she has always found him heart and hand with the popular party—until he was called to the throne, when he left his principles to the next heir, to play the same game over again. By this ingenious political hedging, royalty makes so safe a book, that it can trim the odds to meet any human contingency.* Such were the balanced politics of St. James's Palace and Carlton House. The prince bestowed himself upon the Whigs. Every triumph they achieved in the senate or on the hustings, was followed by an ovation in Pall-Mall; and the jubilee was taken up in Devonshire House and Lower Grosvenor Street, and throughout the principal houses of the aristocracy, until it went the whole round. These assemblies presented irresistible charms to the younger branches of the nobility, and unclaimed country gentlemen, through whose unconscious agency the opposition wisely and untiringly laboured to augment and consolidate their strength. Nor did they rely solely upon the admitted supremacy of their intellectual resources—the wit of Selwyn and Sheridan—the inexhaustible pleasantry of Hare—the universality of St. Leger, embalmed in the prince's joke, that he was " open to all *parties*, and influenced by none," alluding to his indiscriminate enjoyment of the hospitalities of both sides—the irony of

* It is worthy of note that the very first time the Prince of Wales (afterwards George IV.) spoke in the House of Lords, he announced himself as a friend of the people, and solemnly declared that he would never abandon them! This was in 1783. " I was educated in the principle," exclaimed his Royal Highness, " and I shall ever preserve it, of a reverence for the constitutional liberties of the people, and as on those liberties the happiness of the people depend, I am determined, as far as my interest can have any force, to support them. .... I exist by the love, the friendship, and the benevolence of the people, and them I never will forsake as long as I live." Let history draw the moral.

Curran—the racy eloquence of Erskine—or the versatility of Fox, more wonderful than all the rest. They brought still more captivating sorceries into play—an artillery of eyes, a thousand times more effective and convincing than all the logic of parliament or the seductions of place, if they had it to bestow. The Duchess of Devonshire, renowned for her charms and her wit, and the beautiful Mrs. (afterwards Lady) Crewe, immortalised in the poetical gallantries of Fox and Sheridan, were the enchantresses who presided over these bewitching scenes. This ascendancy in the literary and political circles is attested by many memorable incidents, and it was preserved by a zeal, activity, and address, which can scarcely be appreciated in these days of comparative quietude. They lived in the storm and daily struggle of contending factions—they took part in the agitation, and contributed largely, by the refinement and irreproachable purity of their lives, to elevate and dignify the cause to which they were devoted. They served the Whigs, not only by gathering together their scattered forces, and inspiring them with union and confidence, but by drawing in new and available talent wherever it appeared. To the influence of the Duchess of Devonshire is attributed the accession of Lord Grey, who had just arrived at his majority, and was irresolute which side to take, but inclined to the ministry, when her grace determined his doubts, and won him over to Fox and his party. The prize was a jewel of price! He was only twenty-two when he entered the Commons, and his first speech—the initiative step of a long and distinguished career of statesmanship—is still the greatest first speech upon record. By such signal instances of well-directed social power, the Duchess of Devonshire acquired that devotion from her contemporaries, so happily expressed in Fox's charade;* but her domestic character displayed traits of tenderness, which in any circumstances must have commanded their admiration.†

Mrs. Crewe was the reigning toast of the Whigs, a distinction gracefully conferred upon her by the prince himself; and whenever the banquet reached its culminating point of complimentary effervescence, the homage,

"To buff and blue,
And Mrs. Crewe,"

was never forgotten.‡ She was the most beautiful wo-

---

* The occasion is well known. The duchess asked Fox to write a charade. He requested to be supplied with a subject, when she suggested *herself*. The impromptu charade was written in pencil on the back of a letter.
"My first is myself in a very short word,
My second's a play-thing,
And *you* are my third." (*Idol.*)

† She was the first lady of rank in England who nursed her own children. When Roscoe translated the "Balia" of Luigi Tansillo, he requested permission to introduce her name into the poem in reference to that circumstance, as the poet himself had introduced those of the noble ladies of his own country—
"Le Colonne, le Ursine, le Gonsaghe;"
and she consented without hesitation, in the desire of extending the practice by the force of her salutary example.

‡ The origin of the toast was an entertainment in celebration of Fox's return for Westminster in 1784. The prince had given a sumptuous fête at Carlton House in the morning which was followed up on the same night by an assembly at Mrs. Crewe's, in Lower Grosvenor-street. Every person present was dressed in the colours of the party, buff and blue (from whence the "Edinburgh Review" subsequently adopted its livery), and after supper his Royal Highness concluded a speech, sparkling with gallantry, by proposing, amidst rapturous acclamation:
"Buff and blue,
And Mrs. Crewe."
To which the lady merrily replied:
"Buff and blue,
And all of you."
The anecdote is preserved by Wraxall. "Posthumous Memoirs," i., 17. The dress was a blue coat, orange collar, and buttons with "King and Constitution" upon them. This was the costume Horne Tooke, Hardy, and the reformers, used to wear, for the wearing of which, or for what it implied, they were indicted as traitors only ten years afterwards.

man of her time,* possessed great conversational vivacity, and frequently made it tell with the liveliest effect upon the vulnerable points of Toryism. " So Pitt means to come in," she exclaimed to Wilberforce, when Lord Temple resigned in 1783 ; " well, he may do what he likes during the holidays, but it will be a mince-pie administration, depend upon it." And the *mince-pie administration* immediately became the bye-word of the clubs.

The Duchess of Portland—doomed not very long afterwards, unfortunately, to rat with her husband—took a conspicuous part in these dazzling entertainments ; which also derived an irresistible charm from the musical talents of Mrs. Sheridan; " the elegance of whose beauty," says Madame d'Arblay, " is unequalled by any I ever saw, except Mrs. Crewe."† The Tories spared no outlay or artifice to subvert the popularity of their rivals. They

* Madame D'Arblay visited her at Hampstead in 1792, when she had passed her zenith, and was still perfectly lovely. " The room was dark, and she had a veil to her bonnet, half down, and with this aid she looked still in a full blaze of beauty. I was wholly astonished. Her bloom, perfectly natural, is as high as that of Augusta Lock when in her best looks, and the form of her face is so exquisitely perfect that my eye never met with it without fresh admiration. She is certainly, in my eyes, the most completely a beauty of any woman I ever saw. I know not, even now, any female in her first youth who could bear the comparison. *She uglifies every thing near her.*"—" Diary," v. 313.

This remarkable woman was the only daughter of Fulke Greville, Esq., for some time British Minister at the Court of Munich. She was married, in 1766, to Mr. Crewe, who was raised to the peerage by Fox, in 1806. After a life spent in the most brilliant society, through which she moved to the end without a whisper of scandal, she died at Liverpool at an advanced age in the winter of 1818, and was interred in the family vault at Barthomley, near Crewe Hall, county of Chester.

† There was considerable hesitation at first in the introduction of Mrs. Sheridan into fashionable society, on account of her previous professional associations. When the Duchess of Devonshire first met her, she felt some scruples about asking her to Devonshire House ; but Sheridan's growing celebrity soon overthrew all conventional difficulties. It was no small compensation in kind afterwards, that the talents which originally stood in the way of her reception, became one of the leading attractions in those very circles from which they had threatened to exclude her. Mrs. Sheridan's singing was a principal feature in the evening wherever she went.

threw open their saloons with a publicity which startled the habitual exclusiveness of the old aristocracy; and, seeing that office itself had paled its attractions before the brighter lures of wit and beauty, they set up the Duchess of Gordon—a bold masculine woman—and the pert Lady Salisbury, as opponents to the Duchess of Devonshire and Mrs. Crewe. But it was a conspicuous failure. The fashion had set in with the prince and his friends, who carried every thing before them; and who possessed an overwhelming advantage in being enabled by the popular tone of their politics to cultivate a certain freedom of intercourse, which the hereditary reserve of the opposite party prohibited.

While the upper classes were thus engaged, the body of the people was convulsed by a fiercer movement, down to the very dregs of the population. The alehouse and the workshops were crowded by as anxious faces as the ball-room or the antechamber, but with a darker and more earnest meaning in them. That which was but the silken dalliance of party to the one, was a life and death struggle to the other. A new sense of public wrongs had gone forth, and was no longer to be baffled by perfidious or ignorant legislation. The people were unrepresented in parliament: an old grievance, as common as air in the mouths of men, but now strangely, for the first time, laid open in its naked injustice to the meanest apprehension. The remedy was clear enough; but the way to it was full of danger. The path was beset at every turn by monsters and dragons of evil power, and he who should undertake the desperate adventure, must be armed by the good genius of heroic patience, or add another victim to those who had before essayed the enterprise in vain. The fear was that in some sudden access of popular fury, the great opportunity would be lost.

The press teemed with warnings and appeals. The booksellers' counters groaned under the weight of new views of the state of the representation, theories of reform, and philosophical treatises on the constitution. Every day brought forth its bundle of pamphlets and broad sheets. Every man who had any thing to say, or nothing to say, put it into print. The shops of Ridgway and Debrett were crowded every morning by politicians on tip-toe for the last rumour.* And in the midst of this shoal of minor speculators, suddenly appeared a great leviathan in the shape of Godwin's " Political Justice." The sensation excited by this book was unparalleled. At any other period it might have been read by a few sublime dreamers like himself, and put away on the topmost shelves of the library, with Hobbes, and Shaftesbury, and Brown, and others possessed of a like gorgeous thinking faculty; but it came out at a moment when the whole nation was intent upon that one idea which the book undertook to develop, and it was seized upon with universal avidity. The doctrines it enunciated alternately perplexed, delighted, and terrified its readers.† The enthusiasm it produced might have resolved itself into some awkward exhibition of popular absurdity, were the English as explosive as the French; but after a temporary blaze it went out into total darkness. People began to see that it was transcendental and impracticable, and that it made demands upon human perfectibility, which in no age of

---

* Debrett's was the principal rendezvous. Holcroft, who kept a diary, begins his entries generally by a regular call at Debrett's, to hear the gossip of the day.

† Fox received the work from his bookseller, ran through half a dozen pages in the middle (his custom with modern publications), did not like it, and sent it back.

the world, either of action or repose, could find adequate response. Yet it had its effect at the time, became a text book with thousands, and divided with Paine the glory of making a profound impression upon those who least understood the mysteries of abstract philosophy.*

The formation of societies for the attainment of parliamentary reform, was the natural consequence of all this uneasiness—the rational and legal way of looking for redress, to which the people were accustomed. The London Corresponding Society set about doing that through its affiliated branches, which the Anti-Corn-law League is now doing with impunity—the collection of information throughout the country bearing directly upon its avowed object. Other societies were got up under other names, the most conspicuous of which were the Constitutional Society, and the Society of the Friends of the People, all having the one distinct ultimate purpose of acting upon the legislature, through the legitimate channels of public opinion. Every one of these societies declared themselves and their purpose openly. But the ministry insisted that parliamentary reform was only a mask for the secret design of destroying the British Constitution; and Mr. Windham, of all men, went so far as to express his astonishment

---

* Holcroft wrote a notice of the "Political Justice" in the "Monthly Review;" a sneaking, shuffling analysis, in which he begged the question between his hire and his conscience to oblige Griffiths, who was afraid to commit the review to extreme opinions. The "Monthly Review" was on the side of reform, but Griffiths was such a contemptible trader that, whenever he found the *commonplace* character of the work endangered, as Hazlitt says, he shifted about, and escaped through some shabby recantation. But Godwin had Roman stuff in him, and bore the cowardice of the reviewers with as much indifference as their abuse. The world looked for a more majestic issue to all that grave and solid magnanimity. No man ever excited so much attention as Godwin, and lived to excite so little. He not only outlived his fame, but suddenly fell into oblivion. For many of the latter years of his life, nobody knew, or ever thought to ask, whether he was dead or alive—he who once could not walk the streets without being gazed at as a wonder!

in the House of Commons, that any body could be found so credulous as to suppose any thing else. The poor constitution—how often it has been destroyed! What a cat's life, with a lease of cats' lives renewable for ever, this same constitution must have.

But this was the way reform had always been evaded, —treated as a plausible means to some monstrous end, and stifled. Mr. Pitt said, " It is not Reform they want, but revolution;" and under this wily pretence, the right of the people to be heard, for good or evil, was annihilated. It never occurred to him to ask, " Is there any reason in this thing for which they are clamouring north, east, west, and south, and which they call Reform? Before I punish them for asking for one thing and meaning another, let me demonstrate to the world that the thing they ask for has no foundation in justice or necessity." The meetings that were taking place all over the country, and the bold language of the speakers, favoured this hypocrisy. " This is what they mean," exclaimed the minister, " to re-act the sanguinary atrocities of the French Revolution, to murder the king, and establish a republic;" and so he suspended the Habeas Corpus Act. Resolved not to be betrayed into the snare, they lay a petition before the legislature, explaining what it is they do mean; but he will not hear them. Their petition is dismissed with contumely. When they complain and agitate out of doors, it is sedition; when they come to parliament, according to the usages of the constitution, the door is shut in their teeth.

Pitt's conduct throughout this crisis was insincere. It was worse—it had none of that high courage, in which, on other occasions, he was not wanting. Had he relied on the country, he might have spared us the war and the debt, and all the political immorality through which both were contracted. As it was, he displayed neither the experience nor the heroism of a statesman. The argument that the people made use of Reform as a pretext, were it true, was the best possible argument for meeting them boldly on the ground they had themselves chosen. But it was false; and he showed that he knew it was false, by never bringing it to the test of inquiry. Had it been true, nothing could have been easier than to have sifted the pretended grievance, and shown that it was hollow, and there was an end; for no popular agitation can long be sustained upon a bubble. Fire cannot burn without fuel. The discontents of a people must be fed by wrongs, or no human machinations can keep them alive.

Had there been any real danger of a revolution, the measures of the government would have assuredly brought it to a head. But the English are not revolutionary, and least of all for a theoretical end. Could they ever be induced to leave their ploughs and shuttles, and get up an insurrection on a respectable scale, it would be for food. The old generals who served in the continental wars knew well what a belligerent provocation an empty stomach used to be to the English soldier.

Pitt, however, insisted that there was a conspiracy hatching against the institutions of the country, and men were arrested in their houses without bail or mainprize, under the authority of the minister, who was too secure in his majorities, not to be quite at his ease about an act of indemnity. The constitution itself was violated to protect it against outrage; an operation curiously described by the Attorney-General, as " a temporary sacrifice of a small portion of our liberties, for the permanent preservation of the whole,"* like cutting off a man's nose to preserve his profile.

The mere fact that men who asked nothing more than a reform in parliament, a demand which had Mr. Pitt's zealous support in former days, should now be arraigned by Mr. Pitt himself as traitors designing to " compass the king's death," ought to have exposed the hypocrisy. But the French Revolution threw its lurid shadows over men's minds, and they took in all impressions through that distorting medium.

The effect produced by the Revolution in the first instance, before it was degraded by hideous criminalities, was that of almost universal sympathy. It was hailed with enthusiasm in England. Some of the societies carried their admiration so far, as to congratulate the Convention on its success, and the early struggles against a tyranny which had brought discredit upon the monarchical principle all over Europe, was regarded with secret interest even by the most steadfast Church-and-State Tories. The event in fact was hailed by both parties as an effort towards the establishment of good government, neither of them anticipating the horrors of its progress.

The mass of the reading, writing, and speech-making public thought of nothing else, and during the first stages of the Revolution, the valour and devotion of the republicans furnished the grand theme of admiration every-

---

* The exact words as reported in the published trial of Thomas Hardy. "This act," said the learned gentleman (afterwards Lord Eldon), "was no infringement on British liberty. It had frequently been adopted on former emergencies. It was, and ought only to be considered, as a temporary sacrifice of a small portion of our liberties for the permanent preservation of the whole." The sacrifice of a portion of our liberties was no infringement of our liberty, because it had frequently been adopted before. By the same rule you might revive the Star Chamber.

where, in all companies, especially in the numerous debating societies, which at this period were the vents and safety-valves of opinion. The young and unoccupied intellect of the inns of court found congenial employment in these stormy discussions, and here some apprentice politicians, who afterwards won a wider celebrity, first tested their powers, and plumed their wings for more ambitious flights.*

Amongst them was a student of pale and thoughtful aspect, who brought to the nightly contests unusual fluency and grace of elocution. He, too, along with the rest, had been inspired by the heroic spectacle, had pondered upon its causes, and exulted over its prospects. His head was full of constitutions; for his studies lay amongst the elementary writers, rather than the special pleaders and form-mongers of the law. And after a morning of close reading and severe reflection, he would wend his way in the evening to one of these debating-rooms, and taking up his place unobserved, watch the vicissitudes of the discussion, noting well its effect upon the miscellaneous listeners; then, seizing upon a moment when the argument failed from lack of resources, or ran into sophistry or exaggeration, he would present himself to the meeting. A figure slight, but of elegant proportions; a face poetical in repose, but fluctuating in its expression with every fugitive emotion; a voice low, clear, and rich in modulation; and an air of perfect breeding, prepares his hearers

* In such mixed meetings, where the young speaker is brought into direct collision with a variety of character and rougher natures than his own, many of our distinguished men trained their faculties for debate. In Addison's time, a gathering of this kind was held at the Three Tuns, in Hungerford Market, and was constantly attended by the future secretary, Steele, and others. Burke made some of his earliest essays at the Robin Hood, in Wych-street; and Garrow and Dallas distinguished themselves at Coachmakers' Hall, and the Westminster Forum.

for one who possesses superior powers, and is not unconscious of them. He opens calmly—strips his topic of all extraneous matter—distributes it under separate heads—disposes of objections with a playful humour—rebukes the dangerous excesses of preceding speakers—carries his auditors through a complete syllogism—establishes the proposition with which he set out—and sits down amidst the acclamations of the little senate. Night after night witnesses similar feats; at length his name gets out; he is talked of, and speculated upon; and people begin to ask questions about the stripling who has so suddenly appeared amongst them, as if he had fallen from the sky.

But he does not confine his range to the debating societies, which he uses as schools of practice, and as places in which the nature of popular assemblies may be profitably observed. He is frequently to be found in the soirées of the Whig notabilities, where the aristocracy of his style is more at home than amongst the crowds of the forum. Here his cultivated intellect, and fastidious taste are appreciated by qualified judges; and these refined circles cry up his accomplishments as eagerly as the others have applauded his patriotism. Popularity besets him on both sides. The societies look to him as a man formed expressly for the people; and the first Lord Lansdowne (stranger still) predicts to Mr. Bentham that this stripling will one day be prime-minister of England! He is plainly on the high-road to greatness of some kind; but how it is to end, whether he is to be a martyr or a minister, is yet a leap in the dark. The crisis approaches that is to determine the doubt.

While he is revolving these auguries in his mind, and filling his solitary chamber with phantoms of civic crowns and strawberry-leaves, flitting around his head in tantalising confusion, a note is hurriedly put into his hand, with marks of secrecy and haste. It is from one of whom he has but a slight personal knowledge, but whose notoriety, if we may not venture to call it fame, is familiar to him. The purport of the note is an intimation that the writer desires a confidential interview on matters of importance, and will breakfast with him on the following morning. The abruptness of the self-invitation, the seriousness of the affair it seems to indicate, and the known character of the correspondent, excite the surprise of the law student, and he awaits his visiter with more curiosity than he chooses to betray.

A small fresh-coloured man, with intelligent eyes, an obstinate expression of face, and pressing ardour of manner, makes his appearance the next morning at breakfast. The host is collected, as a man should be who holds himself prepared for a revelation. The guest, unreserved and impatient of delay, hastens to unfold his mission. Amongst the speculators who are thrown up to the surface, in great political emergencies, there are generally some who are misled by the grandeur of their conceptions; and who, in the purity and integrity of their own hearts, cannot see the evil or the danger that lies before them. This was a man of that order. He enters into an animated description of the state of the country, traces the inquietude of the people to its source in the corruption and tyranny of the government, declares that they are resolved to endure oppression no longer, that they are already organised for action, that the auspicious time has arrived to put out their strength, and ends by the astounding announcement, that they have selected *him*—this youth who has made such a stir amongst them—as the fittest person to be placed at the head of the movement.

Miracle upon miracle! The astonishment of the youth who receives this communication may well suspend his judgment: he requires an interval to collect himself, and decide; and then, dismissing his strange visiter, shuts himself up to think. In that interval he takes a step which commits him for life. It is but a step from Lincoln's-inn to Downing-street. His faith in the people is shaken. He sees in this theory of regeneration nothing but folly and bloodshed. His reason revolts from all participation in it. And the next chamber to which we follow him, is the closet of the Minister, to whom he makes his new confession of faith, and gives in his final adherence.

Reader, the violent little man was William Godwin, the author of the "Political Justice," and the convert was George Canning.*

There are other versions of the way in which Mr. Canning was brought over to Toryism and Mr. Pitt; but none of them are so circumstantial, or have such a colour of authenticity or likelihood in them as this.† Mr. Moore, in

---

* Scott has preserved this anecdote in his diary. "Canning," he adds, "himself mentioned this to Sir W. Knighton, upon occasion of giving a place in the Charter-house, of some ten pounds a year, to Godwin's brother."—"Life of Scott, ix. p. 230." Sir W. Knighton's memoirs are silent on a circumstance which, doubtless, had never been communicated to the editor.

† The change in Mr. Canning's views from the bar to the senate is said to have been adopted on the advice of Mr. Burke. But he never sat down to the law with any intention of studying it as a profession. Respecting the more important change which took place at the same time in his position, we have the following clumsy circumstantial fabrication in a memoir of Mr. Canning, published in Paris, in 1828. "During the chancellorship of Lord Loughborough, upwards of thirty years ago, his lordship directed a gentleman, holding an official situation, to convey personally a letter to *a* Mr. Canning, of whom all which was known was, that he resided in one of the inns of court! The bearer commenced his search, and after some time, found Mr. Canning at chambers in Paper buildings, Temple. The object of the letter was to convey an offer of the post of Under-Secretary of State, and he to whom it was addressed was the late Premier." The inventor of this anecdote ought to have understood his craft better than to make the Lord Chancellor usurp the functions of the First Minister of the Crown.

his "Life of Sheridan," suggests that this alteration in his views may, probably, be accounted for by his association with Mr. Jenkinson ; or by his unwillingness to appear in the world as the pupil of such a man as Sheridan, whose irregular life had in some degree placed him under the ban of public opinion ; or by the difficulty of rising to eminence under the hopeless shadow of the Whigs. If these motives, which amount to nothing more or less than a calculation of advantages in the choice of a party, ever presented themselves to his consideration, they could scarcely have decided him, unless at the same time his opinions had undergone a total change ; and that they had undergone such a change is evident, from the fact that he had previously declined a seat in parliament, which was offered to him by the Duke of Portland, then at the head of the Whigs ; and from his refusal to join the society of the Friends of the People, although repeatedly urged to do so. If he had been determined by mere expediency, the weight of the argument was obviously in favour of that party with whom he had been all along connected— and through whose influence he might naturally have looked for an introduction to public life. His strength lay there, where he was wooed by every temptation short of office; with the certainty that whenever they came into power, his fidelity would be remembered. But the truth was, that *his genius assimilated more nearly with that of the opposite party*, and he only found it out when he was brought face to face with the necessity which decided him.

It has been stated that he confidentially consulted Mr. Sheridan on this momentous passage of his life ; and, according to one account of the transaction, Mr. Sheridan had the dishonesty to advise him to abandon his liberal notions, and devote himself to the Minister, as the only chance a poor man had of making any market of his talents. According to another account, Sheridan laughed outright; and betraying his friend's secret before a large party at supper, made a humorous appeal to Mrs. Crewe at whose house it happened, to decide the important dilemma of a young man who did not know upon which side he ought to bestow his lustre. Both these stories are mere fabrications, but the latter comes nearer to Sheridan, and lies more like truth than the former ; for into whatever social transgressions his high animal spirits may have hurried him, his political integrity was above suspicion. Had poor Sheridan traded upon his extraordinary powers, he would not have been found so often struggling on the floor of the House of Commons, against overwhelming majorities; augmented occasionally by deserters from those ranks, which, in the worst of times, he never forsook.

The supposed connexion with the Sheridans, so often alluded to, and to which all such idle gossip may be traced, rests upon no better foundation. Sheridan was intimate with Mr. Stratford Canning's family, and was constantly in the habit of meeting Mr. George Canning in the circles which, at this period, they both frequented; but no strictly private intercourse was ever kept up between them.*

* A report appears to have obtained currency that Sheridan was instrumental in some way to Canning's education ; and Wilberforce, who merely echoed what he had heard, alludes to it with ludicrous commiseration. "Poor fellow," says Wilberforce, "he had neither father nor mother to train him up. He was brought up, I believe, partly with Sheridan. *I always wondered he was so pure.*"—"Life," iv. 370. One can forgive the pity for the sake of this tribute to the purity of Canning's life :—for assuredly it was no easy matter to come up to Wilberforce's notions of purity. But the report was wholly unfounded. Sheridan contributed nothing to Canning's education ; and had nothing to do with it beyond the interest which he may have taken in the early promise of a youth whom he often met at his friend's house. The

Mr. Therry assigns a somewhat different origin to the interview with Mr. Pitt.* He says that the celebrity of Mr. Canning's talents reached the minister, who communicated through a private channel his desire to see him; a desire with which Mr. Canning, of course, very readily complied. That Mr. Pitt, upon their meeting, said that he had heard of Mr. Canning's reputation, and that if he concurred in the policy of the government, arrangements would be made to bring him into parliament; and that after a full explanation on both sides, Mr. Canning accepted the offer.† There can be no doubt that Mr. Pitt sent for Mr. Canning, for it is extremely improallusions to the name of Canning, in Moore's "Life of Sheridan," have probably led to some mistake as to the intercourse of the families. Thus, in 1784, Mrs. Sheridan in a letter from Putney, speaks of Mr. Canning having been with her; but as George Canning was then a schoolboy at Eton, the reference is clearly to his uncle. In 1792, also, Sheridan is said to have been on a visit somewhere in the country with Mrs. Canning and her family; but this must have been the widow of Mr. Stratford Canning, as George Canning's mother had changed her name long before. As to any pecuniary obligations between them, the only one that ever took place was shortly after Canning's return from Lisbon, when Sheridan, ill in bed, wrote to him to the House of Commons to ask the loan of £100; a request which was immediately complied with.

* " The Speeches of the Right Honourable George Canning," i. 17.

† Lady Hester Stanhope, if her memory may be credited (which is doubtful), appears to have been present at this interview; and to have taken an aversion to Mr. Canning, founded upon a peculiar theory of personal appearance, by which she was always guided in her likings and dislikings. "The first time he was introduced to Mr. Pitt," she tells us, "a great deal of prosing had been made beforehand of his talents, and when he was gone, Mr. Pitt asked me what I thought of him. I said I did not like him; his forehead was bad, his eyebrows were bad, he was ill-made about the hips; but his teeth were evenly set, although he rarely showed them. I did not like his conversation. Mr. C. heard of this, and some time after, when upon a more familiar footing with me, said, 'So, Lady Hester, you don't like me?' 'No,' said I; 'they told me you were handsome, and I don't think so.'"—" Memoirs of Lady Hester Stanhope," i. 311. A good " woman's reason" for an invincible personal antipathy. Mr. Pitt told her that she must like him. And she said, " If I must, I must," but she never did. Lady Hester had the Pitt blood at perpetual fever heat. She sometimes hated people without a reason, sometimes against reason, and always hated them the more when the cause was slight. She hated them most when there was no cause at all.

bable that Mr. Canning would have gone to Mr. Pitt without knowing beforehand how he was likely to be received. But it is still more improbable that Mr. Pitt would have sent for Mr. Canning without being perfectly secure of the result. How such confidences are brought about it is unnecessary, as it would be quite fruitless, to inquire. The invisible agency is always tenaciously guarded by the honour of both parties, and the public are interested only in the result. Certain it is, that when Mr. Pitt and Mr. Canning entered into this arrangement, their friends supposed them to be strangers to each other; for, at a dinner which was given at Addiscombe House, by Lord Liverpool, for the express purpose of bringing them together, it was discovered, greatly to the amazement of the whole party, that they were already well acquainted.

That Mr. Canning passed over, at once, from the one party to the other, cannot be denied. Nor was he alone in this transition; for many others, of greater weight in the country, and who had committed themselves deeply to the party they relinquished, passed over at the same time, from undisguised apprehensions at the progress of revolutionary principles. But so far from having been " ravished from the opposition for his talents," as Peter Pindar said, he joined the Tories from deliberate conviction. Some writers have been at great pains to prove that the French Revolution, which, according to Mr. Burke's sophism, was not to be tried by any known principles, had already disturbed his opinions by its eccentric terrors, before he became acquainted with Mr. Pitt. Explanations of this sort look very like apologies, and there never was less need of one than in this instance. The adoption of Tory principles, when such events were pressing him to a decision, was the only honest and conscientious conclusion at which

Mr. Canning could have arrived. It was thoroughly consistent with the character of his mind, which was essentially *prudential*. His genius might have been generally disposed to take the imaginative side of a question; but his understanding, stronger than his genius, invariably took the English side, whichever that happened to be. His theory was liberty, which he inspired like poetical air from the heights of Parnassus; but his practice was the constitution. The French Revolution was not a matter of classical sympathy with him, but of plain reason. He began to look upon it, and upon its growing power over the credulity of his countrymen, through the eyes of his English judgment; and, once he had fixed it there, his decision was clear and inevitable.

Besides, it may be fairly doubted whether we have any right to raise an argument upon the opinions Mr. Canning entertained before this time, still less to describe any change in them as a desertion of his party. He was not bound by any overt act to any party. That he was claimed in the House of Commons by the Whigs, before he appeared there to answer for himself, is evidence of the importance attached to his opinions, not of any obligation on his part. He had not yet begun public life: his political responsibilities were yet to be incurred. A line must be drawn somewhere, to limit the right of inquiry into the fluctuations of a man's opinions; and it cannot be placed anywhere with such obvious propriety, as at that point of time when he first avowed them.

We must not confound changes of this kind with the tergiversations which occur later in life, in the midst of suspicious circumstances, after pledges have been ratified, and connexions formed, and acts done, which tie men up with a party, and which cannot be renounced without treachery and disgrace. Let us take an illustration from one of Mr. Canning's immediate contemporaries.

Amongst the most furious supporters of the Society of United Irishmen, which grew out of the discontents of 1792, was a young nobleman belonging to a rich and powerful family in the North, who had given a remarkable proof of his patriotism only the year before by the expenditure of no less than 30,000*l.* on a contested election. If he were not actually a member of that formidable body (which there is much reason to believe he was) he at least rendered himself notorious by his open advocacy of its principles. Nothing was too desperate for the ardour of his nationality. He was the intimate friend of the Sheares, who were hanged in the rebellion, and was himself so deeply implicated in the movements which preceded that catastrophe, that he was supposed to be quite ready at any convenient opportunity to "cut the painter." All this time he was in the Irish Parliament; but Mr. Pitt, discerning his uses, drew him over to England, and in 1795 he took his seat, for the first time, in the English House of Commons. And now it was that he performed the most wonderful evolution—the cleanest psychological summersault—ever witnessed in the legislative gymnasium. The firebrand of the Irish opposition seconds the English address—the fomenter of the rebellion becomes the avenger of the law—the suspected abettor of separation becomes the agent of the Union. All of a sudden, to borrow an expressive image of his own, this political *Scapin* turned his back upon himself. He not only abandoned the party upon whose shoulders he had clambered into power, and which was called into existence to vindicate the liberties of the country, but he handed over the country itself, bound neck and crop, to the

British minister. He was not satisfied with breaking the vow, but he must complete the sacrilege by breaking the altar too.

Lord Castlereagh and Mr. Canning were about the same age, and entered public life about the same time. The one commanded a county, with which he bribed the minister; and, after having identified himself for four years with a party whose excesses he encouraged, took office and apostatised. The other belonged to no party, until he went into parliament; he then avowed his principles, and maintained them, through good and evil, to the end of his life.

IV.

FIRST START IN PARLIAMENT. THE WAR. SUSPENSION OF THE HABEAS CORPUS ACT. THE UNDER-SECRETARYSHIP.

Mr. Pitt lost no time in availing himself of the talents of his new adherent. A borough was placed at his disposal by the obliging zeal of Sir Richard Worsley, who retired for the purpose ; and, in the session of 1793, Mr. Canning took his seat in the House of Commons, for Newport, in the Isle of Wight.

Never did an administration stand so much in need of young blood. Nearly the whole weight of the debates in the Lower House fell upon Mr. Pitt. He had nobody to help him but Dundas. Rose, punctual and prosy, was little better than a stop-gap ; and good old Lord Liverpool was fast sinking into a Downing-street Polonius.*

---

* Mr. Pitt, at one time, contemplated a new order of merit, and requested the opinion of the ministers upon the colour of the ribbon. Lord Liverpool prepared his with considerable care, and came by appointment to show it. " You see," said he, with much self-complacency, " I have endeavoured to combine such colours as will flatter the national vanity : red for the English flag, blue for liberty, and white for purity of motive." Lady Hester Stanhope, who was present, burst out into a fit of laughter, and, to his infinite mortification, showed him that it was the exact pattern of the tri-coloured flag. His lordship had quite overlooked that. " What am I to do with it?" said he ; " I have ordered five hundred yards." " Tie up your breeches with them," replied Lady Hester, " for you know you have always such a load of papers in your pockets, that I quite fear some day to see them all tumble out." " This

The new Whig recruits rendered very inefficient and equivocal aid, where aid was most wanted; and, with the exception of Windham, who was reconciled to an inferior office by a seat in the cabinet, none of them had the slightest chance in confronting the able and indignant opposition. Even Windham, under any circumstances, must have felt himself placed at an enormous disadvantage in his new position—a position in which candour was difficult, and in which all useful progress as a public man was vexatiously impeded by the eternal necessity of explaining, qualifying, and protesting; but pitted against such overwhelming odds as Fox, Sheridan, and Erskine, with their troop of interrogatory followers, who were perpetually pressing the most disconcerting questions, his situation was not only onerous and embarrassing, but frequently humiliating and hopeless. But, worse than this, and apart from personal perplexities, the coalition itself was unpopular, as all coalitions must be; for, let the expediency or justification be what it may in reference to points of agreement, it is impossible to persuade the people that such unions can ever be effected without a compromise of principle on points of difference. And this coalition was particularly unfortunate in one respect, that it placed in a position of apparent, if not real, antagonism to popular principles, men known to be lovers of constitutional liberty, whose authority thus came to be cited for the sanction of abuses which they never could have deliberately approved. The Whig members of the coalition were so engrossed in the contemplation of what they regarded as the paramount

was his way," adds Lady Hester; "he used to ram his hands into his pockets, first on one side and then on the other, searching for some paper, just as if he was groping for an eel at the bottom of a pond."— "Memoirs of Lady Hester Stanhope," i., 217-18.

danger, that they overlooked every other; and, in the desire to prevent the pre-eminent evil of anarchy, they threw open the door to a series of minor evils scarcely less fatal to the liberties of the people. Scared at the prospect of a revolution, they took refuge in a system of ministerial despotism. Had they contented themselves by frankly giving their support to the minister on the imminent matters on which they differed from their former colleagues, reserving to themselves the right of exercising an independent judgment on all other points, they might have effected their main object without risk or opprobrium; but the acceptance of office and honours, by binding them to the whole future course of a party whose general policy they had hitherto uniformly resisted, exposed them not only to open distrust, but to a loathing suspicion of their motives. Sheridan denounced the coalition as a piece of wholesale corruption. His hits against the leaders told with prodigious effect upon the House. " 'I will fight for nobility,' says the viscount; 'but my zeal would be much greater if I were made an earl.' 'Rouse all the marquis within me,' exclaims the earl, 'and the peerage never turned forth a more undaunted champion.' 'Stain my green ribbon blue,' cries out the illustrious knight, 'and the fountain of honour will have a fast and faithful servant.'"

But Pitt cared little for the ridicule of Sheridan, which he always affected to treat with the most dignified contempt. He was too much impressed with the urgent necessity of drawing in all the assistance he could get, upon any terms, to be turned aside from his purpose by derision or invective. He was constantly on the look out for fresh accessions, from whatever quarter they could be procured; and no manager of a metropolitan theatre ever watched the dawning talent of the provincial boards with more anxiety than Mr. Pitt noted the rising men of his day. Foremost amongst these were Jenkinson and Canning, whom he had already secured, and Lord Castlereagh and Huskisson, who were brought in soon afterwards. They were all of the same standing,* and promised to become valuable auxiliaries in different ways. Jenkinson, without a ray of eloquence, was safe and respectable. Huskisson had a great practical capacity; and Castlereagh, although he was always blundering, and never could draw up an official paper which Mr. Pitt did not find it necessary to alter, was ready and expert at a parliamentary altercation. Canning was the greatest acquisition of all; the variety of his powers and accomplishments, his knowledge, judgment, and facility, gave him immediate ascendancy in the bureau and the senate; and while the others were gradually acquiring reputation by repeated efforts, he may be said to have stepped into his fame at once.

Jenkinson and Castlereagh were no sooner fairly launched into Parliament, at one or two-and-twenty, than they took a conspicuous part in the proceedings; the one with a clearness and moderation which satisfied the confidence of his friends; and the other with a spanking intemperance which fore-shadowed the rashness and mistakes of his career. But it was in the nature of Mr. Huskisson's genius to demand time for its mature development. Oratory was not his forte, and he hesitated long before he addressed the House. Even when he had acquired considerable confidence in speaking, he rarely ventured beyond that class of subjects over which

* Huskisson, Canning, and Jenkinson, were born in 1770; Lord Castlereagh in 1769.

his laborious researches and the analytical character of his mind had given him a complete mastery.

Friendships are commonly formed by contemporaries thus starting into life under the same auspices; sometimes from force of circumstances, and sometimes from force of sympathy. But between Lord Castlereagh and Mr. Canning neither of these influences appear to have operated. Flippancy, pretension, and zealotry could not by any process be brought to mix up with calm reason and good taste. There was nothing in common between them. The early intimacy with Mr. Jenkinson, on the other hand, was now improved and cemented by a union of sentiments upon public affairs, and by the absence on both sides of all paltry passions and false enthusiasm. Mr. Jenkinson began the world like a man of the world, and displayed a great deal of common sense in his intercourse with it; and the friendship that existed between him and Mr. Canning, although it suffered the usual fluctuations of the party thermometer, was never seriously damaged by political differences. With Mr. Huskisson there was a closer affinity: his comprehensive views upon commercial policy, the solidity of his judgment, his close powers of statement, and the masses of information he marshalled into his arguments, early attracted the regards of Mr. Canning, who, from the commencement of their intercourse, entertained for him that feeling of admiration which subsequent years heightened into the strictest attachment.*

* Mr. Canning became acquainted with Mr. Huskisson in 1793, shortly after the return of the latter from Paris, where he had resided from the age of fourteen with his great uncle, Dr. Gem. During the last two or three years of his residence there, he filled the office of private secretary to Lord Gower (afterwards Marquis of Stafford), who

To Mr. Canning's connexion with the Tory party may be ascribed that progressive modification of its more violent tenets, and that infusion of liberalism into its practice which has been ever since gradually cancelling, one by one, its most objectionable tendencies. It is no less certain also, that Mr. Huskisson exercised a moderating influence in other directions, and that although his principles were never fully carried out, they were so far admitted in small details, as to break down the outworks of that antiquated system by which we were already insulated in the midst of advancing civilisation. Wherever either of them might have taken up his stand, singly he must have effected important ameliorations; but thus united, and acting with a party which had hitherto kept itself aloof with a high hand from all popular approaches, they drew the administration nearer to the people, and opened a new era in the history of Toryism.

was then the English ambassador to the court of France. This was the foundation of his subsequent fortunes. At Lord Gower's table in England, Mr. Huskisson had frequent opportunities of meeting Pitt and Dundas; and one day the conversation turned upon the necessity of creating an office under the new Alien Bill, by which its provisions might be properly carried out, and the claims of emigrants examined without delay. It was necessary that the person filling this office should be a good man of business, a gentleman in manners, and a perfect master of the French language. Lord Gower immediately suggested the employment to Mr. Huskisson, who accepted it, although its harassing and common-place duties were far below his talents. But it was the first introduction to the ministry, who soon discovered his abilities, and made use of them in a higher sphere. In 1795, he was appointed Under Secretary of State in the department of War and Colonies; and towards the close of 1796, he was brought into Parliament for the borough of Morpeth, under the patronage of Lord Carlisle. He made his first speech in February, 1798.

Mr. Huskisson was present at the taking of the Bastille, and exhibited so hearty a zeal in the cause of the Republicans, that he was frequently accused of having been a member of the Jacobin Club. But this was not true, as the only society with which he connected himself, was the '89 Club. In defending himself against this charge, he cited the example of Mr. Pitt, who even up to 1792, saw so little danger to other states from the changes taking place in France, that the speech from the throne in that year declared that there was nothing in the condition of Europe which was likely to involve this country in hostilities!

The entrance into Parliament is an event of incalculable magnitude in a man's life. It unfolds before him a world of experiences, of which he could form no adequate conception from theory or description. He finds the assembly not only different from what he expected, but from any thing he had ever imagined to exist. The dream of legislative sobriety and responsible statesmanship dissolves before the reality. He is surrounded by the most incongruous materials, whose natural discordance is rendered still more glaring by the strife of factions and the extraordinary inequality of talents. He finds certain models set up whom he is expected to imitate or obey as the oracles of the senate; he is to be tried by standards of excellence of which he had no previous warning; there are exactions to be satisfied, which put his generosity, if not his integrity itself, to the severest test; qualifications to be established, which had never entered into his calculations; and critics to be appeased, whose judgment he may be well disposed to hold in contempt, but which it would be ruin to dispute. The danger is, that in accommodating himself to these exigencies, his originality may be paralysed; that in endeavouring to suit himself to his audience, he may be restrained from giving full scope to his energies; that in lowering himself to the requisite formulæ, he may cease to cultivate higher sources of success; and that with the noblest ambition, and powers equal to its achievement, he may sink at last into the common mediocrity. Mr. Canning was too conscious of all these obstacles, and of the anticipations his reputation had excited, not to choose his occasion carefully. Throughout his first session he resisted all the temptations which the anxious topics before the House presented to him. He was determined not to fail;

and before he invoked the criticism of the Commons—always ready to cry down new merit, to terrify it by savage contumely, or abash it by supercilious derision—he resolved to take the measure of all its moods and usages.

He delivered his first speech on the 31st of January, 1794, selecting for his subject Mr. Pitt's motion for a subsidy to the King of Sardinia. The specific objection to this motion was, that it gave 200,000*l.* a-year to the King of Sardinia, and got nothing in return; the general objection was to the war itself, which the subsidy was intended to support. Mr. Fox and Mr. Grey had both spoken before Mr. Canning rose; and from the structure of his reply, it was evident that he had carefully prepared all its main points, which were less remarkable for eloquence or originality, than for dexterity of arrangement. It was the speech of a clever tactician. The most practised debater could not have conducted the argument with greater adroitness. He divided all the objections against the subsidy into two propositions: 1st. That it ought not to be entered into at all; 2nd. That, acknowledging such a subsidy to be proper in principle, this particular subsidy was disadvantageous in details. It will be seen at once that the whole question was enclosed in the first proposition, which in point of fact involved the second; but with the expertness of a well-trained logician, Mr. Canning took the first for granted, as a matter upon which there could be no difference of opinion, and proceeded to discuss the merits of the second, as if it were the vital topic; then, having succeeded in engaging or entangling attention on subordinate considerations, he suddenly reverted to the original question, and wound up with a general defence of the war.

The house was taken by surprise. It expected something highly inflated from the new speaker: the opposition looked for a display of exuberant enthusiasm which might damage a cause that required to be trimmed with the utmost caution and subtlety; and the ministers may probably have had some slight apprehensions of a similar result. Both were disappointed. The speech discovered complete knowledge of the artifices of debate, and was of too close a texture to be easily picked to pieces. The topics insisted upon were old and exhausted. Every thing that could be said on behalf of the war had been already said; but these commonplaces were here put together with such compactness and rapidity of illustration, as to strike the mind with condensed force, if not with actual novelty. It had been urged, for instance, over and over again from the ministerial benches, that the war was absolutely necessary to prevent the spread of revolutionary principles; but Mr. Canning placed this contingent terror in a more startling aspect, by asserting that we had to thank the war that we had still a government, that the functions of the house were not usurped by a corresponding society, and that instead of sitting in debate as to whether or not they should subsidise the King of Sardinia, *they sat there at all.* In the same way, upon a subsequent occasion, in the same session, he defended the Alien Bill, and the act for protecting French property in our funds, by observing that if it had not been for such measures, our towns would have been filled by French citizens, and instead of English notes, our cities would have swarmed with French assignats. The merit consisted in bringing the argument home to the very doors of the people, in reducing speculation to reality, and resolving a sounding generality into palpable images. This was a great merit; it gave an articulate tongue and intelligible shape to the vague bugbear of national alarm, and made it tell with distinctness on the nerves of his hearers. It was like the sudden challenge of a trumpet at the gates of the Council.

This speech squared wonderfully also with the prejudices of the audience. It was a common thing to say, for example, that the French were a parcel of madmen, and to describe the Revolution as an outbreak of insanity. Nobody minded such frothy declamation; but Mr. Canning knew how to give point to the extravagance. "If," he exclaimed, "it had been a harmless, idiot lunacy, which had contented itself with playing its tricks and practising its fooleries at home; with dressing up strumpets in oak-leaves, and inventing nick-names for the calendar, I should have been far from desiring to interrupt their innocent amusements; we might have looked on with hearty contempt, indeed; but with a contempt not wholly unmixed with commiseration." It is easy to understand how such allusions would act upon the sturdy Protestantism of an English House of Commons—how this artful method of dramatising the superstitions of our neighbours, would throw the unguarded audience into roars of applause.

The effect, upon the whole, was considerable, although not exactly of the kind anticipated. But Mr. Canning took an early opportunity of vindicating his reputation for eloquence, which this subject, hackneyed and narrow, scarcely afforded him.

In his next speech—on Major Maitland's motion of inquiry into the causes of the failure of Dunkirk, and the evacuation of Toulon—delivered in April, he made the first experiment of his powers of sarcasm. This is always dangerous in a young member, who is sure to be reminded of the respect he owes his elders; to be told to go back to his books, and study the laws and constitution of the country, of which, of course, he is profoundly ignorant; with a great deal of good advice to the same purpose, highly flavoured with contempt. Mr. Canning did not escape this inevitable lesson. Mr. Francis administered it with the usual square-toed solemnity; but had scarcely got so far as to inform " the young gentleman who had just escaped from his school and his classics, and was not yet conversant in the laws and constitution of his country, that he had imprudently delivered sentiments which tended to degrade him in the opinion of the world," when he was suddenly called to order. The house did not see any thing in Mr. Canning's "sentiments," which should exactly degrade him, and so the young orator had the full benefit of the laugh.

It seems to have been Mr. Canning's manly determination to avail himself, in this session, of every proper occasion which offered, for making a clear declaration of his principles, on all the great questions which were then before the country. He left nothing in doubt as to the course which he felt it his duty to pursue; and even they, who dissented most strongly from his opinions, were compelled to applaud the candour and integrity with which he avowed them. He spoke only three times during the session: the first time on the subsidy to the King of Sardinia; the second, on the review of certain circumstances in the campaign just then closed; and the third, on the suspension of the Habeas Corpus Act. The first and second may be taken as declarations in favour of the war;

and the third, as the announcement of his determination to support Mr. Pitt in any measures which he should consider necessary for its maintenance.

The war question was then at its height. It dazzled many people; and had especially in its favour the traditional fanaticism which used to set up hostility between France and England as a sort of law of Providence; and the capacity of one Englishman to beat six Frenchmen as an article of faith. It required little excuse, or none, to engage the people in a war with France. We were too ready at all times, shut up in ill-humours and animosities as we were, to shoot our quills at the least alarm from that quarter. There was no great difficulty, therefore, in the first step—the puzzle was to justify it when taken.

We were already at war when Mr. Canning entered parliament. He had nothing to do with the origin of the war; his province was to maintain the necessity of prosecuting it, which was easier, and more reconcileable with reason, than any defence which could be made for having begun it. There were half a million of soldiers on the frontiers of France, a great many more training in the interior, and a fleet at Brest: here were the elements of the argument—the rest was left to fancy or inspiration.

The most remarkable peculiarity of this war was, that nobody could tell exactly what it was for. Ministers and their adherents differed amongst themselves in assigning an object to it. Like the *melée* in the burlesque, it exhausted all the ingenuity of conjecture:

> " To it they goes;
> But what they're all fighting for, nobody knows."

Mr. Burke declared, that the object of the war was the restoration of the ancient monarchy of France, and that it ought to be openly avowed. Mr. Pitt denied that such was the object,* declaring that the restoration was only a means to an end, the end itself being peace.† Mr. Canning, Mr. Jenkinson, and others asserted that the legitimate aim of the war was the destruction of the Jacobin party, and that it could never be brought to a termination until that was accomplished—a view of the case which was adopted in the king's speech of 1794, with as little ambiguity as could be fairly expected in a king's speech.‡

* This denial on behalf of ministers was perfectly explicit, on the occasion of Mr. Tierney's motion for peace in 1798 (as it had been on several previous occasions), when Lord Hawkesbury (afterwards Lord Liverpool) took extraordinary pains to disclaim, on the part of ministers, any such design as that of restoring the monarchy in France. Yet it is a curious commentary on this disclaimer, to find Mr. Pitt, in 1801, when all chance for the Bourbons was at an end, betraying the desire which he had all along secretly nourished, and diligently concealed. His words are remarkable : he said that " he gave up his hopes of restoring the ancient monarchy of France with the greatest reluctance ; and he should, to his dying day, lament that there were not, on the part of the *other* powers of Europe, *efforts corresponding with our own*, for the accomplishment of that great work. There were periods, during the continuance of the war, in which he had hopes of our being able to put together the scattered fragments of that great and venerable edifice—to restore the exiled nobility of France—but that had been found unattainable."

† " Gifford's Life of Pitt," iv. 310. The facts are to be found scattered through the numerous debates which were raised on this subject ; but it is well to confirm them by the evidence of a thorough-paced partisan like Gifford, who would certainly admit nothing to the prejudice of his own side of the question which he could avoid.

The jesuitry of Pitt comes out boldly in the audacious quibble, that the restoration was to be considered merely as a means to an end. The end was to be peace, yet he would not negotiate with the existing government, who were willing enough to make terms ; and with this profession on his lips, which every day falsified, he meant to carry on the war until the Bourbons, with whom alone he would negotiate, were re-established ! The proper way to describe it would be, by direct inversion— the pretence of peace being really used as a means to the true end, the restoration of the monarchy.

‡ It is really curious to trace through the interminable debates on the war, the anxiety of the opposition to extract from the ministry some explanation of their objects, and the obstinate determination of the ministry not to give any. Night after night this harassing question was sure to be agitated in one shape or another, but all to no purpose. Mr. Canning, before he was sufficiently habituated to the ways of the house

It was admitted by every body, that no country has a right to interfere with the internal government of another. Pitt was unusually explicit on this point. He granted in full the right of the French people to set up their own government; but he refused to recognise it when it *was* set up. This was the Pitt policy in every thing. The abstract principle was always admitted; but the moment it came to be applied, there was sure to be some plausible pretext for rendering it impracticable. The Pitt ministers pursued this huge fraud upon so grand a scale, and with such systematic action, that they imposed to an incredible extent upon the good-nature of the people; who, like a dog that is soothed by words of endearment, at the same moment that some urchin is pinching its tail, were so puzzled, that they hardly knew whether they ought to be pleased or vexed.

The peace which Mr. Pitt professed was unique. It was to be brought about by much the same sort of agency which used to be so effective in establishing quietness at an Irish pattern. England went to war with France to secure peace to Europe; and when it was urged, over and over again, especially by Wilberforce, in his humane, persevering way, that the obvious mode of getting peace was to open negotiations and stop the war, Pitt would still insist that the best possible way to insure peace was to keep up the war as long as we could.

to bear such tantalising scrutiny with due parliamentary patience—a thing, indeed, which his temper and his candour could never, at any time, have endured—broke out into a burst of petulant ridicule on this point. " 'But what,' say the gentlemen on the other side of the house, ' is the distinct *object* for which we are engaged ?'—Gentlemen put this question, as if an *object* were a corporeal substance, as if it was something tangible, something that could be taken in the hand and laid upon your table, and turned round and round before them for accurate, ocular examination. In this sense I profess myself perfectly unable to satisfy them."

As to negotiations, that course was repudiated at once. Pitt, while he allowed that the French people had a right to set up their own form of government, insisted that the new government possessed no authority to give stability to its treaties. He admitted the general proposition, that the people had a right to frame any government they thought fit; but denied the irresistible corollary that they were bound by its acts. This refusal to negotiate with the republic was practically equivalent to a declaration of war against that particular exercise of a right, which even they who made war upon it, admitted in full. Of course, ministers endeavoured to evade any direct acknowledgment that such was the state of the case, and tried to escape from it by general declamation upon the insecurity of things in France, the fall of assignats, and the crippled condition of the population; but no equivocation could conceal the fact that this was literally a war of principles.

Mr. Canning alone, of all the supporters of the ministry, was candid enough to defend the war on that special ground. " Distinction had been taken," he observed, " by gentlemen on the other side of the house, between the progress of the arms of France, and the progress of her principles. The progress of her arms, it was admitted, it had been, and would always be, our right and our policy to oppose ; but we need not, and we ought not it seems, to go to war against her principles. He, for his part, could not see such fine distinctions. Admitting that the aggrandisement and aggression of France must naturally be the objects of our jealousy and resistance, he could not understand that they became less so, in proportion as they were accompanied and promoted by principles destructive of civil society." The concluding sentence is a little obscure, and partakes of the mystification which was commonly resorted to in the application of general doctrines to particular cases. Aggrandisement and aggression certainly could not become less the objects of jealousy and resistance, because they were accompanied by pernicious principles; seeing that they had already become so without any accompaniment. But that was not the question, which simply concerned the distinction that had been drawn by the opposition between the progress of arms, and the progress of principles; and in admitting that he could see no such distinction, Mr. Canning, in effect, took his stand upon the very intelligible ground that one government is justified in going to war with another because it disapproves of its principles.

Mr. Canning did not in so many words enunciate this doctrine, but the argument he employed bears no other construction; and the fact, that he applied it practically to the war with France is only one instance out of a multitude which might be cited, of the false political morality into which ministers were driven in their defence of that measure.

That peace was not the object of the war is sufficiently disclosed by the strenuous opposition of ministers to every effort that was made for its attainment. If they had been sincere, they might easily have secured an honourable peace. But peace was the last thing they desired. They even went so far as to declare that the consequences of peace would be worse than the continuance of war. "In the event of a peace," exclaimed Mr. Windham, "the intercourse between the two countries must be opened, when the French would pour in their emissaries, and all the English infected with French principles, whom we had now the means of excluding, would return to disseminate their abominable tenets among the people." Here was the secret let out ; and yet all this time, ministers were guilty of the transparent hypocrisy of pretending that they were seeking to re-establish the peace of Europe.

In one thing alone, Mr. Pitt was sincere. He never disguised his determination to prosecute the war at any cost, shuffle as he might about his motives. To be sure, concealment on that point was not very easy, as he was constantly making new demands upon the industry of the people to sustain the tremendous expense of troops and subsidies. What with new taxes upon every conceivable article of taste, necessity, or pleasure, the wants of man and the gifts of heaven, the people must have been more obtuse than the tax-collector usually finds them, if they were not thoroughly convinced that he was in earnest ; and, that, while the resources of the country lasted, he was resolved to persevere. And that was exactly what he meant. He went upon the exhausting process. It was like a profligate competition between two trading rivals, carried on at a daily loss, with the desperate certainty that the one or the other, beggared and undone, must abandon the field to his adversary at last. Mr. Pitt avowed this part of his policy frankly enough, and openly boasted, during one of the thousand and one discussions which took place on this subject, that Great Britain had expended on the prosecution of the war no more than 25,000,000*l*. per year, while the outlay of France amounted to 97,000,000*l*. per month, or 324,000,000*l*. per year. The inference was, as his historian, with incredible candour, observes, that we should exhaust her in the long run.* And this was the war for which we are to this hour labouring under the weight of a national debt,

* " Gifford's Life of Pitt," iv. 292.

from which no prophetic trance of the imagination can foresee the date or the means of our extrication.

But this very debt was a significant and powerful agent in bringing round the results Mr. Pitt aimed at. It would be difficult to hit upon a more effectual method of preventing the people from cultivating French principles, or any other kind of principles. To use their own descriptive phrase, it kept their noses so close to the grind-stone, that there was no time for any thing but work. They were compelled to work double-tides under the pressure of the war taxes, which were raised to pay the interest of the debt, while the debt itself crushed the independence and silenced the complaints of the monied and property classes, whom it enslaved, as a matter of pure necessity, to the will of the minister. The debt was not only the instrument by which he over-awed public opinion at home, but the fulcrum by which he moved the whole of Europe.

Had the war even been successful (poor satisfaction as that would have been to a tax-crushed country) the event might have furnished some fortuitous vindication of all this ruinous outlay; but it was more disastrous in its progress, and exhibited more extraordinary failures in the " long run" (the final test to which ministers pointed on every fresh mortification, or whenever more money was wanted) than any known war in the history of the world.* There was

* Mr. Pitt openly declared to the house, that we had failed in our efforts against France, and that the objects of the war were frustrated in the sequel. " Disappointed in our hopes of being able to drive France within her ancient limits," he observed, " or even to raise barriers against her farther incursions, it becomes necessary, with the change of circumstances, to change our objects : for I do not know a more fatal error than to look only at one object, and obstinately to pursue it, when the hope of accomplishing it no longer remains." This was when the war was over, and peace concluded with France.

H

not a single point to which the administration nailed their colours from which they were not ultimately beaten down.

After this Pitt ministry had pledged itself in the most solemn manner that it would never negotiate with a new-fangled government of French manufacture (a sly hint that they were only awaiting the legitimate advent of the Bourbons), Pitt himself endeavoured to effect a sort of underhand negotiation with the Convention,* and Lord Hawkesbury actually entered into a treaty with Buonaparte.† On this latter occasion, the noble lord was severely taken to task for condescending to reduce himself in his own office in Downing-street, to the level of the " citizen" minister, with whom he signed the preliminary articles. It seems that it was considered an indispensable condition of diplomatic etiquette that the rank of the agents should be equal ; which was about as reasonable, said Mr. Sheridan, as if Lord Whitworth were to be sent to Petersburg, and told that he was not to treat but with some gentleman six feet high and as handsome as himself !

The project of entering and occupying France was constantly declared to be on the eve of accomplishment. "We have reason to hope," exclaimed Mr. Jenkinson, in 1794, "that we shall be able to penetrate the interior of France in the present campaign ;" and his biographer congratulates him upon the fact, that although he was incessantly baited in the House of Commons upon this and other equally sagacious prophecies, he had the satisfaction of seeing the idea realised at last, by the entry of the allies into Paris, twenty-one years afterwards.‡ A

* In 1796. † In 1801.
‡ "Memoirs of the Public Life and Administration of Lord Liverpool," p. 83.

man who bet upon the Epsom, might as well claim the stakes because his horse happened to win at Newmarket. The consequential connexion between the entry of the allies into Paris, in 1815, and Mr. Jenkinson's campaign in 1794, or the war of which it formed a forlorn fraction, is just about as obvious.

The conquest of France was treated as a thing not to say practicable, but certain. It was "hey, presto!" and you might look for France in Pitt's waistcoat-pocket. Well might Mr. Fox cry out, "Oh, calumniated crusaders, how rational and moderate were your objects! Oh, tame and feeble Cervantes, with what a timid pencil and faint colours have you painted the portrait of a disordered imagination!"*

The restoration of the Bourbons was another vaticination, and like the rest it was signally falsified; with this aggravating difference that a second revolution, completing the imperfect issues of the first, has shown, in its immediate results and distant influences, that these costly crusades, instead of crushing the popular principle, only submitted its vitality to the most triumphant test it is in the nature of human circumstances to afford. In the meanwhile the world has gained some wisdom, and will never again, we may venture to predict, behold such an iniquitous league hounded on by the criminal passions of despotism, in the pursuit of objects so utterly hopeless and unjust.

It was the last misfortune of this war against France, that, well inclined as the bulk of the population might have been at other times to embark in such an enterprise, out of false notions of glory, or jealousy, or national pride, they were so averse to it at this period, that they suffered

* Letter to the Electors of Westminster.

no opportunity to escape without testifying the abhorrence in which they held it. When the king was going down to parliament to open the session, the mob surrounded his coach, shouting " No war!" in his ears (some add " No king!"), clamouring for cheap provisions, and demanding with furious gestures the dismissal of Pitt. This was a plain indication of the lowest stratum of public opinion. The opposition declared their belief that it was only a plot to terrify the people into weak compliances, planned and executed by ministers themselves, for the maintenance of their power.* But if it were a plot, it was so clumsy that it defeated its own purpose. If it supplied an excuse for fresh severities against the people, it also betrayed the unpopularity of the war, and the condition of want to which a large section of the population was reduced. This was proving too much for ministers, who were too cunning to cast nets in the dark for catching their own feet.

The discontents were real. There was no fiction or masquerade in the sufferings or resentments of the poor. They had the gratification, however, of learning from the lips of the minister, that they never before enjoyed such astonishing prosperity; that although the National Debt had been doubled and quadrupled, the Sinking Fund was flourishing; and that although taxation was grinding them to the earth, there was no diminution in the exports.† These consolatory facts were brought before the House of Commons with such a display of unanswerable figures, that even the starving mechanic, if he had the least

* Speech of the Marquis of Lansdowne, October 20, 1795.
† The advance in the exports in the war-time was repeatedly put forward as a proof of the prosperity of the country—a fallacy which to this hour is fallen back upon, whenever it can be made use of to serve a purpose.

candour, or was at all open to conviction, must have been shaken in his belief in the existence of hunger.

The people never know when they are well off; and sometimes, in spite of the most encouraging increase in the quarter's revenue, they cannot be persuaded that they are a whit wealthier than before.* So, notwithstanding these proofs of their happy condition, the turbulence and the distress, and the demand for a reform in Parliament, grew deeper and louder; and ministers who had made up their minds not to open the question of reform under any extremity, took a short cut to suppress the agitation, by seizing upon some of the most conspicuous members of the Corresponding Society, and demanding on the same day an act of indemnity from Parliament. Mr. Pitt moved for a suspension of the Habeas Corpus Act, to enable the king to secure and detain persons suspected of having designs against the government. Had Mr. Pitt proposed to lock up the doors of the House and fling the keys into the river, he could not have created more amazement amongst the members of the opposition. They were required on the sudden, without time for reflection, for evidence, for the expression of public opinion, to pass an act to annihilate the liberties of the subject, not by speculative and indirect approaches, but by direct and forcible deprivation. The people demanded time—it was refused; it was even declared that no mass of petitions could affect, right or wrong, the inflexible course the ministers were resolved to take in this exigency. The pilot was weathering the storm, and he must weather it in his own way. A secret committee was appointed; they made their report

---

* The increase in the revenue is the ordinary surface-evidence of a thriving state of things; although in the majority of cases, it is solely referable to increased taxation and improved modes of collection.

on the next day but one; and the bill was hurried with indecent expedition through the Commons, and passed into law with still more alarming alacrity by the Lords—amidst the execrations of the multitude.

This was the first violently drastic measure of Mr. Pitt's new system of treatment. The experiment was accompanied by great danger to physician and patient; and it was essential on this occasion, beyond all others, that the supporters of the minister should rally round him with unflinching resolution. Mr. Canning was deeply impressed by the difficulty of Mr. Pitt's position, and the imperative necessity of sustaining him through it; and, boldly facing the storm of invective, indignation, and opprobrium by which the Treasury benches were assailed, he delivered a defence of the measure and the minister, which was more to be applauded for courage and zeal, than for discretion or judgment.

The defence of the measure rested exclusively on the plea of necessity. The necessity, however, being rather obstinate of proof, the readiest course was to take it for granted, and wonder how people could be so blind as not to see it. " Good God !" exclaimed Mr. Canning, with that admirable air of astonishment which became him so well, and looked so real, " how *can* gentlemen oppose a measure that is so obviously necessary?" The opposition had menaced them with petitions, but neither he nor Mr. Pitt were to be intimidated by petitions so long as they felt that they were conscientiously discharging their duty to the country. This was at least carrying the wrong with a high and fearless hand, and imparting a tone of pomp and authenticity to a palpable outrage on the constitution.

Mr. Pitt had been taunted by Mr. Grey for his apostacy

on the question of parliamentary reform; an apostacy rendered the more glaring on this occasion by the fact that one of the persons whom he had just dragged to prison for agitating that question—John Horne Tooke— had formerly been his own associate in the very same cause. "William Pitt, the reformer of 1782," exclaimed Mr. Grey, "was now the prosecutor, ay, the persecutor of reformers."* There was no possibility of turning aside this accusation. It was drawn from circumstances too notorious to admit of evasion. Mr. Canning met it boldly, and declared that he entirely agreed with Mr. Pitt, that though such a reform might not be improper for discussion in time of peace, yet it was a proposition that ought not to be agitated in times of tumult and storm. As to the change in opinion, he had no hesitation in saying that if Mr. Pitt in future should return to his former opinion, *it was probable that he might again agree with him.*

These declarations on the part of Mr. Canning, extraordinary and extravagant as they are, can scarcely be regarded as involving any specific principles. They must be looked upon rather as declarations of adhesion to Mr. Pitt. He felt himself bound to support the ministerial policy as a whole ; that was essential to what he believed to be the true interests of the country; and he knew that

* In 1782, Mr. Pitt brought forward a motion in the House of Commons, for a plan of parliamentary reform, by which he proposed to buy up the boroughs, and transfer the right of election to the freeholders of the counties at large, or to certain districts. In 1794, he was called as a witness upon Horne Tooke's trial, and compelled to convict himself of his former participation in the agitation for reform, and of his recommendation to the people to pour in petitions in favour of it, from all parts of the country ;—the very thing, distorted by indictment into treason, for which Horne Tooke and the rest were placed in the dock at the Old Bailey.

the slightest misgiving, the least wavering, or exercise of individual judgment, might be productive of the most serious misfortunes. The practical question arising out of such a line of conduct, concerns, in effect, not the particular vote, but the obligations understood to be imposed by all party alliances.

The character of the compact is clear. We have seen the ministerial majority turned round, like a troop of horse in the amphitheatre, upon the selfsame question, and revoking their own decision of the night before, at the bidding of the minister.* This is an extreme case (such a one as it is reasonable to hope, for mere decency, may never happen again); but it illustrates the action, and discloses the real nature of a party compact. The united body must move together—there must be no straggling—no hanging back or breaking line for the pursuit of honest crotchets—there must be a total surrender of opinion—a tacit submission to orders—no man must think for himself—individual convictions must be sacrificed to unity of purpose. It is upon this principle the papal power has maintained itself so wondrously against the broken and scattered assaults of independent reason, pushing its conquests silently by the mere force of the wedge, which keeps its place because there is no equal and uniform pressure by which it can be dislodged. To this principle the Tory party owe every thing:—to the absolute impossibility of acting upon it, consistently with the higher obligations of conscience, the Liberal party may attribute their weakness and dispersion.

Mr. Canning approved of the war, and voted, as a

* This (happily unprecedented) exploit occurred in the session of 1845.

matter of course, for the measures which Mr. Pitt declared indispensable to its prosecution. The overwhelming magnitude and importance of the object absorbed his scruples, if he had any, about the means. But Mr. Canning's political life yielded some memorable proofs that he did not hold this doctrine of passive obedience, as being binding at all times, and under all circumstances, and that he insisted upon the right of standing sometimes upon exceptions, and broad exceptions, too; *and by these exceptions, and not by the rule of Toryism, he won his illustrious fame.*

The devotion, ability, and fearlessness displayed by Mr. Canning throughout this arduous session, marked him out at once for distinction ; and he was selected by Mr. Pitt, on the opening of the next session, in December, 1794, to second the address which was moved by Sir Edward Knatchbull. His speech upon this occasion was directed principally to the one question upon which all other questions turned; and he traversed over again, without much freshness and novelty, the old reasons for not seeking or inviting negotiations for peace. But there was a deficiency of parliamentary tact in the treatment of his topics. He was much too clear and sturdy for an address on a king's speech. There was no attempt at conciliation, and as to the requisite vagueness and mystification, it seemed as if he had not the least suspicion that it was necessary to shirk or mystify any thing. He certainly began with the standing phrase which from time immemorial has followed all king's speeches, like a wailing spirit waiting to be laid, that " he hoped for one night gentlemen would consent to lay aside their differences;" but he immediately added that he did not expect any thing of the kind, and took care before he had done, to prevent the possibility of its consummation.*

The tone of defiance that breathed through this speech (although it was not more warlike, after all, than that of his majesty), called up a new and unexpected antagonist in the person of one of Mr. Pitt's most indiscriminate admirers. Really alarmed at the menacing character of the ministerial manifesto, and with the best intentions in the world, Mr. Wilberforce moved an amendment; taking occasion to review and condemn the sanguinary conflict in which we were engaged, and telling Mr. Canning that, hurried away by his eloquence (a complimentary way of describing an oratorical indiscretion), he had made assertions which it was impossible to maintain, and asked questions which it was unfortunately but too easy to answer. The opposition were thrown into ecstasies. Mr. Pitt, deeply moved at the defection of an ally whose odorous reputation was so desirable at such a moment, did not hesitate to confess his mortification—and the discussion passed away amidst a roar of artillery, and ended in smoke. Mr. Pitt, who apologised to the House for the emotion he betrayed under these painful circumstances, had a majority of 173.

Mr. Fox brought forward his motion on the state of the nation, in the following March. It was introduced by a

* Mr. Therry, referring to this speech, says, that "Mr. Pitt, in the circle of his private friends, spoke of it, and of the admirable address with which it was delivered, as one that afforded an indication of even greater abilities than fame—which had been busy in Mr. Canning's praise —had hitherto awarded him."—"Speeches, I. 22." From an allusion which Mr. Therry makes to a particular passage in the speech it is quite evident that there is a mistake in the description, and that Mr. Pitt's eulogy was intended to apply to a speech made by Mr. Canning upwards of three years afterwards. There was, undoubtedly, nothing in the speech on the address to justify such an encomium.

speech of transcendent power, which extorted even from Pitt a burst of admiration. The domestic questions it embraced, chiefly relating to Ireland, required to be met with great reserve, and Mr. Canning, who followed Mr. Sheridan, was careful not to commit himself. In this alone consisted the excellence of his short and emphatic speech. The object of the opposition was to obtain enquiry—that of the ministry to prevent it: the former wanted to compel or entrap the government into admissions or declarations upon certain topics—the latter to resist discussion without betraying any opinions whatever. Mr. Canning conducted his share of the debate with infinite skill. He said very little, but it was to the purpose—or, more correctly, to no purpose. He assured the House that "he was far from contending against the right of the English Parliament, to call the ministers to account for their conduct with respect to Ireland; but he *did* mean to say that he had strong doubts of the policy and propriety of exercising that right at a period when it could not be exercised without reducing us to the dilemma either of discussing what we had no power to decide, or of deciding what we had no right to enforce." Nothing could be clearer than the general right—and nothing, as usual, more doubtful than the exercise of it.

Mr. Canning's accession to some appointment under the administration, was now looked upon as the natural consequence of the position he had already acquired; and before the close of the session of 1795, he vacated his seat to accept the office of Under Secretary of State for the Foreign Department, the seals of which were then held by Lord Grenville. In the following session he took his seat for Wendover, in the County of Bucks, and appeared for the first time in the House of Commons, as a member of the government.

The opposition of that day had a great horror of placemen—as all virtuous oppositions have until they get into power themselves; and Mr. Canning, having already excited envy and jealousy enough by his talents, could hardly expect to escape a little odium for the official eminence to which they had so rapidly promoted him. He was not suffered to enjoy his honours very long, until one night, in a fit of economical indignation, the appointment was impugned on the ground that Mr. Aust, his official predecessor, a person represented to be eminently qualified, and as fit for business as ever, had been removed merely to provide for Mr. Canning. The accusation was the luckiest thing imaginable. It reduced a hundred pointless and malicious inuendos to a distinct shape, and enabled Mr. Canning to show at once that it was founded on a total misconception of the facts of the case. The truth was that the "eminent" Mr. Aust (who gained more by the affair than any body else, since it will surely send him down to posterity immortally linked with Mr. Canning), had been advanced to more lucrative offices, while Mr. Canning had been put into his former place, so that the public had neither been burdened by one shilling of additional expense, nor, which was probably of more consequence, deprived of the invaluable services of Mr. Aust. "If sordid views had been my object," said Mr. Canning, "I would rather have accepted the offices Mr. Aust now holds, than the station which I fill."

Incidents must not be looked for in the life of a young minister, whose apprenticeship in the bureau is too laborious to admit of much external variety. In the next two years, 1796 and 1797, Mr. Canning devoted himself assiduously to the business of his office, and rarely took any part in the discussions in Parliament.

V.

THE ANTI-JACOBIN.

ABOUT this period, a phrase got into use, which seems to have been perfectly well understood by every body, but which, at this distance of time, does not appear to convey a very accurate idea of any thing. It led to unexampled confusion in the country. Had a raging plague gone forth sweeping the land's breadth, it could not have produced more desolating effects; some people were cowed and struck dumb at its approach; others, inspired with a sort of frenzy, defied it to come on, as if it were an incarnate fiend; and the government, impressed with a proper paternal responsibility, took every possible precaution that could be devised for averting this alarming visitation.

It is not to be hoped that any body in the nineteenth century will be much enlightened as to the terrible cause of this national fright, by being informed that it bore the name of *French principles*. That was its name, whatever its nature might have been; and the administration, in their urgent anxiety for the public safety, thought of nothing, night, noon, or morning, but how they should keep it out of the country. There are some French articles—such as fans, gloves, blonde, and the like—which can be excluded without difficulty; and should it ever be considered desirable to prevent their admission into England, we know exactly how to do it, by setting them down in the tariff at a prohibitory duty. But it was not so easy to describe French principles in the tariff, or to get revenue officers to seize and confiscate them at the ports.

Spanish mahogany is intelligible. If we were told that there was an extraordinary supply coming across the seas to us, we might probably anticipate a derangement in the timber market. But we should have no such uneasiness if we heard of a shipment of French principles. Judging from the nature of principles in general, we should be disposed to imagine that the cargo must be rather volatile and harmless. Nevertheless, the bare suspicion of such an importation threw the established authorities of this island into an agony of apprehension.

Mahogany can be cut, and sawed, and seasoned, and made into chairs. Not so a principle, which having no physical attributes whatever, bears a nearer analogy to the object of the war, which Mr. Canning declared could not be taken up in gentlemen's hands and turned round and round upon the table. But how this intangible and elemental thing—the common property of the reason and imagination of all nations—could be called French any more than Russian, or Hanoverian, it is hard to say. If any one were to speak of a Hottentot principle, he would be set down as an egregious blockhead, yet we cannot, for the life of us, see why there should not be Hottentot principles as well as French principles.

Still, notwithstanding the incomprehensibility of the thing, true it is, that for a long and dreary season multitudes of honest people, who had caught up this cuckoo cry about French principles, used to quake in their shoes at the bare thought of their spreading into this happy country; as if no such principles had ever found their way here before; or, as if, being dressed up in the French fashion, they had become odious to our English taste. The difficulty of understanding is great, how it came to pass, that we, the people of this country, ever could have been afraid of such a phrase; or, how we could have suffered it to fly about in books, newspapers, state documents, and common conversation, with some direfully mysterious meaning attached to it over and above that of mere revolution—we who had beheaded one king, and driven out a race of kings for betraying their trust—we, whose living dynasty was placed on the throne by a revolution.

This mad panic was foolish and unreasoning, not alone in attributing peculiar danger to the circulation of these principles, but in presupposing (for otherwise there could have been no danger) that the people were inclined to lay violent hands on the monarchy, or to disturb in the slightest degree the integrity of our mixed and balanced constitution. We have the express declarations of all the popular leaders to the contrary, and their recorded testimony in favour of a limited monarchy, as the mode of government which presented, above all others, the most perfect safeguards for public liberty. In fact, so far from entertaining any desire to destroy the constitution, the aim of the reformers was to purify and invigorate it. And had they entertained such a design, they neither could have been prevented from effecting it by the suppression of these French principles, nor furnished with a solitary additional reason for prosecuting it by their most active diffusion.

But, giving the government full credit for the best intentions, was there ever such a stark staring absurdity as the notion that they could check the admission into this country, or the propagation in it of political doctrines of any kind? How could they do it? By calling out the militia? By putting a tax upon reading and writing? They might as well have talked of keeping out the sun, or stopping the course of the winds. And all the time that this folly was showing itself through all sorts of actual precautions on the part of the executive, the press was disseminating the poison as fast as hands could distil and distribute it through every nook and cranny of the kingdom; and parliament was accelerating its consumption by eternally analysing and discussing its miraculous properties, and serving it out gratis to the poor in infinitesimal doses. The danger was held to be so great that there was nothing else talked of; until at last the curiosity of fear was wrought up to such intensity, that there was not a man, woman, or child, from the Land's End to John o' Groats, who was not as well acquainted with the doctrines of the revolution as the French themselves. To say that the minister did not restrain the diffusion of French principles would be saying little;—he not only did not restrain them, but by betraying the impotent desire to do so, he stimulated their circulation to an extent incalculably greater than they could have attained under any other possible circumstances.

It used to be said—but the saying is fast dying out—that had it not been for the vigorous measures of Pitt, the populace would have taken up the doctrines of the revolution. The reverse of this good old saying happens to be true. In consequence of the vigorous measures of Pitt, the populace *did* take up the doctrines of the revolution; but in consequence of their own good sense—they laid them down again. Instead of congratulating ourselves, therefore, on the vigilance of Pitt, it would be more consonant with justice to acknowledge what we owe to the virtue of of the people.

While Pitt and Grenville were carrying on the war with remorseless energy abroad, Canning was employing a much more effective instrument than the sword in combating the progress of revolutionary principles at home. That instrument was ridicule; and if the ministry had been content to leave French principles to its tender mercies they would have witnessed their extirpation by a surer process than riot-acts and state trials. The " Anti-Jacobin" was a much more formidable prosecutor than the attorney-general.

The first number of the " Anti-Jacobin," or " Weekly Examiner," was published on the 20th of November, 1797. The avowed purpose of this journal was to expose the vicious doctrines of the revolution, and to turn into ridicule and contempt the advocates of them in this country. The work originated with Mr. Canning, who wrote the prospectus, and contributed some of its ablest articles. Mr. Gifford was the editor, and amongst the writers were Mr. John Hookham Frere, Mr. Jenkinson, Mr. George Ellis, Lord Clare, and Lord Mornington, afterwards Marquis Wellesley.* It occupied the opposite ground to that which had formerly been taken up by the " Rolliad" and the " Probationary Odes," but " with a difference." The wit and vigour (and scurrility) of the " Anti-Jacobin" left behind,

* The author of a Biography of Mr. Huskisson says, that " there is no entire article in the ' Anti-Jacobin' to which even conjecture has ever affixed the name of Mr. Huskisson."—" Speeches of the Right Honourable W. Huskisson," i., 42. It might be inferred from this that Mr. Huskisson had contributed parts of articles to the " Anti-Jacobin;" but we believe it may be confidently stated that, although intimate with the writers, he had no share whatever in the work, direct or indirect.

I

at an immeasureable distance, the gentlemanly satire of the Whigs.*

Wherever the wit of the " Anti-Jacobin" is irresistible, the reader may conclude that he has detected the hand of Canning ; but there was such a copartnery in these things, and such a disinclination to separate each person's share, even were it possible to do so, that, with some marked exceptions, the authorship cannot now be ascertained with certainty. The work closed in 1798, and during its brief existence, Mr. Canning wrote largely for it. His connexion with it was well known at the time, nor was he ever disposed to disavow it. He declared in Parliament, ten years afterwards, that he had no other source of regret for the share he had in it, except the imperfection of his pieces. But what that share was is to a great extent a matter of conjecture, to be determined by internal evidence.

* The " Rolliad" and the " Probationary Odes" appeared about the spring of 1785. Lord Rolle was the nominal hero of the former, but the satires generally were levelled against Pitt, Dundas, and Lord Liverpool. The reputed author was a Mr. Joseph Richardson of one of the Inns of Court ; they were really written by Burgoyne, Fitzpatrick (to whom some of the happiest things are attributed), Townshend, Tickell, Pretyman, and Dr. Lawrence. Sheridan was suspected of having contributed, but he denied it in the House of Commons when charged with the authorship by Lord Rolle.

Mr. Moore, in his " Life of Sheridan," says : " The ' Rolliad' and the ' Anti-Jacobin' may, on their respective sides of the question, be considered as models of that style of political satire, whose lightness and vivacity give it the appearance of proceeding rather from the wantonness of wit than of ill-nature, and whose very malice, from the fancy with which it is mixed up, like certain kinds of fireworks, explodes in sparkles." This playful description may be allowed to apply with sufficient accuracy to the " Rolliad;" but it is suggested, with deference, that it can hardly be considered applicable to the " Anti-Jacobin," which was so full of base personal invective, so coarse and even indecent, that it gave great offence to some of the minister's strongest supporters. Wilberforce always spoke out against it. "I attacked Canning," he says, " about the ' Anti-Jacobin,' at dinner at Pitt's."—" Life of Wilberforce," ii., 334. The " Rolliad" *did* expire in sparkles ; but the ' Anti-Jacobin' belonged to a different sort of fireworks, had more of an incendiary spirit in it, and might be more properly compared to a firebrand.

The poem of " New Morality " is on all hands ascribed to Mr. Canning; and his exclusive title to it appears to admit of little doubt. This satire, as the name implies, is aimed at the false philosophy of the day, but, hitting beyond its proposed mark as the theme rises, it strikes at the Duke of Bedford, Southey, Coleridge, Godwin, and several other minor celebrities. The passages, which are clear of scornful personalities, are written with that unmistakeable polish which at once declares the authorship; and even where he flings his arrowy contempt upon Thelwall, Williams, and the small fry of democratic agitators, we fancy we can still trace him in the refinement of the points.* But it was not in weighty or savage satire that Mr. Canning's strength lay—the tomahawk of right belonged to the author of the " Baviad" and " Mæviad," who wielded it with the rude force and ruder courage, befitting such a weapon. Canning's more civilised taste delighted in handling lighter instruments; and the sphere of operations in this rampant journal was accordingly extended to accommodate him.

It must be confessed there was a large field for ridicule in the literary as well as the political fashions of the day. The " Sorrows of Werter" had done its work upon the maudlin tenderness of the English public; Darwin had transferred to the vegetable world the affected sensibility of the boarding-school; Southey was bringing out his English Sapphics; and Sheridan and Holcroft were doing their best to naturalise upon the English stage, the false sentiment and bad fine writing of the German playwrights.

* It is in this poem of " New Morality" the following lines occur, which have since become so familiar to the public :
" Give me th' avow'd, the erect, the manly foe,
Bold I can meet,—perhaps may turn his blow ;
But of all plagues, Good Heaven, thy wrath can send,
Save, save, oh ! save me from the candid friend !"

Here were tempting topics for the " Anti-Jacobin," all legitimate topics, too; coming in luckily enough to give an aspect of justice to its foul partisanship.

So far as the literary offenders were concerned, the " Anti-Jacobin" had not only justice on its side, but the thanks of every person of good taste. We may be assured it had no heartier reader—if we could find it out —than Fox himself, who despised all false styles, and must have enjoyed the good things of these slashing critics to the top of his bent, stopping short only at their politics, which were evil in thought and utterance. It would have been well if the writers had stopped there, too. The " Anti-Jacobin" has grown into a vague sort of fame by the assent of thousands who take it upon report, and who are ready to transmit its reputation to posterity, without any better knowledge of its deserts. But it is right that people who receive and forward this judgment should know something of the grounds on which it originally proceeded.

When the " Anti-Jacobin" was started, the available talent of the Reform party, in and out of Parliament, greatly preponderated over that of its opponents. An engine was wanted that should make up, by the destructiveness of its explosions, for the lack of more numerous resources. That engine was planned by Mr. Canning, who saw the necessity for it clearly. But it required a rougher hand than his to work it—one, too, not likely to wince from mud or bruises. The author of the " Baviad," and "Mæviad," was exactly the man—hard, coarse, inexorable, unscrupulous. He brought with him into this paper a thoroughly brutal spirit; the personalities were not merely gross and wanton, but wild, ribald, slaughtering : it was the dissection of the shambles. Such things had their effect, of course, at the time, and they were written for their effect; but they exhibit such low depravity and baseness—violating so flagrantly all truth, honour, and decency, for mere temporary party objects, that we cannot look upon them now without a shudder. Fox was assailed in this journal as if he were a highwayman. His peaceful retirement at St. Anne's Hill was invaded with vulgar jibes, and unintelligible buffoonery; Coleridge, Lamb, and others were attacked with extravagant personal hostility ;* and there was not an individual distinguished by respectability of character in the ranks of the Reformers, who was not mercilessly tarred and feathered the moment he ventured into public. Such was literally the " Weekly Anti-Jacobin ;" but time, which has bestowed so much celebrity upon it, has also made an equitable distinction in the verdict. The scurrility which, at the moment of publication, stung the town to madness, has long since lost all power of exciting attention; it sank into oblivion with its subjects, the wonder and contempt of a day. The prose papers, written in the ferocious vein of the Jacobins, whose criminalities they scourged, are gone down into darkness, and nothing has survived of the " Anti-Jacobin " but its etherial spirit, in the shape of its poetical burlesques and *jeux d'esprit.* That spirit was animated by Mr. Canning. His responsibility was always understood to be confined to the

* Coleridge was stated by these calumniators to have been dishonoured at Cambridge, for preaching Deism, at a time when, he tells us, he was absolutely decried as a bigot by the proselytes of the " French philosophy," for his ardour in the defence of Christianity. The " Anti-Jacobin " also accused him of having abandoned his native country, and deserted his wife and children. " Is it surprising," exclaims Coleridge, " that many good men remained longer than perhaps they otherwise would have done, adverse to a party which encouraged and openly rewarded the authors of such atrocious calumnies?"—" Biographia Literaria," i., 17.

airy and sportive articles, for he cannot be suspected of having intermeddled with the lower necessities of the work. It is to his contributions, assisted by his personal friends, that the "Anti-Jacobin" is indebted for being still remembered and talked of; and some of them—not all—are worthy of the distinction.*

As long as the English language lasts, "The Friend of Humanity, and the Needy Knife-Grinder" will last too. This is monumental brass of the true metal. The irony is exquisite, and, which cannot be always said in such cases, just. It ridicules at once the Sapphics and the politics of Southey, who was just getting into notoriety for the extravagance of his tenets under both heads. No man ever out-Heroded Herod with such verse or such doctrines. At that time he was violently democratic, for the reader need not be reminded that Southey, like Titian, began in one style and ended in another. No two Titian-Venuses can afford a more instructive contrast than Wat Tyler and the Book of the Church. But let that rest—for it is a compensation to know that Southey's genius was as versatile as his faith.

In the creed of the day, every rich man was an oppressor and every poor man a martyr. All such generalisations are fair game for the satirist, who pushes the argument to its extremity in the case of the Knife-grinder. He supposes that "a human being in the lowest state of penury and distress is a treasure to a reasoner of this cast," and that he " refrains from relieving the object of his

* There was an attempt made to revive the "Anti-Jacobin" in 1827; and, strange to say, the venom of the work was concentrated on Mr. Canning himself! It was called, unfortunately for the foolish speculators, the "New Anti-Jacobin," which suggested comparisons not particularly favourable to its reception. Besides, there were no longer any Jacobins to fall foul of, and so the project perished.

compassionate contemplation, well knowing that every diminution from the general mass of human misery must proportionably diminish the force of his argument." The colloquy in which this philanthropic principle is illustrated possesses immortal merit as a piece of imitative versification; showing Mr. Southey's Sapphics in all their varieties, from the dancing rhythm with its fine swing of melody to the break down into flat ambling prose. As this poem may be considered Mr. Canning's *chef-d'œuvre* in this way, and is now rarely to be fallen in with, it is inserted here. But in order to quicken the enjoyment of its skilful wit, it is preceded by a specimen of Southey's Sapphics duly accentuated, as it was introduced by the author in the "Anti-Jacobin."

" Cōld wăs thē nīght wīnd : drīftĭng fāst thĕ snōws fĕll,
Wīde wĕre thē dōwns, ānd shĕltĕrlēss ănd nākĕd :
Whēn ă poōr wānd'rēr strŭgglĕd ōn hĕr joūrnĕy
    Wēarў ănd wāysōre."

THE FRIEND OF HUMANITY AND THE KNIFE-GRINDER.

" Needy Knife-grinder ! whither are you going ?
Rough is the road, your wheel is out of order—
Bleak blows the blast ;—your hat has got a hole in't,
    So have your breeches !

"Weary knife-grinder ! little think the proud ones,
Who in their coaches roll along the turnpike-
-road, what hard work 'tis crying all day, ' Knives and
    Scissars to grind O!'

" Tell me, Knife-grinder, how came you to grind knives?
Did some rich man tyrannically use you?
Was it the squire? or parson of the parish ;
    Or the attorney?

" Was it the squire, for killing of his game ? or
Covetous parson, for his tithes distraining?
Or roguish lawyer, made you lose your little
    All in a lawsuit?

("Have you not read the 'Rights of Man,' by Tom Paine?)
Drops of compassion tremble on my eyelids,
Ready to fall, as soon as you have told your
   Pitiful story."

     KNIFE-GRINDER.
" Story! God bless you! I have none to tell, Sir,
Only last night a-drinking at the Chequers,
This poor old hat and breeches, as you see, were
   Torn in a scuffle.

" Constables came up for to take me into
Custody; they took me before the justice;
Justice Oldmixon put me in the parish-
   -stocks for a vagrant.

" I should be glad to drink your Honour's health in
A pot of beer, if you will give me sixpence;
But for my part, I never love to meddle
   With politics, sir."

     FRIEND OF HUMANITY.
" *I* give thee sixpence! I will see thee damn'd first—
Wretch! whom no sense of wrongs can rouse to vengeance;
Sordid, unfeeling, reprobate, degraded,
   Spiritless outcast!"

Kicks the knife-grinder, overturns his wheel, and exit in a transport of republican enthusiasm and universal philanthropy.

The dactylics also came in for a fling in some lines which are described as " the quintescence of all the dactylics that ever were or ever will be written."

" Sorely thy dactylics lag on uneven feet;
Slow is the syllable which thou wouldst urge to speed,
Lame and overburthened, and ' screaming its wretchedness!'"

An " Elegy on Jean Bon St. André," a French republican, who was put to death by the Dey of Algiers, and an inscription for the cell of Mrs. Browning, the 'prenticide, a parody on Southey's inscription for the cell of Marten the regicide, are also attributed to Mr. Canning, although the exclusive right in them is said not to be vested in him. Indeed, all the poems in the " Anti-Jacobin" are supposed to be the common property of a joint-stock company of wits; a circumstance to which the inequality so remarkable in most of them must be ascribed.

Various scattered touches seem to indicate a more brilliant source than the rest, and are likely on that account to be assigned to Canning as the most celebrated of the contributors. It is also known that he was the largest contributor, and for that reason, if there were no better, he has the best right to the advantage of the doubt. The prisoner's song in the " Rovers," and parts of the dialogue of that capital satire on the German drama; snatches here and there of the " Loves of the Triangles" (which is too laboured, as a whole, to have sprung from Canning); and some of the best lines in the " Progress of Man;" come within this speculation.

No authentic edition of Mr. Canning's poems has ever been published. He did not write much verse, and that which he did write was either intended merely *pour l'occasion,* or was too slight for the purposes of a collection. His early pieces—of which some specimens are published in this volume for the first time—were dispersed in MS., and never resumed by the author, who would probably have been sufficiently unwilling to see them drawn out from their private depositaries. Poetry seems to have been rather a toil than a pleasure to him, if we may judge from the scantiness of his productions in this way, and the severity with which they are finished. It was only when some happy inspiration came that he cared to throw the thought into the shape of verse, and even then it was too brief and subtle to reward him for the trouble it gave. He had too large a critical faculty, and too small a creative power, to have been a great poet. But why should we look for miracles? Who wonders that Demosthenes could not write odes like Horace?

In endeavouring to trace through private channels any fragments of his poetry that may yet chance to survive, it is very tantalising to find odds and ends of numerous pieces (the originals of which are probably lost), carried away in fleeting memories here and there, with only enough of accuracy to make us impatient to get the remainder, and always accompanied by an assurance, that what is forgotten was so much better than what is remembered! Mr. Canning wrote a great number of political pieces, now destroyed or irrecoverable. Lady Hester Stanhope speaks of some verses he wrote on Mr. Pitt, in which he compared him to a chained eagle, and which were so "fine" that Lord Temple wanted to steal them, and actually ran off with them into the street without his hat, but was pursued and captured, and so the verses were restored; this is all we hear about them. Mr. Canning seems to have been very careless of his rhymes, and not only to have cast most of them heedlessly upon the waters, but to have cast off many of them anonymously.

Notwithstanding, however, that he took so little pains to establish his authorship of the pieces he really did write, other people have been at considerable trouble to confer upon him the authorship of pieces which he certainly did not write. One of the most conspicuous instances is that of a clever *jeu-d'esprit*, which appeared shortly after the battle of Waterloo, entitled "An Epitaph on the Marquis of Anglesea's Leg." This was suspected to have been written by Mr. Canning, and not only went the round of the newspapers, but was actually transferred to the pages of a biography, which appeared after his death, where he was announced as the author, with this very grave rebuke for the bad taste of jesting on such a subject: "Some minds," says the writer, "are so constituted, that they throw an air of pleasantry over the most serious misfortune, and extract from pain itself the jest of the *bon mot!*" But this epitaph thus authoritatively asserted to be the production of Mr. Canning, was written by a gentleman well known in the world of literature and the public journals.*

The "Loves of the Triangles" is also given to him in a Paris edition of his poems, although it is one of the composite pieces of the "Anti-Jacobin;" and other things are ascribed to him in various collections, of a no less apochryphal character. Beyond these productions, veritable and spurious, nothing remains of Mr. Canning's poetry to which any further reference need be made, except two or three pasquinades, which will be noticed in the places to which they refer.

* Mr. Thomas Gaspey, author of the "Life of Lord Cobham," "The Lollards," "George Godfrey," and numerous works of fiction and facetiæ.

VI.

THE DOWNWARD STRUGGLE OF THE WAR QUESTION. THE UNION WITH IRELAND. DISSOLUTION OF THE PITT MINISTRY. MR. CANNING'S MARRIAGE.

HITHERTO we have seen, in Mr. Canning's parliamentary career, little more than the close and watchful subtlety of the partisan. The statesman was yet to come. His early speeches, acute and brilliant upon small points, and discovering considerable ingenuity in the art of presenting a question in its most specious and favourable aspects, are deficient in grasp and largeness of purpose. The argument is everywhere minute, compact, clear—never comprehensive; it is the dialectician, not the reasoner, who charms you so cunningly. We miss in these speeches all the great attributes for which he was afterwards famous—generalisation, intellectual beauty, and sustained eloquence; but we have in them some minor qualities no less characteristic—delicacy and refinement of diction, almost amounting to prudery, sentences of most musical structure, the happiest wit, the keenest sarcasm.

The first great occasion on which he put forth his powers, was that of Mr. Tierney's motion, on the 11th of December, 1798, recommending negotiations for peace. The subject had been repeatedly before the House during the last two years—two years so crowded with distracting events that it is wonderful how Mr. Canning kept silence.

The activity of the opposition was unparalleled. No sooner was one motion overthrown by an overwhelming majority, than another was ready to fill its place. They seemed to acquire fresh vigour from defeat, and, like Antæus, to rebound from every fall with renewed elasticity. Ministers had scarcely an hour's repose, and, if they slept at all, it must have been to fight Sheridan and Tierney over again in their dreams. That phalanx was awful to gaze upon, arrayed before the Treasury-benches in implacable hostility, and invincible resolution; and bringing forward night after night a succession of accusations against the government, which no conviction of numerical weakness could prevail upon them to abandon or abate. Motions for the impeachment of ministers; for addresses to remove them; declarations of distrust; and open charges of corruption and perfidy, were of perpetual recurrence. Motions for negotiations with France were proposed and thrown out, and re-proposed, and thrown out again, regularly every session. The question of Parliamentary Reform was brought forward with the same uniform determination, and met the same invariable fate. And all this time incidents were occurring in doors and out of doors, which considerably heightened the flurry and dramatic interest of public affairs. Mr. Fox and his friends, wearied out by the hopelessness of making any impression on the government, seceded from their attendance at the House, for which Pitt's friends blamed them severely; but, speedily returned again, for which Pitt's friends blamed them still more. The French were victorious everywhere, and fresh taxes were laid on, including the income-tax, to a prodigious amount, to enable us to assist them to further triumphs. The discontents of the navy broke out in a mutiny at the Nore. Ireland, goaded by ill-usage, plunged into a sanguinary rebellion; and Mr. Pitt and Mr. Tierney, having had a slight difference of opinion in the House of Commons, referred the dispute to Wimbledon Common, where they fought a duel on a Sunday morning, *while divine service was going on in the church.**

Throughout these agitations Mr. Canning never spoke in Parliament, except to answer some question connected with his department, or to explain something in the absence of a minister. But it must not be forgotten that his official duties involved the heaviest and most responsible functions of the administration; and that, however much he was wanted in the House of Commons, he was wanted still more in the Foreign Office. He had more than enough to do between Pitt and Lord Grenville, men of totally opposite tempers. The icy haughtiness of Lord Grenville chilled even the premier, who was not very remarkable for warmth himself. There was none of that freezing pride about Pitt which made the manners of Lord Grenville so oppressive to his inferiors. Pitt, habitually cold, was at least distinguished by a plainness and simplicity, which put the stranger at his ease.

---

* Pitt, who had given the provocation, received Tierney's shot and fired in the air. Wilberforce was so shocked at this occurrence, that he gave notice of a motion about it, which he would have actually brought on if Pitt had not written him a private note to say that it would render his resignation inevitable.—" Wilberforce's Life," ii., 282. Pitt's want of religion was a source of great trouble to this good, importunate man. Whenever he went to any of Pitt's parties, he used to come away quite in low spirits. "My heart," says he, "has been moved by the society of my old friends at Pitt's. Alas! alas! how sad to see them thoughtless of their immortal souls; so wise, so acute. I hope I felt in some degree properly on the occasion and afterwards," ii., 334. He dines at Dundas's on Pitt's birthday, and declares that he cannot "assimilate." Lady Hester Stanhope says that Pitt was an infidel, and that the account which Gifford gives of his death-bed is absolutely false.

Lord Grenville's stately isolation, on the contrary, was inexplicable for a man in his situation. Windham said that he knew nobody, and that nobody knew him. It has been observed that his fine understanding redeemed his *hauteur;* but as fine understandings do not enter into the details of daily official intercourse, and the *hauteur* generally does, it must be concluded that Mr. Canning had a task of no common difficulty in keeping his immediate chief, and the head of the government, on tolerable terms with each other.

There was no novelty in Mr. Tierney's motion. Similar motions had been thrown out over and over again. But circumstances were changed. Ministers, hunted down by the most persevering of oppositions, had been making secret attempts to bring about a negotiation for peace, although they publicly resisted every suggestion of that kind in both Houses of Parliament. Their argument was this—that peace or war lay in the province of the crown, and ought not to be interfered with by Parliament; and that it would be unwise to affirm any resolution on the subject of peace, until it had been first ascertained what prospect there was of obtaining just and honourable terms. With a view to discover the disposition of the Directory on this momentous question, they had taken sundry steps to sound that body, through Lord Malmesbury, and other agents in Switzerland, Paris, Lisle—all failing from the duplicity and over-reaching spirit with which they were conducted.

It would be a wilful injustice, with the information before us which the lapse of years has permitted its possessors to reveal, not to relieve Mr. Pitt from the exclusive responsibilities of these double-dealings. He was guilty, in the main, only of being a consenting party; but, considering that he was prime minister, the guilt of yielding to a system of deception at such a moment was hardly less culpable than that of having originated it. Pitt was forced into acquiescence by Grenville, in whose department these delicate diplomacies lay. The inflexible, overbearing Whig insisted upon a peace, which he *knew* the French Directory would never grant. *He never intended that the negotiations should end successfully.* Pitt, on the contrary, was becoming every day more and more anxious for peace—having at last discovered the necessity for it—and would have effected it (Lord Malmesbury testifies that it *could* have been effected) but for the obstinacy of his unbending colleague. " It is the fault of the French," says Canning, in a private letter to George Ellis, hinting at Pitt's real disposition, "if they have not a peace as good as to terms as they can reasonably desire."* If Pitt could have ventured to risk an open difference with Grenville, the matter might have been settled in the usual way, by an imperative action in the cabinet; but he was not in a position to make or to betray a disagreement with his dictatorial allies. He could not afford it. This state of things placed Lord Malmesbury (then conducting the negotiation at Lisle) in a most painful situation. " You must have perceived," he observes, in a confidential communication to Mr. Canning, " that the instructions and opinions I get from the minister under *whose orders I am bound to act*, accord so little with the sentiments and intentions I heard expressed by the minister *with whom I wish to act*, that I am placed in a very disagreeable dilemma." But this was not the worst. It was not merely that he was required to act in a spirit averse to his inclinations and convictions, but *averse to the object*

* " Diaries of Lord Malmesbury," iii., 433.

which he was to pretend to promote. The passage which unveils this fraud (divulging the true secret history of the failure) is remarkable. After stating that he had no objection to persevere steadily in pursuit of his object till it was either attained, or demonstrated to be unattainable, so long as the original purpose with which he was commissioned, (for it seems that Lord Grenville broke his designs to him only by wary degrees) was to be sought with sincerity; he goes on: " but if another opinion has been allowed to prevail—if the *real* end is to differ from the *ostensible* one—and if I am only to remain here, *in order to break off the negotiation creditably, and not to terminate it successfully*, I then, instead of resigning my opinion, must resign my office."

Canning was the sole depository of this piece of state perfidy. He stood between Pitt and Grenville, and between Malmesbury and both, and prevented the rupture, which, with less discretion, must have placed the government in a serious difficulty. The country was indebted to his judgment, temper, and tact, that no worse consequences ensued from these dangerous confidences than the frustration of the mission. But the management of the ministerial intrigues greatly increased the harassing nature of his duties.[*] The only breaks of sunshine he appears to have enjoyed were in corresponding with his uncle Legh, or with his old friend George Ellis, who was attached to Lord Malmesbury's embassy (a correspondence, however, which was so full of the subjects on which they were both engrossed, that it consisted of little else than French politics melted down into private disclosures); an occa-

[*] Although he bore with Lord Grenville wonderfully to the end, winning the admiration of every body by his self-control, he several times contemplated a retreat from the Foreign-office, and once told Lord Malmesbury that he hoped to effect a change to the India Board.

sional run down to Hollwood or Dropmore, or a stray half-hour of a morning with the Freres or the Lavingtons. His time was almost exclusively passed between his house in Spring Gardens (where Pitt used frequently to dine with him) and Downing Street.

The period occupied by these negotiations was one of intense anxiety to the government. "No messenger yet from Lisle," writes Mr. Canning to a private friend. "It is an interval of anxiety and impatience, such as makes it impossible to think, speak, or write upon any other subject. I get up, go to bed, eat, drink, sleep, walk, ride, with nothing but the messenger in my head, and I hear nothing all day long, but 'Well; not come yet? when will the messenger come, and what will he bring? Peace?'" The fact was that, although for prudential motives they still maintained "the fiery front of war" in the face of Europe, ministers (at least Pitt and those who originated the war) were secretly more desirous of peace than the opposition themselves.*

To return to Mr. Tierney's motion. The main points on which he rested were these: that the European confederacy against France was already, to all intents and purposes, broken up, that we could no longer pursue the war with

* During the difficulties and delays which arose throughout these negotiations, Lord Grenville suspected Pitt of getting up opinions out of doors and in the newspapers, to fortify himself in the cabinet; and in order to *tie up his tongue*, he got a resolution passed pledging the cabinet to secrecy respecting these matters. To Canning and Hammond were confided the duty of opening and answering the despatches, and none but the copies made by Hammond, who wrote an abominable hand, were shown to the subaltern ministers, hoping that they would not take the trouble to decipher them. See the "Malmesbury Diaries." Such was the mystery observed respecting Lord Malmesbury's negotiation, that the whole cabinet, with the exception of Pitt and Grenville, were kept in the dark about his despatches; and he was obliged to prepare one for general purposes, besides his special despatch to Lord Grenville. The most secret revelations, however, intended neither for the public nor the minister, came out in the private letters to Canning, who was the recipient of the complaints and contentions on all sides.

the remotest hope of driving back France to her ancient limits; that in six years we had increased our debt by one hundred and fifty millions, adding eight millions to our annual burdens (a sum equal to our entire expenditure when George III. ascended the throne); and that our domestic situation, with the Habeas Corpus Act suspended, Ireland in rebellion, and enormous establishments to support, rendered it imperative upon us to leave Europe to herself, and look to our own interests at last. As to the objection that the crown alone had the undoubted power of making war or peace; he balanced it by the constitutional right of the Commons to grant or refuse the supplies. The speech was sensible and to the purpose, but languid and ineffective, and deficient in the caustic acerbity which usually distinguished Mr. Tierney. No great wonder—the subject was thread-bare, and every body knew its agitation to be a mere waste of lungs.

Mr. Canning rose to reply, and delivered a speech which for compass of reasoning, and masterly elocution, might well have drawn an expression of admiration from Mr. Pitt. This magnificent display of eloquence fairly electrified the House—the previous dullness disappeared —members crowded in—and the orator held the senate suspended in wonder and delight. It is not too much to say of this speech, that it is one of the greatest—in some respects the most complete, that was delivered on the ministerial side in reference to the war. We had at that time, too, passed out of the mere abstract question: it was no longer speculation; experience had thrown unexpected lights upon the subject ; we had tested our strength through triumphs and reverses; we had tested our alliances also, and found some of them frail, selfish, and cowardly; Austria and Prussia had at different times made peace with France, in violation of their engagements with us; Spain, Holland, and Sardinia, were overawed by the arms of the republic; our situation was no longer the same as when we commenced the crusade, and that which was at first a question of policy, open to doubts and difficulties, had now become a point of honour with ministers —a calculation in which they were to strike the balance between glory and shame.

Mr. Canning's reply was the best argument for the prosecution of the war which could be built upon this altered state of things. The defection of allies was only an additional reason, if any were wanted, for the observance of good faith towards those who still remained true to their engagements; and the wanton horrors which everywhere tracked the progress of the French arms, furnished another reason for pursuing hostilities, until such a peace could be effected as should repose upon a basis wide enough to include and indemnify all interests. A separate peace for England would be inadequate for this purpose. The war was European—the settlement must be European too.

The ingenuity of this view of the case consisted in assuming a chivalric motive for not doing a very hazardous thing. The opposition wanted ministers to enter into a separate peace with France, without reference to the situation or prospects of other powers. That circumstances would have justified such a course, was perfectly true; at least true to the extent of supplying undeniable precedents. But the contingencies of a separate peace were more dangerous than the war itself. In the first place, it would have been impossible to obtain singly as good an arrangement as if the united powers coalesced in their demands; and, in the second place, if it could be obtained, it would have been impossible to render it secure. In the last place, it was quite certain that the moment we retired from the field, France, relieved of her most formidable adversary, would overrun the continent, and ultimately compel us to the defence, at a great disadvantage, of whatever rights we might have acquired by such a treaty. There were, therefore, many prudential reasons for keeping together as long as we could the elements of resistance, even at the risk of prolonging the war indefinitely. Mr. Canning was careful not to betray to the world—especially to the republic—the fact that his real motive for continuing the war was the impossibility of establishing a safe and honourable peace; he put it upon higher and more popular grounds—the alliances by which we were still bound, and the duty imposed upon us, as the guardians of freedom and civilisation, to succour and redress the countries which were trodden down by the hoofs of French despotism. This sort of appeal to the integrity and humanity of England never failed; but it was enforced on this occasion with such power, that it roused the country into a fit of enthusiasm.

Ministers had latterly spoken of the deliverance of Europe (referring to the superfluous atrocities of the French) as the purpose to which they directed their efforts; but Mr. Tierney rejected the expression with ridicule, as conveying no determinate idea whatever. Mr. Canning's exposition of its meaning is one of the happiest passages in the speech. Its effect on the public mind was extraordinary. It served as a text for every body who declaimed about the war, and converted many to that side of the question who had never before been brought to consider so closely the magnitude of the French aggressions.

"I cannot undertake to answer for other gentlemen's powers

of comprehension. The map of Europe is before them. I can only say that I do not admire that man's intellects, and I do not envy that man's feelings, who can look over that map without gathering some notion of what is meant by the deliverance of Europe. I do not envy that man's feelings who can behold the sufferings of Switzerland, and who derives from that sight no idea of what is meant by the deliverance of Europe. I do not envy the feelings of that man who can look without emotion at Italy—plundered, insulted, trampled upon, exhausted, covered with ridicule, and horror, and devastation; who can look at all this, and be at a loss to guess what is meant by the deliverance of Europe? As little do I envy the feelings of that man who can view the people of the Netherlands driven into insurrection and struggling for their freedom against the heavy hand of a merciless tyranny, without entertaining any suspicion of what may be the sense of the word deliverance. Does such a man contemplate Holland groaning under arbitrary oppressions and exactions? Does he turn his eyes to Spain trembling at the nod of a foreign master? and does the word deliverance still sound unintelligibly in his ears? Has he heard of the rescue and salvation of Naples, by the appearance and the triumphs of the British fleet? Does he know that the monarchy of Naples maintains its existence at the sword's point? And is his understanding, is his heart, still impenetrable to the sense and meaning of the deliverance of Europe?"

It seemed as if people had no suspicion of the extent of the French conquests, or as if they could not realise the idea of the carnage and oppression by which they were accompanied, until this picture—so crowded, yet so distinct,—was thus brought suddenly before them. Then the whole terrible truth became apparent, and then, for the first time, they began to comprehend the shape which this question of war was taking under the influence of such events. The forced alliances, or cowering submissions, into which the French compelled the weaker states to enter, were scarcely less dreadful to bear than the sacking of towns, the violation of women, and the other barbarities which descended upon such as had the heroism to resist; so that even the friendship of the Directory was as fatal as its enmity—another reason against being too eager about peace. All this was touched upon with striking effect by Mr. Canning in his allusion to the allies of France, especially the Cisalpine Republic, upon whom she was making experiments in the theory of government; and Sardinia, whom she had reduced to a mere mockery of a kingdom. The description of the position of the King of Sardinia is a masterly piece of history-painting.

"By what ties of gratitude is the King of Sardinia bound to his ally? The King of Sardinia, it is true, has not yet been precipitated from his throne; but he sits there with the sword of a French garrison suspended above his head. He retains indeed the style and title of king; but there is a French general to be viceroy over him. A prisoner in his own capital, surrounded by the spies and agents, and hemmed in by the arms of the Directory; compelled to dismiss from his councils and his presence all those of his servants who were most attached to his person, and most zealous for his interests; compelled to preach daily to his people the mortifying and degrading lesson of that patience and humility of which he is himself a melancholy example, to excuse and extenuate the insults offered by his allies to his subjects; to repress, even by force, the resentment of his subjects against his allies. Is this a situation in which the King of Sardinia can be supposed to derive comfort from the alliance of France, and repay it with thankfulness? Would he not, even if this were to be the extent of his suffering and degradation; would he not, if he inherits the spirit of his great ancestors, if their blood flows in his veins; would he not seize, even at the risk of his crown and of his life, any opportunity that might be afforded him, to emancipate himself from a connexion so burdensome, to shake off the weight of a friendship so intolerable."

The Cisalpine Republic, shuddering under the hands of the operator, is equally forcible.

"Are we to look for attachment in the Cisalpine Republic, whom, in preference to the others, France appears to have selected as a living subject for her experiments in political anatomy; whom she has delivered up tied and bound, to a series of butchering, bungling, philosophical professors, to distort and mangle, and lop, and stretch its limbs into all sorts of fantastical shapes, *and to hunt through its palpitating frame the vital principle of republicanism.*"

This speech established Mr. Canning's reputation. It placed him in the highest rank of parliamentary orators, and the few who were close enough to observe accurately now began to look to him as one who promised at no remote day to take a lead amongst our statesmen. Others, of the class which is always jealous of rising men, could not conceal their vexation at his success. A contemporary meets him at dinner about this time, and exclaims, "What envy I saw of him universally." We learn also that when he used to get up in the House, Grey, Tierney, and others generally went out. The Whigs, of course, disliked him; but the feeling was not confined to them. The Tories were incensed at the favour bestowed on him by Pitt; they used to say that Pitt encouraged him too much, and that he was too flippant and ambitious. The secret of all this is penetrated at a glance.

He spoke on other subjects during the sessions of 1799, and 1800; principally old topics reproduced in new shapes—the war question argued over again in new disguises. He made a speech in defence of bull-baiting, which threw poor Wilberforce into an agony of distress; but "to do him justice," says the good man, "when I showed him an account of the cruelties that were practised he was quite ashamed of himself!"* Canning had too much real regard for Wilberforce to be offended at his well-mean but rather officious advice. He would have dealt with most other people under like circumstances, as he did with Courtenay in the debate on the suspension of the Habeas Corpus

* "Life of Wilberforce," ii., 366.

Act, when he told him " to keep his humanity for Smith and Bains, his religion for Newgate, and his jokes for the hackney coachmen."

The only great questions to which he addressed himself during this period, were the slave-trade, and the union with Ireland. The former may be deferred for later consideration;—but the latter, having led to the dismemberment of Pitt's administration, requires to be treated at some length.

On the 22nd of January, 1799, Mr. Dundas brought down a message from his majesty, setting forth that our enemies were plotting the separation of Ireland from the rest of the kingdom, and recommending to Parliament the consideration of the most effectual means for defeating so heinous a design, and for improving and perpetuating a connexion essential to the common security of the whole British empire. This message was vigorously debated both in England and Ireland, and ended in the Act of Union, which was finally passed in the following year.

The first thing that must strike the mind of a foreigner upon opening this passage of our history is the curious fact, that England should never have thought of this act of incorporation before. It cannot fail to appear very surprising that upwards of six hundred years of settlement and possession, chequered by feuds that ought to have furnished significant hints, should have elapsed before the necessity of such a step—saying nothing about its wisdom—happened to strike the government of this country. And surprise will be worked up into wonder, " with hair on end," by the discovery that, within a century, Ireland had actually begged for this same legislative union as a boon, and had been refused!* England

* The English Parliament had so frequently over-ruled the de-

was always smitten with suspicion and indecision in her dealings with Ireland, acting as one would do who was making bargains with an usurer: always afraid of appearing too liberal—always afraid of bidding for the affections of the people, in the apprehension of raising their terms—always withholding what they asked for, thinking there must be some sinister design in it—and always forcing upon them what they abhorred, for the same excellent reason.

The consequence was, that as she would not hear of a union when the Irish wanted it; so when she saw fit, for her own safety, to seek it, the Irish refused their consent: the common fate of all legislation that waits upon necessity. An act that might have been performed with grace, was at last effected by fraud and violence; and instead of being carried with the good-will of the people, was forced upon them by bribes and bayonets.

The policy invariably applied to Ireland was the policy of fear. Nothing in the way of justice was ever done to the country, unless there happened to be a pressure of some kind which rendered it also a matter of prudence. The experiment of justice, for its own sake, was never yet tried upon Ireland; whenever justice did chance to take that direction, it was for the sake of England. There was some fear of disturbances at home, some suspicion of a

cisions of the Irish Parliament, that in 1707 the Irish Commons made a proposal, in an address to the queen, for a legislative union between the two countries; and this proposal the English government treated with scorn. Upwards of four hundred years before, so strong was the desire of the Irish to participate in the advantages of the English government, that *they offered to pay for permission to live under the English law;* but although the king was well disposed to favour so rational a request, his intentions were intercepted and frustrated by the English lords settled in Ireland. They thought it was their interest to keep the two races apart, and laboured hard for that end, and it must be admitted, succeeded to admiration.

descent from abroad, some want to be supplied—money or soldiers—and then Ireland was sure to be smiled upon by British justice, but never till then. On the other hand, when England was prosperous and secure, Ireland was coerced; her conflicting interests set up against each other, her wrongs re-opened, her prejudices excited, her old animosities exasperated anew, and every means resorted to, through the intricate machinery of bad government, to break her spirit and repress her advancement. It was not an idle figure of speech by which Grattan described these crimes of choice and virtues of necessity, when he said, that " England's weakness was Ireland's strength."*

This is an old story. But it is a true story, nevertheless, and must be heard for its truth, as well as for its intimate bearing upon things as they are. Indeed, the Past cannot be divorced from the Present and the Future of Ireland. Unhappily for all parties, there can be no oblivion of bitter memories which are still kept alive in their visible effects. That which we see in Ireland to this day is not a new birth of human folly, but the direct consequence of acts which were done in Ireland in former days. "Let by-gones be by-gones" will not hold here. The connexion between existing evils and continuous misrule is that of cause and effect; and it is impossible to legislate for evils of this nature, without a complete knowledge of their lineage.

Yet there are people—hundreds of thousands on this side of the channel—who do not believe one word of this old story; who regard it as a mere raw-head and bloody-bones. People who judge of Ireland from passing manifestations and first impressions, who see the social ruin plainly enough,

* Speech on moving an Address to the Crown, 1782.

but throw it all upon the want of nationality, of energy, of any thing and every thing, in the Irish themselves rather than upon England. They find it no easy matter to carry their imaginations back into the history of the past, and to conjure out of its dismal depths the ghastly bigotries that once ruled the realms of life, and swayed the courses of man. They cannot get out of the sunshine of the English homestead, fenced round by paternal institutions, and connect with it in any way the black midnight of the Irish hovel, and the children of famine who stalk about its unsightly heaps. They cannot comprehend the existence of a political hypocrisy so monstrous as that which, creating free institutions with one hand, was no less actively employed in fomenting anarchy, and abetting despotism with the other. They do not see this going on now, in the old wholesale bare-faced way:—they do not believe, therefore, that it ever did go on. If you relate to them particular facts, well attested, of singular tyrannies—such as that of giving rewards for shooting an Irishman, instead of hanging the perpetrator as we should now do; or of making the nurture of an English infant by an Irish nurse high treason by law;[*] they will treat them as they would ghost-stories, which *you* may believe if you are fool enough to put any faith in such absurdities, but which *they* have *rather* too much sense to swallow.

Nine-tenths of the people of England are ignorant of the demoralising atrocities which have been inflicted in their name, upon Ireland; and the remaining tenth do not believe in them. The only comfort to be extracted from this is, that it is creditable to the humanity of to-day to disbelieve in the inhumanity of yesterday; and that there

See "Davis's Tracts"—Plowden.

is, consequently, some hope that it will act better to-morrow.

The Englishman of to-day sees in Ireland the sister Cinderella (*in her servitude*) of the British islands, and thinks that it is her own fault she should be such a thankless drudge. He sees her in serge and coarse stockings (or none); while her more fortunate sisters are flaunting in lace and satin; and attributes all to sloth and poverty of spirit. He has not witnessed the slow harassing unintermitting process of domestic slavery, by which she has been reduced to this; he only sees the miseries of her condition, and satisfies his sense of justice by blaming her who *suffers* them. He sees in Ireland, fine harbours and no ships; spacious docks, grand custom-houses, and no commerce; a region proverbial for fertility, and a starving population. He thinks that these anomalies must be the fault of the people themselves; as if *that*, were it true, would not be the greatest anomaly of all!

To suppose that any race of human beings would voluntarily starve in the midst of plenty; go voluntarily half-clad, in the midst of their own wool; wilfully lie down to sleep on stones and dream of devouring them, when they might have pillows and visions of roast pig if they would; is a stretch of fancy that considerably transcends even the poetical faculty of the Irish themselves.

There is no country in the world which exhibits in its actual condition, and in direct circumstances, possessing present power over that condition, such irresistible deductions from historical facts as Ireland. Every person who has taken the trouble to investigate the subject has been compelled by the force of evidence to refer the evils under which Ireland labours, in the past and in the present, not to any incomprehensible waywardness in the people, or mysterious malediction in the climate, but to a long course of blind misgovernment. The social disorganisation of sects and parties is a legacy of that misgovernment; the curse of absenteeism is a legacy of that misgovernment; the double curse of sub-letting and middlemen, a consequence flowing out of absenteeism and other causes, themselves the effects of misgovernment; want of profitable employment, a consequence of want of capital, produced by this conspiracy of impoverishing circumstances; low wages, thinly scattered at broken intervals, over some millions of working men, a consequence of scanty employment; periodical famine, periodical typhus, constant misery, constant complaint, constant outrage, hopelessness and indifference to life, the natural results of these complicated and ravelled grievances; all having their common source in an infatuated system of misgovernment; prolonged in defiance of experience, in defiance of justice, in defiance of the general safety. Whoever would discover the real causes of Irish anomalies, must look for them in Irish history; and it is because the influences of time are thrown out of the calculation, that some people are eternally disappointed at not finding temporary and special remedies panaceatic in their effects. These are the class of people, ignorant of her history, and of its action upon passing events, who are always so ready to throw up Ireland as a confounded bore and a hopeless case; and who think that the best thing that could happen to her, would be just to sink her under water for four-and-twenty hours.*

The historical origin of Irish evils has been acknow-

* It is a strange thing, and somewhat awful to think of, that poor Sir Joseph Yorke, who made use of this wild observation, was drowned in the Southampton Water.

ledged by every politician who understood the problem involved in them. "It is impossible," observes a recent writer of great intelligence, "to form a fair and impartial judgment on Irish affairs, or to arrive at sound conclusions upon present political questions, without knowing and keeping studiously in view the whole course of Irish history."* Mr. Pitt bore testimony to the chronic character of the disease, when he stated in the debate on the Union that for one hundred years England had pursued a narrow, jealous, and selfish policy towards Ireland; although he might have extended his range a little further, like Bushe, who declared, that for centuries Great Britain had kept Ireland down, shackled her commerce, paralysed her exertions, despised her character, and ridiculed her pretensions to any privileges, commercial or constitutional; "she never conceded a point to you," said that brilliant orator, on the floor of the Irish House of Commons, when this question of the Union came before it, "she never conceded a point to you which she could avoid, or granted a favour which was not reluctantly distilled."

But the Union was to atone for all past mischiefs, and to prevent the recurrence of new ones, by drawing Ireland into such close connexion with England, as to identify their interests. This was the avowed purpose, and, it is charitable to hope, the real desire of Pitt. Unfortunately, something more was required to crown this union with the desiderated felicity, than the mere ceremony of pronouncing the bans.

There was scarcely any thing in common between the two countries. The bulk of the Irish even spoke a different language.† On the one side was prosperity, on

* "Past and Present Policy of England towards Ireland," p. 14.
† See "Ireland—Past and Present," a pamphlet published in

the other wretchedness, inherited generation after generation, and leaving its impress, mental and physical, behind. With the English, the sense of security in wrongs; with the Irish, the rankling feeling of wrongs suffered and unappeased. There were different meanings attached to the same things in the two countries—different manners, different habits, growing out of circumstances as contrasted as jocund Plenty and haggard Want. In England there was a public opinion, which restrained the powerful within the limits of defined rights; in Ireland, there was no public opinion, it was extinguished under an indefinite ascendancy. That which was in England a source of pride—her bold peasantry—was in Ireland a source of shame. In England, men were protected by the law; in Ireland, the law was either not executed at all, or used only as an agent of terror. These things, and a thousand more, were to be reconciled by Act of Parliament.

But this was not all. The people had been divided amongst and against themselves, and they were to be blended into one. Various conflicting castes were to lie down together in amity under the roof-tree leaves of this Act of Parliament. There was the English settler, who had never yet mixed himself up with the Irishry, and who, to all intents and purposes, inhabited a Paradise of the Pale of his own; there was the settler who, through intermarriage and other commerce with the natives, stood mid-way in the shadows of the two camps, and hardly knew to which he

Dublin in 1808. This pamphlet excited considerable attention at the time from its terse and glittering style, and the apparent impartiality with which it held the scales of party. But, like most specimens of medium politics, it left all the vexed questions exactly where it found them. The most interesting point about the *brochure* is that, although never avowed, it was the first political production of the Right Honourable John Wilson Croker.

belonged; then there was the pure Catholic, who had never mingled with the Sassenach, and who represented in its integrity the sentiment of national resentment; the wavering Catholic, who was fluctuating between his interests and his conscience; and the reprobate Catholic, who had already gone over to Protestantism and sinecures, with a mental reservation which rendered him as dangerous to his new profession, as he had already been faithless to his old one;—and all these discords were to be reduced to harmony by Act of Parliament.

It may be added that the situation of the Catholics at this crisis was calculated to kindle novel jealousies, and to furnish peculiar pretences for depriving this measure of all its healing and conciliatory properties. They had recently obtained certain ameliorations of the Penal Code, and one of the inducements held out to them for agreeing to the Union was, that it would facilitate the repeal of the remainder. Now this reason, so tempting and plausible on the one side, was the most unfortunate that could be resorted to on the other. It wounded the Protestants on the most tender point—it suggested the only conceivable ground on which they could seek or discover a pretext for opposing the Union, which in all other respects was quite consonant with their English sympathies. There was nothing which the Irish Protestants were not ready to sacrifice rather than consent to the relief of the Catholics. It was not merely that they hated Popery intrinsically, but because every diminution of the thraldom under which it groaned, would have been a deduction from their own ascendancy. And whoever is learned in Irish history, and knows what that terrible Protestant ascendancy was in the fulness of its power, will be at no loss to understand why they who lived by the breath of its

L

nostrils, should have been so reluctant to grant the smallest fraction of human freedom to the Papists. And this ascendancy, haughty from long impunity, and formidable from long possession, was now to be brought round to the support of a measure which indirectly menaced its very foundations. How was this to be accomplished?

Mr. Cooke, the Under-Secretary for Ireland, published a pamphlet to prove that the Union would be equally beneficial to both parties.* The argument was at least recommended by being thoroughly Irish. It fairly cut the ground from under its own feet. To the Protestants it offered this lure, that the Union was the only chance they had of resisting the claims of the Catholics, through the overwhelming influence and known character of the British Parliament; while to the Catholics it declared that the only hope of emancipation lay in this same measure of Union which would release them from local tyranny, and facilitate their admission into the British Constitution.†

It was plain, however, that subterfuges of this kind, like Macheath's *asides* to his two mistresses to make them believe that he was in love with them both, could not deceive the vigilance of the country; and the Cabinet found it necessary to try more effective arguments. In short, they bought up both parties—the Catholics by

* "Arguments for and against an Union between Great Britain and Ireland considered." Dublin, 1798.
† Lord Castlereagh employed the same jesuitical reasoning in his speech on the Union, in the Irish House of Commons, Feb. 5, 1800. "This measure is one," he observed, "that by uniting the Church Establishments, and consolidating the legislatures of the empire, puts an end to religious jealousy, and removes the possibility of separation. It is one which places the great question, which has so long agitated the country, *upon the broad principle of imperial policy, and divests it of all its local difficulties.*" This was the snare which entrapped the Catholics, eager to catch at any thing that promised to float them into the harbour of the constitution.

promises of emancipation,* the Protestants by peerages and places, strengthened in all instances of official dependence, by threats of dismissal.

The fact was that the salvation of the British Empire depended at this moment upon the Union, which was to be carried at any cost by fair means or foul. Pitt was not the minister to hesitate in such a juncture, and he had an agent in the person of Lord Castlereagh, who was ready to second him to the last extremity. The "undertakers" of Ireland—the two or three families who were perched upon the apex of Protestant ascendancy, that *imperium in imperio* which drove out Lord Fitzwilliam, controlled the law, and overawed the government itself—had only one vulnerable spot, and that spot was struck by Pitt. The sacrifices were of incredible magnitude—sacrifices of gold, of honour, of character, of every thing that ordinarily renders life and station desirable to men of integrity; but the enemy was at the gates, and such sacrifices alone could save the country.

The moment was ill chosen—but it had the excuse of

* Some of the more sincere Protestants, who were perfectly guileless in their horror of contracting promises and engagements with the Catholics—clean-hearted men who lived up to the very letter of the Penal Code—were so shocked at the Machiavelian conduct of the government in this crisis, that they did not hesitate to complain of it openly. One of them, in a pamphlet, entitled " Orange Vindicated," (Dublin, 1799,) reproves the government for holding out false hopes to the Catholics, and hints that such dishonest policy may cost them the allegiance of their best friends. "I will conclude," says this bold, good man, "by warning the government against a practice which has been too common amongst the parties of this country, namely, that of treating and parleying with the Catholics as a political body, and making stalking-horses of them and their claims, *for the purpose of mutual embarrassment and vexation*. This weak and wicked policy feeds, and has fed, unjustifiable pretensions. This has been a sort of game; but *hæ nugæ seria ducant in mala*." This worthy pamphleteer was evidently ignorant that this "sort of game," of setting "both your houses" by the ears, had been the state policy of England towards Ireland from the very beginning of their connexion.

being also inevitable. If the Union had been proposed in a season of peace and prosperity it would have been free from suspicion, and might have been consolidated without disgrace. But it followed upon the smoking track of a rebellion, and was forced upon the people. It was not a measure of deliberate benefit, but of sudden and violent expediency. Like all other Irish measures, which, however good in themselves, did not come recommended by their goodness, but, by their necessity, the Union was an exigency, not a concession—it was dictated by England's difficulty, not for Ireland's advantage. But it settled for ever the question which was then taking a palpable and menacing shape—namely, whether Ireland was to become British or French.

Upon this question the Irish themselves never wavered. They have an instinctive antipathy to foreign connexions. But it was rapidly ceasing to be a matter of choice. They might at any time be overborne by events; and although no country can be reasonably expected to prefer a neighbourly despotism to a distant rule, there is no doubt, that the Irish would have borne much injustice from England, and did bear it, rather than suffer the intervention of strange hands between them. Had Ireland ever fallen under the dominion of France—should she ever be lost to England—it would not have been, it will not be, her own seeking.

The expression of opinion in Ireland against the Union was universal and intense. "It is the most barefaced, undisguised assault upon our honour, dignity and character, as a nation, and our liberties, as a people, that has yet been attempted," said a Protestant writer, who belonging to neither extreme, represented the moderate and rational of all parties.* One leading objection to the measure was, that it destroyed the independence of the country—another, that it violated the arrangement of 1782, by which that independence was guaranteed. Both objections were true—but the need was imperious, and they were overruled.

It was said of Mr. Grattan by whom the freedom of Ireland was achieved in 1782, that "he sat by its cradle —he followed its hearse." The phrase depicts the feelings with which the Union was regarded. It was looked upon as the grave of Irish liberty. Yet, honestly carried out, a legislative Union would seem to be the natural issue of the relations in which the two countries stood towards each other. It is more reconcileable with the principles of natural justice that England and Ireland should be bound up under the same laws, the same government, and the same system of representation, than that there should be separation without independence, or connexion without the benefits of reciprocity.

Whether the Union *has* been honestly carried out, is a different consideration.

In the *management* of the question, the worst feature of all was the use that was made of the recent rebellion. It was assumed as a pretext for hurrying forward the Union, before the people could give vent to the feelings it provoked. Yet there were not wanting persons who accused the government of having fomented the rebellion themselves for that very purpose. But the English cabinet, whatever final responsibility may attach to them, were hardly answerable for the hideous details of that insurrection. The blood-guilt belonged to the Irish Executive

* "First Letter to a Noble Lord on the Subject of the Union." Dublin, 1799.

alone; it was the furious spirit of implacable faction usurping the functions of authority. Pitt was ignorant of the iniquitous severity with which the general instructions of the government were carried out in Ireland. He appears to have had no notion of the extent to which the system of torture was prosecuted for the discovery of concealed arms, and when these atrocities came out in discussion, and Lord Clare attempted some sort of reply to the charge, without being able to deny it, " I shall never forget Pitt's look," says Wilberforce ; " he turned round to me with that *high indignant stare* which sometimes marked his countenance, and walked out of the house."*

That the settlement of the Catholic claims was intended by Pitt to follow the Union is now matter of history. In private he was quite open on the subject—in public guarded as to details, but unequivocal as to the principle. He distinctly gave the Catholics to understand that he contemplated their emancipation as a consequence of the Union ; and he assured the Protestants that the concession would no longer be dangerous after the Catholics had become incorporated with the whole population of the empire. He won the Catholics by promises of equality, and wooed the Protestants by promising to swamp the Catholics.

These views were illustrated by Mr. Canning in two speeches—the one on the king's message in January 1799, the other on the address in April. He showed that the Popery code (as it was called) took its rise from the rejection by the British government of a proposal for an union from Ireland ; and that, the contrary course holding

---

* "Life of Wilberforce," ii., 327.

good, the adoption of an union would lead to the relaxation of that code.

"If it was in consequence of the rejection of an union at a former period, that the laws against Popery were enacted, it is fair to conclude that an union would render a similar code unnecessary; that an union *would satisfy the friends of Protestant ascendancy*, without passing laws against the Catholics, and *without maintaining those which are yet in force.*"

It must be remembered that the treasury benches were nearly filled with Protestant ascendancy men, and it required some tact to indicate to them that their bigotry should be in some sort respected; and to convey at the same moment a little hope to the Catholics. The necessity of caution on this vital point was over-ruling; for had the minister spoken out he would have roused into fury the prejudices of his supporters, and been compelled to abandon a measure upon which, as upon a thread, hung the existence of the government. In his second speech Mr. Canning again urged the same considerations, but still clothed in the most careful language. He showed that the Irish parliament, instead of losing something of its power by incorporation, would be better qualified to adjust the animosities arising out of religious differences, by being removed out of the reach and influence of every varying gust of popular frenzy.

"Instead of being committed as a party, it becomes an impartial judge of the conflict, when it is placed in a situation which enables it to weigh every claim with dispassionate calmness and dignity, to resist what may be extravagant without the appearance of severity, *and concede to the Catholics what may remain to be conceded,* without the appearance of intimidation, and without hazard to its own authority and power."

So far as ministerial *hints* at any time, or under any circumstances, can be considered binding, such passages as these must be allowed to have been broad enough to pledge the administration to the Catholic question. Mr. Pitt thought so himself, although his ultra-tory friends thought differently. The greatest misfortune Mr. Pitt laboured under through his life (and his reputation after his death) was that of having friends—warm, enthusiastic friends—who insisted upon worshipping him for opinions and intentions, which he not only never professed but earnestly disclaimed. It would be impossible, for instance, to conceive any set of notions more unlike Mr. Pitt's, than the general run of the sentiments of the Pitt Club. The members of that lively institution have made him responsible for principles so utterly at variance with his convictions, that Mr. Pitt, as some one said, could not with any decency dine at his own dinner.*

Upon this question of emancipation, Mr. Pitt's biographer states, that "no pledge or promise whatever was made by Mr. Pitt, or by his authority, directly or indirectly, to the Romanists of Ireland, that the *few* restrictions under which they still laboured, and forming the *only* bars to a full participation of political power, should be removed, if they would give their consent to the Union."† The *italics* are not Mr. Gifford's; but they ought to have been. How scornfully such men look down upon the wrongs of others, from their heights of power and impunity! These *few* restrictions, which appeared so contemptible to Mr. Gifford, were all sufficient,

---

* It is only fair to observe, that the Pitt Club was not always so perverse and intolerant. That section of the Tories who would have nothing to do with it at first, have since become its most zealous members ; not by conforming to the principles in celebration of which it was established, but by setting up a new set of principles in their place. The Pitt Club originally held liberal doctrines on some leading questions, especially Catholic Emancipation.

† "Gifford's Life of Pitt," vi., 234.

nevertheless, to shake the tranquillity of every succeeding cabinet for thirty years; and to compel a confession at last, which must have thrown Mr. Gifford into fits, if he lived to witness it—that the government of the country could not be carried on till they were removed! Even then it was not the fault of ministers that the Papist was let loose from his bonds. They would have kept him in chains if they could: but events pressed, and they were forced to choose between that old rank antipathy and a civil war.

According to this authority, Mr. Pitt never encouraged the Catholics to expect that their political disabilities would be repealed, if they would consent to the Union.

Mr. Pitt unquestionably possessed, in almost supernatural perfection, the art of appearing to say a great deal, without saying anything. His wonderful fluency, when he had any point to seem to clear up, but really to confuse, had the effect of filling the ear without conveying one positive idea to the mind. Great was his skill in creating a dubious impression, which might be admitted or denied at convenience. He was so wonderfully *safe* in this way, and had such a miraculous gift of no-meaning, that Windham once said that " he verily believed Mr. Pitt *could speak a king's speech off-hand.*" It must be allowed, therefore, that if any man could have successfully produced an universal conviction that he meant to do a certain thing, which he had not the slightest intention of doing, without committing himself to a single act or expression that could ever be brought in evidence against him, Mr. Pitt was unquestionably that man. But as he could not have done so in this case without being guilty of an extraordinary and cruel stretch of duplicity, we have to decide which is the more likely—that Mr. Pitt acted in this perfidious spirit, or that Mr. Gifford's statement is untrue.

There is no doubt that Mr. Pitt held language calculated to suggest and nourish such expectations in the Catholic mind. There is no doubt that similar language was held by Canning, Dundas, Windham, and other recognised members and organs of the government. There is no doubt that these ministerial manifestoes, which were neither pledges nor promises, but something a thousand times more binding in honour and conscience, were actively circulated all over Ireland, and used as a decoy for the Catholics. If Mr. Pitt meant nothing by all this, but merely to carry his object—if he were ready to avail himself of the want of distinctness on this special point in his own speeches, or to repudiate, as lacking his sanction, the too much distinctness of others—it is clear that Mr. Pitt must have been a man of remarkable hardihood of a certain kind. But we prefer the other horn of the dilemma; and circumstances fortunately enable us to go just far enough to rescue Mr. Pitt from the ruinous friendship of his biographer.

The Union was carried, and became the law of the land in 1801. The moment was now come for keeping faith with the Catholics. Mr. Pitt applied to his majesty, urged upon him the imperious necessity of adjusting these claims, and intimated the impossibility of remaining in office unless his majesty empowered him to carry out the terms upon which he had been enabled to accomplish the Union. George III. however was of opinion that the coronation oath was an eternal impediment to the royal assent; entreated Mr. Pitt not to urge him on that point; and offered, as the story-books say, to do anything for him, except emancipation, if he would stay in office. Mr. Pitt resigned.*

Nothing can be much clearer than this. Mr. Pitt resigned because he could not carry Catholic Emancipation. Now unless he acknowledged to himself (although it seems he never communicated his impressions to Mr. Gifford) that he had led the Catholics to agree to the Union, on the pledge or supposition that their disabilities should be removed, why should he resign upon that question?

The act of resignation was the only saving grace in the matter, for it is not to be concealed that Mr. Pitt ought to have ascertained his majesty's opinions before. Nor will posterity believe that he was not already acquainted with them when he promulgated the scheme of the Union.† If the great measure was a great hypocrisy, it was not because he did not deceive the Catholics by false promises, but because he deluded them by promises which he knew at

---

* See a correspondence between the king, Mr. Pitt, and Lord Kenyon, published in 1827 by Dr. Philpotts. This correspondence was published in the hope of annihilating the Catholic claims for ever, but it had the unlooked-for effect of materially accelerating their settlement.

† However this may be, great blame was cast on Pitt by the court party, and even by some of his own friends. It was said that he took his majesty by surprise. "Mr. Pitt," says Lord Malmesbury, "either from indolence, or from perhaps not paying always a sufficient and due attention to the king's pleasure, neglected to mention *ministerially* to his majesty, that such a measure was in agitation, till he came at once with it for his approbation."—"Diaries," iv., 1. The enemies of the measure —including the two Chancellors of England and Ireland—took care, however, that the king should know Pitt's intentions, and in a way the most likely to displease. The consequence was, that the day after it was formally proposed (28th January) the king declared he would consider any man personally indisposed towards him who voted for it. Canning suspected Lord Westmoreland to have been at the bottom of this cabal. Hawkesbury, who took office under Addington, is also open to suspicion. It is satisfactory to know, however, that Auckland, who was one of the chief plotters, got nothing by it, and that Loughborough, who moved conspicuously in it, overreached himself, and lost the chancellorship—the lucky circumstance which lifted Eldon to the woolsack.

the time he could not fulfil. There is too much reason to believe that the latter is the true version.*

If Mr. Pitt had been firm, the court faction must have yielded, and emancipation might have been carried within a year of the Union. His resignation threw it back indefinitely; and honourable as that resignation was, its lustre is much diminished by his consenting to take office three years afterwards under the same sovereign, not only without any stipulations on behalf of the Catholics, but with the knowledge that he must abandon them. It is notorious that during the life-time of the king, Mr. Pitt was resolved never to bring forward the Catholic question; in fact, he bound himself to sacrifice it to the good old intolerance of George the Third. All this goes a great way to reduce the merit of Mr. Pitt's resignation, if it does not destroy confidence in his sincerity altogether.†

* Some light is thrown upon this suspicion from a very unexpected quarter. In an article in the "Anti-Jacobin," said, we know not upon what authority, to be written by Mr. Canning, it is very clearly stated that the king had never given his ministers the smallest reason to believe that he would sanction measures of relief for the Catholics ; but that on the contrary, nearly three years before, his majesty had declared his determination never to consent to them, feeling that such consent would involve a violation of his oath. Yet, notwithstanding their private knowledge of his majesty's fixed resolution, ministers held out positive hopes to the Catholics. Mr. Canning stated in his speech on the Catholic Claims in 1812, that ministers all along led the Catholics to believe that their Emancipation was to follow the Union. He disclaimed any direct "promises," but allowed that the Catholics were encouraged to expect a release from their disabilities. "As to promises," he said, "there have been none; but as to expectation, there certainly has been a great deal. *Expectations have been held out, the disappointment of which involves the moral guilt of an absolute breach of faith.*"—Speech on Lord Morpeth's Motion, 3rd. Feb., 1812.

† It is now known that Pitt did voluntarily offer to sacrifice the Catholic question to the disordered bigotry of the king. The subject was submitted to his majesty towards the close of January ; about the middle of February his majesty betrayed the first symptoms of his malady ; for a fortnight or so he got worse and worse, but recovered again early in March, sufficiently at least to be conscious of all that had passed, and capable of talking about it. In this state of temporary restoration, he desired Willis, his medical attendant, to write to Pitt.

From that moment his course ran through crooked paths, and was no less unfortunate in its progress than disastrous in its close. Every thing failed with him. His next administration was formed of materials so weak, that he was obliged to do all the work himself. His coalition projects led to fresh disappointments and distrusts, and the glory of Trafalgar only shed an expiring gleam on his last hours. When he died, the feeble remains of his cabinet fell to pieces without a struggle.

Mr. Canning was too closely identified with Pitt not to participate in his fortunes at a juncture of such imminent importance. He followed him into retirement.* Mr. Huskisson also resigned. Mr. Pitt had a few close friends who were superstitiously devoted to him. With the desperate attachment of Hindoo widows they insisted upon being buried in his grave. The breaking up of his administration was a sort of political suttee.

So far as Mr. Canning was individually concerned, the respite from the labours of his office was not altogether undesired on private grounds. A few months previously he had changed his condition by an alliance which, fortunately, in addition to the first essential of mutual attachment, united all the elements his utmost ambition could desire—connexion and fortune. On the 8th of July 1800, Mr. Canning was married to Miss Joan Scott, daughter and co-heiress to General Scott, and sister to the Marchioness

"Tell him," said he, " I am now quite well, *quite* recovered from my illness; but what has *he* not to answer for who is the cause of my having been ill at all?" Willis wrote as he was commanded, and Pitt sent a reply full of regrets and repentance, and offering to *give up the Catholic question to please his majesty.* In fact he did give it up. He always spoke of it afterwards as given up. It was plunged into the ministerial *oubliette.*

* Mr. Canning resigned his under-secretaryship, and no longer formed a part of the administration. But he kept the place of Receiver-General of the Alienation Office.

of Titchfield, afterwards Duchess of Portland. General Scott is said to have been a man of peculiar habits and eccentric character, who possessed considerable wealth, which he left tied up by some very singular and stringent conditions.

Miss Scott's fortune was large, and placed Mr. Canning at once in a position of independence. The union was in every point of view a source of mutual happiness. The unsullied purity of Mr. Canning's life, and his love of domestic pleasures (for, after his marriage, he seldom extended his intercourse with general society beyond those occasions which his station rendered unavoidable), were rewarded by as much virtue and devotion as ever graced the home of an English statesman.

In an antechamber in Mr. Canning's house there used to hang over the mantel-piece a painting of two female figures—the Duchess of Portland and her sister. The duchess, who was many years the elder, is represented leaning over her sister, and caressing her with an expression of affectionate emotion. From the history attached to the picture, we learn that this attitude was chosen by the duchess herself, as a memorial of a somewhat romantic circumstance in the lives of the sisters. It seems that General Scott made the principal part of his fortune by play, to which he was passionately addicted, and which in his time ran high in the fashionable world. He was remarkable for many personal singularities, odd tastes and antipathies; and, amongst the rest, he conceived an extraordinary aversion to the aristocracy. He carried this feeling to such an extreme, as to resolve that neither his family nor his money, if he could prevent them, should ever be found shining under a coronet; and in order to secure this object he inserted a strict condition in his will, that if either of his daughters should marry a nobleman her moiety of a sum of 200,000*l.*, which he divided between them, should devolve upon her sister. The Duchess of Portland was the first to disobey this testamentary injunction; but her sister, refusing to take advantage of the will, insisted upon an equal division of the legacy. She saw no reason why, having married a lord for love, the duchess should not at least be as rich as if she had married a commoner upon compulsion.

The picture illustrates with touching simplicity this little episode of magnanimous love.

VII.

THE ADDINGTON ADMINISTRATION. THE RETURN AND DEATH OF PITT.

PITT resigned in March, 1801. There were various rumours about his successor—some named Grenville; others Dundas; Auckland, says one of his contemporaries, named himself. But there never was any real hesitation as to who should succeed. Pitt named Addington, then Speaker of the Commons; and Addington succeeded accordingly. The Addington administration was merely a fantoccini ministry, of which Pitt worked the wires.

There was another reason, besides the Catholic Question, why Pitt so precipitately quitted office—the impossibility of extricating himself with credit from the war. He wanted to throw upon Addington the ignominy of patching up a disgraceful peace, and then, when fresh difficulties arose, to return to office again, " amidst thunders of applause," as the only man who could save the country. His strategy was betrayed plainly enough in the last verse of Mr. Canning's famous Pitt lyric:

And, oh! if again the rude whirlwind should rise!
    The dawning of peace should fresh darkness deform,
The regrets of the good, and the fears of the wise,
    Shall turn to the Pilot that weathered the storm!*

* "The Pilot that weathered the storm," was written for the first

But power once relinquished is not so easily recalled. Followers and parasites have an ugly way of forsaking the retiring patron, and trooping round the in-coming minister. Even so it fell out with Pitt, who was excluded from the government for upwards of three years, by this obstacle of his own making.*

meeting of the Pitt Club, which originated under Mr. Canning's auspices, and was founded by him immediately after Mr. Pitt's retirement from office. The object of the Club was of course to celebrate the glories of the late minister, and it is a significant and very curious fact, that not one of the members of the Addington administration joined it, although their successors were the persons of whom its meetings were afterwards chiefly composed, and who gave such an unexpected direction to its enthusiasm. The song was written with great skill for the end it was designed to serve; on other grounds its merit is not above the average of most patriotic effusions stuffed with stock sentiments and huzzas disguised in heroic metre. But it answered its purpose effectually, and produced a sort of national *furor* as long as the war-fever lasted. Lord Brougham objects to this song that it treats as a "fall" Pitt's sacrifice of power to principle, when by retiring from office he earned the applause of millions. His lordship ascribes this to Mr. Canning's early official habits, which seem to have given to place an aspect of power essential to one who would serve his country. "Historical Sketches of Statesmen," p. 279. But it was not necessary to go so far out of the way to discover why Canning treated Pitt's retirement as a "fall"—

Admired in thy zenith, but loved in thy fall—

Or why he described him in his retirement as

Virtue, in *humble resentment* withdrawn.

He wanted to get up a party for him as a *martyr* to his own integrity and the king's intolerance. He wanted to keep him alive in the generous sympathies of the people. Something must be allowed for political songs that are only written to serve an occasion. "The Pilot that weather'd the storm," was not intended to be submitted to the criticism of posterity. It may be much more seriously questioned whether Lord Brougham's opinion, that Pitt *did* sacrifice power to principle on this occasion, is founded upon a correct estimate of all the circumstances of his retreat from office.

* "The baseness and ingratitude he found in mankind," says Lady Hester Stanhope, "were inconceivable. All the peers that he had made deserted him, and half those he had served, returned his kindness by going over to the enemy."—"Memoirs of Lady Hester Stanhope," iii., 167. The close of all was still more terrible. Mr. Pitt died in the villa on Putney heath; his corpse lay in one of the rooms for a week. "It is a singular and melancholy circumstance," says Lord Brougham, "resembling the stories told of William the Conqueror's deserted state at his decease, that some one in the neighbourhood having sent a message to inquire after Mr. Pitt's state, he found the wicket open, then the door of the house, and nobody answering the bell, he walked through the rooms till

M

All Pitt's friends were opposed to his resignation. There was no apparent excuse for it. The Catholic Question had been already abandoned in the Cabinet, although set up as a pretext for history. This was so well understood, that Lord Cornwallis wrote to Lord Castlereagh immediately upon hearing of the resignations, to say that as the Catholic Question had been " given up," it would be highly criminal at such a moment to desert his majesty.* But Pitt was resolved, and everybody thought he was very obstinate, because they could not comprehend *why* he went out, and he would not tell them. He kept his own secret.

On the very evening of his resignation Canning called upon him. They had a long conversation, but it ended in nothing. All that Canning could extract from him was, that he had the greatest confidence in Addington; and wished his party to support him; that, as a private friend he was pleased with Canning for having resigned; but more pleased with those who remained as they were. This was the way Pitt sustained his worshippers. He entreated them all to stay in under Addington, and would satisfy none of them as to the reason why he did not stay in himself. Some did stay in—such as the Duke of Portland, Lord Chatham, Lord Westmoreland; but the strangest circumstance of all was that Dundas went out— that true Scot, to whom place was hardly less vital than the atmosphere.

he reached the bed on which the minister's body lay lifeless, the sole tenant of the mansion, of which the doors, a few hours before, were darkened by crowds of suitors alike obsequious and importunate, the vultures whose instinct haunts the carcases only of living ministers."— "Historical Sketches." There never was a statesman out of whose hands power passed so suddenly and so completely. There was no decline—no transition—no twilight to soften the descent from his meridian glory; but darkness, like night in the tropics, set in upon him at once.

* "Diaries of Lord Malmesbury," iv. 42.

It was suspected that Pitt resigned merely to show his strength, and that he could return to power whenever he wished. For the three years preceding he had been compelled to make so many concessions in the royal closet, and the government had become so weakened by the frequency of this secret control, that he began to feel that he retained only a nominal power, while the real power was wielded by people who influenced the king's mind out of sight. His choice lay between making a firm stand on some great public necessity, or going out and letting his loss be felt. But where was this public necessity to be found? It was idle to think of Catholic Emancipation, as that was one of the subjects on which the royal mind was *unapproachable.* During the king's illness there were two topics for ever present to his distempered imagination — America and the Church. " How can I," he used to exclaim, " *I that am born a gentleman,* ever lay my head on my pillow in peace and quiet, as long as I remember the loss of my American Colonies?" At another time he would mutter, " I will remain true to the Church!" Then back to America—and anon, he would return to the Church; and so swing backwards and forwards between these two points of remorse, until they became an absolute part of his moral existence. The minister who should have attempted to make a stand upon the Catholic Question, under such circumstances, must have been as demented as the king himself; and so having nothing else to go upon, Pitt threw up the seals.

Addington was supposed to be entirely in Pitt's confidence in this move, from the tone he took *at first.* He used to say every where that he was only Pitt's *locum tenens.* This was generally believed in the beginning, and circumstances favoured its likelihood. But as time wore on, and Addington, who was a vain and arrogant man at heart, grew giddy with authority, people began to wonder whether he really was minister or puppet. The mystery became darker and darker. Pitt's conduct throughout this period of anxious suspense was unintelligible. Soon after his retirement, he sold Hollwood, his favourite residence; laid down his carriage and horses; reduced his establishment; and paying off as many debts as he could, took a house in Park Place, where he lived on an income of less than 1000*l.* a year. This looked like a complete farewell to power ; and yet all this time he was advising the ministers secretly at every step: they did nothing without his sanction ; and to ensure them still greater security, he was continually urging his personal friends to support them in their measures.

Canning was distressed and irritated at all this. He could not conceal his vexation that Pitt should sacrifice himself to bolster up an administration which had no sooner made its appearance in Parliament than it was treated by both houses with open derision. There was some personal feeling, also, mixed up in the mortification he felt at Pitt's impenetrable reserve. He thought that he was entitled to a closer confidence than Pitt was willing to extend to any body ; but although he was wounded at this, his friendship was too sincere to be susceptible of the small jealousies which sometimes spring from a suspicion of imperfect trust. His attachment to Pitt was not merely that of the lover, whose imagination exaggerates the perfections of his idol, but rather that of the devotee, who is disposed to believe his idol infallible.

It was from this devotion that, heedless of Pitt's remonstrances, he insisted upon throwing up office ; at a period of life, too, when the objects of his ambition, thus placed within his reach, might naturally be expected to exercise a paramount influence over his decision. His conduct on this occasion contrasts strongly with that of Lord Castlereagh, who professed an equal homage to Pitt. Canning went out—Castlereagh went in. The former felt himself bound to share the adversity of the statesman, who was their common leader—the latter was restless till he got an appointment under the ministry that displaced him. Castlereagh was considered a staunch Pittite, and may have been one. Perhaps he had a peculiar manner of showing his attachments. Like the Irishman who went into the twenty-fourth foot, that he might be near his brother who was in the twenty-fifth, his lordship may have joined Addington for the sake of his love of Pitt.

For the first year of the new ministry, Canning almost wholly abstained from attending Parliament, and, except upon one occasion (his motion respecting the cultivation of Trinidad, 27th May, 1802), he does not appear to have spoken. He pursued this line of conduct out of deference to Pitt, to whom he was indebted for his seat; but when the dissolution of 1802 released him from that obligation, and he was returned on his own account for the borough of Tralee, he felt himself at liberty to oppose an administration he despised.

Trinidad was one of the acquisitions of the war. It possessed two advantages: it was an important naval station and one of the most fertile islands of the West India group. Mr. Canning desired to confer a greater distinction than either upon it, by making it the scene of an initial experiment in the gradual process of extinguishing the slave-trade. The new island—with its breeding climate and luxuriant soil—was to be cultivated. How?—By negroes imported from Africa.—The object of Mr. Canning's motion was to make grants to the planters on the express condition that they should *not* import slave labour. He wanted to make a beginning somewhere, and he thought this a favourable opportunity. His speech, although ostensibly addressed to a general view of the best means of cultivating and turning Trinidad to account, was a powerful argument, enforcing a practical proposition, against the slave trade. The subject was one in which he felt a deep interest. He had spoken upon it in 1799, with a fulness of spirit and beauty of illustration, which, even in his later years, he never excelled. But, rich, various, and powerful as it was, his speech had produced no practical result. The motion on Trinidad also fell to the ground. The time was not yet ripe for this great step in Christian civilisation. But the seed was sowing, and Mr. Canning happily lived to gather in the goodly harvest.

In 1803 a rebellion broke out in Ireland—a direct corollary from the Union. Mr. Canning, in a speech of unusual severity, declared, that the Irish Executive ought to be impeached. But it is only justice to this unfortunate fantoccini ministry to say for them what they had not the courage to say for themselves—that the Irish rebellion was a dying bequest from their predecessors. Everybody wondered how they could have been induced to take out letters of administration!

The worst of all was the necessity of winding up the war. The peace of Amiens was the great end for which the administration seemed to have been called into existence; and, having accomplished its destiny, the astonishing thing is that it did not surrender up its spirit to Pitt. The peace pleased nobody. Windham described it as an armed truce, entered upon without necessity, negotiated without wisdom, and concluded without honour; Lord Grenville denounced it as a national degradation; and the only recommendation it had in Fox's eyes was that it brought the war to an end without restoring the Bourbons.

The peace was negotiated by Lord Hawkesbury, who had committed himself to such exhilarating prophecies of the occupation of Paris; and who now, not content with destroying the hopes he had been all along holding out to his party, added a sort of private sanction to an act of official suicide by accepting a present from the First Consul of a superb service of china.* While the honest advocates of the war were grumbling over the shells, the Foreign Secretary was swallowing the oyster.

There never occupied the Treasury benches an administration so hacked and cut to pieces as this Addington make-shift. Every party assailed it in turn; and there were more party sections than usual, with a greater variegation of political opinions, but all united against the ministry. There was the pure Fox party—the Grenvilles, with their mixed doctrines—the Windhamites, who drew between them—and the Young-Pitt party, whose especial function it was to bring about the restoration of

* The fact is stated by Trotter, "Memoirs of Fox," p. 260. Trotter's book is wretched trash, but it contains two or three small facts that are not to be found elsewhere. He was employed by Fox to copy and read for him, and saw a good deal of his private life, which he mistook his calling in attempting to chronicle. It seems that he expected something would have been done for him, and published the memoirs out of revenge. An observation of Sheridan's upon the proceedings of the Whigs in 1806, applies exactly to Trotter's case. "I have heard," says Sheridan, "of men running their heads against a wall, but this is the first time I ever heard of a man building a wall on purpose to run his head against."

Pitt, even in spite of Pitt himself. Canning was the leader of this section, the most energetic of all.

The inherent feebleness of the ministry supplied their antagonists with perpetual openings for ridicule and defiance. Hawkesbury possessed the most respectable talents amongst them, but he was totally unequal to his position. He had so little influence as Foreign Secretary that the French negotiators heaped repeated insults upon England in their correspondence with him; demanding at one time that he should stop the attacks of the press on the French Government; and at another, that the French Royal Family, and other illustrious exiles who had taken refuge here, should be peremptorily sent out of the country. With a man of known ability or established name at the Foreign Office, such experiments would never have been tried; but Hawkesbury was shy, paltering, and all but unknown. Canning had the lowest opinion of his capacity;[*] Lord Malmesbury spurned his "weakness and timidity;" and the king said, that he had no head for business, no method, no punctuality.[†] Yet, incompetent as he was, and ill as they could spare him from the Commons, they were obliged to send him up to the Lords, where they were still worse off.[‡]

Addington was deficient in every quality necessary to form or control a cabinet. He had no personal weight— no ministerial reputation—even his technical parliamentary habits were against him. Great stiffness, without the

[*] Lady Hester Stanhope, in her hectoring way, says that Hawkesbury was a "fool," and that Canning could not conceal the contempt in which he held him; carrying it so far as to take wine very reluctantly with him at dinner. "Memoirs," I. 316.
[†] "Diaries of Lord Malmesbury," iv. 197.
[‡] Lord Hawkesbury did not on this occasion change his title. He was called to the Upper House, by writ, as a peer's eldest son.

least natural dignity, gave a false lacquer to his manners, which were offensive to men of high breeding; and his attempts to supply the want of discrimination and forethought by an assumption of artificial gravity, only rendered him ridiculous. "My Lord Salisbury," said Fox, in a public company, speaking of Addington, "would make a better minister, only that he is wanted for court dancing-master." Being asked what Addington would do after the peace, Fox replied: "I cannot say; but it will be something which will render him ridiculous to the end of time. If Mr. Addington wishes for supreme authority, let him be King of Bath, if he has interest enough at the rooms; he will find it more pleasant, and, I am persuaded, more to his reputation."* To make matters still more deplorable, he was cut off from the means of strengthening his hands, by a train of greedy expectants, pressing voraciously to be provided for—his brother, Bragge, Vansittart, Bond Hopkins, and a dozen others— all officers and no soldiers.† "No followers," is found an excellent rule in certain situations, and would tell with good effect amongst higher functionaries. It would have saved Addington the necessity of putting his hangers-on into leading appointments, to the exclusion of men who could have brought experience and character to the aid of his administration. He never recovered from this original source of weakness.

* "Circumstantial Details, &c. of the Rt. Hon. C. J. Fox," 1806.
† "Life of Lord Chancellor Eldon." Addington's place-hunting dependents were not forgotten in the lampoons that were showered upon him; especially "Brother Bragge and Brother Hiley."
Each a gentleman at large,
Lodged and fed at public charge,
Paying (with a grace to charm ye)
This the fleet, and that the army.
"Brother Hiley" was provided with the situation of Secretary to the Treasury.

Canning nicknamed him the "Doctor," in allusion to the lucky accident which made the fortunes of his house. Addington's father was a country doctor, and happening to be sent for to attend Lord Chatham's coachman, in the absence of the regular attendant, grew into such favour, that his lordship appointed him his family physician.* The nickname took wings over the kingdom, in the shape of numerous witty pasquinades, some of which were attributed to Mr. Canning;† and it provoked many a hearty roar in parliament, where it was frequently introduced by a humorous side-wind in the debates. On one occasion, when the Scotch members had deserted the government, Sheridan stretched across the table, and cried out to the premier, "Doctor! the Thanes fly from thee!" to the infinite amusement of the house. The "Doctor" stuck to Addington, until he finally sank his patronymic in a title. Dropping one's family name, and taking out a peerage, is in some cases as secure an escape from the odium of a nickname as the grave itself; for nine-tenths of the world lose sight of the commoner in his new glory, as completely as if he were dead. It was probably for this reason Addington felt such anxiety to bury himself in a peerage. He had already chosen a title—Lord Raleigh; an absurdity, probably, which he never would have relinquished but

---

* The anecdote is related on the authority of Lady Hester Stanhope, "Memoirs," i., 217.
† One of them is called an "Ode to the Doctor;" another, "The Grand Consultation;" a third, "Moderate Men and Moderate Measures." The best of them is the second, which opens in this way:
    If the health and strength, and the pure vital breath,
    Of old England at last must be *doctored* to death,
    Oh! why must we die of one doctor alone?
    And why must that doctor be just such an one
                      As Doctor Henry Addington?
These pieces have frequently been printed as Mr. Canning's; but it is doubtful whether he wrote a single line of one of them.

for a jest of Lady Hester Stanhope's, in which he was supposed to be represented in a caricature, side by side with Queen Elizabeth.*

Canning was indefatigable in his efforts to throw out the paltry ministry, and to bring back Pitt. At this time he lived in Conduit-street,† and could scarcely spare leisure, although the strain upon his constitution needed it, to take a little repose in the country, from his constant exertions. The only stolen intervals of rest he appears to have allowed himself was an occasional visit to South Hill (his country house), with Mrs. Canning, whose health had been for some time delicate and precarious.‡ He was incessantly moving about amongst his party, to get up some manifestation of opinion that might bring about a change; driving backwards and forwards from Dropmore to Walmer, and from Walmer to Dropmore; from George Rose to Tom Grenville, from Tom Grenville to Lord Malmesbury, inciting every body to action, and putting every engine he could think of in motion to turn out Addington. All this while, Pitt was as motionless, passionless, and mysterious as a stone sphynx.

Several plans were suggested by Canning for Pitt's restoration. He laboured nearly single-handed, and would have been altogether alone, but for three young friends whom he drew into council with him—Lord G. Leveson, Lord Morpeth, and Mr. Sturges Bourne. These gentlemen were not of sufficient standing to possess

* " Memoirs of Lady Hester Stanhope," i., 216.
† At the house, No. 37.
‡ Mr. Canning's eldest son, George Charles, was born on the 25th of April, 1801, and died on the 30th of March, 1820. William Pitt, the second son, was born on the 27th December, 1802, became a captain in the navy, and died in 1828. It was on the occasion of the birth of her second son, that Mrs. Canning's health suffered.

much public influence; but they were well adapted for the sort of work they undertook. They were perfectly in earnest, had activity and zeal, and enough of prudence not to commit Pitt, which was all they cared about. Failure under such circumstances could recoil only on themselves.

They watched every stir of the government, noted every variation of public opinion, and took advantage of every circumstance that offered for keeping alive the flagging zeal of Pitt's friends; which was more than Pitt himself ever troubled his head about. No man whose ear could be caught in either house, or at the drawing-room, or at a dinner-party, was suffered to go home without carrying away some gloomy hint about the pitiful conduct of ministers, the impossibility of things going on as they were, and the absolute necessity of a change; always ending in the ejaculation that there was only one man in the kingdom who could redeem us from the deep disgrace into which we had fallen. But this tone was taken up here and there only by a few scattered old-school politicians, and even that doubtingly and slowly. There was no combination, no motive-power in the absence of the great leader. In fact it was very difficult to get up a Pitt party. Personally Pitt repelled all enthusiasm; and this movement was entirely a personal affair.

At one time it was suggested that the Duke of York should open the matter to the king; at another time it was proposed that a remonstrance (which was drawn up by Canning) should be presented to Addington, signed by a long list of influential persons, requesting him to resign. But just as these friendly plots were ready for execution, Pitt was sure to hear of them through some meddling, good-natured busy-body, and to put a stop to them at once. He was offended at the officious zeal of his friends; and especially offended with Canning, who sinned in this respect beyond all the rest.*

There was some injustice in the severity with which Pitt regarded these ardent efforts for his recall; but he had a right to judge for himself. Real anxiety for what he believed to be necessary to the salvation of the country may have carried Canning too far, particularly in his speeches. Pitt complained of this as tending to embroil him with the ministry, by the assertion of doctrines and opinions in his name without his authority.† Canning was rash, headstrong, and even presumptuous in the course he took, and persisted in at this period; but it was in the exuberance of feelings that were honourable to his character. Nothing else can explain or excuse the eagerness and *freedom* of his correspondence with Pitt—with a man so lofty, so cold, so remote. He wrote to him constantly; literally fatigued him with long, bold, sincere letters, in which he fairly lectured him upon his ascetic resolution, and tried to argue him out of it. To these letters he sometimes got no reply; sometimes an answer that left him more in the dark than ever, by assuring him of the impossibility of entering into any explanation at that moment; and sometimes a short, freezing, polite acknowledgment that would have been to any other man a discharge in full from all such thankless services. Once, in a perplexity of temper about some unusually urgent matter which had just arisen, he determined

* Throughout all these "loving differences," their friendship continued firm. " My plans," said Pitt, " have not the concurrence of my eager and ardent young friends (Canning and G. Leveson), but we are on the best of terms, and it is much more easy for me to forgive their impetuosity, than for them to be in charity with me for treating office with so little regard, and keeping it at such a distance from those who are disposed to act with me."

† "Diaries of Lord Malmesbury," iv., 127. Pitt's complaints on these points are also alluded to by Lady Hester Stanhope.

to see Pitt, and wrote to announce that he would come down to Walmer; but Pitt wrote back very plainly to decline the visit. Still Canning persevered. But it was all to no purpose. Pitt was stone to the end.

Taking into consideration Canning's youth and position, and the peculiar relation in which he stood to the ex-minister, (circumstances which, after all, furnish the best apologies for his conduct,) it must be frankly allowed that he trespassed beyond his legitimate province, in taking upon himself the responsibility of advising Pitt, against his will, in this crisis; and in endeavouring, whether Pitt liked it or not, to keep together the broken fragments of his party. He had not yet acquired sufficient personal weight to justify the assumption of so prominent a part; and the manner of his interference was not calculated to conciliate the jealousies his prosperity had already created. His bearing was high and authoritative in quarters where, from the force of habit, the assertion of natural advantages over the advantages of birth was resented as an indignity. With a person remarkably handsome, a head of great intellectual power as well as beauty, an aristocratic carriage, which must have been intolerable to such as were envious of his success, brilliant abilities, and a temper a little quickened, and spoiled by the admiration which had strewn his path with chaplets from his boyhood, and rendered his whole life a progress of ovations; it is easy to understand how many persons, and what sort of persons they were, whose self-love he must have offended, by putting himself forward as the active friend of Pitt during this interval of doubt and suspense. That the exigency of the occasion demanded such a man—with all his vehement contempt for the hesitating forms that wait upon convention, letting the tide of circumstance run past—with all his youthful daring, and even his haughty vanity—we can see now clearly enough ; but it was not so apparent then. Dukes and earls and honourables were thinking more of themselves, and of seeing to the pomp that marshalled the approaches to their greatness, than of the one object which night and day consumed *his* spirit; an object which is historical with us, and which was then felt and understood by him alone in its overwhelming importance.

It is true, he did not set about this darling project very coolly. He wondered that every body did not see it as he did, as quickly and as passionately. He had not been accustomed to impediments or hindrances, and he could least of all brook the kind of obstacles that fretted him now: dulness, lukewarmness, reserve, lordly *insouciance*,—he was impatient of all this, and did not hesitate to show it. Lord Malmesbury touches the springhead of these faults of character in Canning, when he says that " he had been forced like a thriving plant in a well-managed hot-house ; had prospered too luxuriantly; had felt no check or frost ; and too early in life had had many and too easy advantages." This was the secret of that confidence, almost amounting to arrogance, which led to so much misapprehension and misjudgment of his qualities; and which prevented him from stooping to a popularity so easily obtained by men of more suppliant dispositions, and immeasurably inferior powers. It was the error of the true nobility of his nature to look upon such popularity as improper to be cultivated by a statesman. He treated with a rigorous dignity, very likely to be mistaken for contempt, the half-informed and class-prejudiced multitude upon which other public men diligently fawned. The chastity of his mind took the colour of disdain. He had won his reputation with such facility—

his good fortune had been so rapid, without a break in its ascent—and he had distanced all his contemporaries so suddenly and completely, with all their advantages against him, that something of the flush of conquest was communicated to his manners. This was sufficient to inflame into open enmity the suppressed spleen by which he was surrounded. His successes were cause enough for malice, without this dazzling air, which looked so like conceit, to recall them at every turn. There is no difficulty in understanding how the action and reaction in this case, as in all others, aggravated the original grounds of resentment on both sides.

But he was not to be discouraged by personal checks. He never relaxed in his exertions to bring back Pitt; although frequently baffled, vexed and dispirited, and doomed to see one scheme after another melt into air. Addington grew firmer in his seat every day, acquiring increased assurance from the failure of the plots that were exploding about him on all sides. Numerous significant hints were thrown out to him, even by some members of the cabinet, Lord Camden, Pelham, and the Duke of Portland. But all in vain. Addington was not to be moved. He was a prodigious favourite at Windsor, and stood upon that. The old king loved him for his anti-Catholicism; and his anti-Catholicism became more and more strenuous for the king's dear love; and he knew that nothing short of the apparition of Buonaparte on the coast, or some equally horrible event, could frighten the king into his dismissal to make room for Pitt, or any one else inclined that way. Of course hints were thrown away upon Addington; and scoffs and jeers were thrown away upon Addington: he bore them all with the unruffled complacency of one who stood well with his lord, the king. In vain Sheridan exhausted his wit upon Addington, and threw the House into convulsions by his parody on Martial:

> "I do not like thee, Doctor Fell,
> The reason why, I cannot tell;
> But this I'm sure I know full well,
> I do not like thee, Doctor Fell."

What did Addington care whether Sheridan liked him or not, so long as he knew the king loved him. He rose with the impunity of possession, and the king's dotage.*

But this could not last. Cardhouses have a capacity of standing only just so long as the air is perfectly motionless around them. The moment a breath comes, they tumble down. Such was the fall of the Addington ministry.

On the 23rd of June, 1803, Colonel Patten brought forward a motion of want of confidence in the administration. Pitt, to avoid an expression of opinion either way, moved the previous question; and on this occasion, for the first and only time in his life, Canning voted against him. He declared that he could not conscientiously vote otherwise; that the conduct of ministers was as disgraceful to themselves as it was mischievous to the people; that they had either duped England into a peace, which had turned out to be mere waste paper, or had themselves been duped by France; and that they were utterly incapable of administering the affairs of the country, which could no longer be intrusted with safety to their hands. Pitt's amendment was negatived; and he and his friends walked out of the house. Fox and his supporters refused to vote; and the original motion was lost by a large majority. But the debate disclosed a state of opinion

* Lord Malmesbury says, "that he latterly persuaded himself he had actually saved the king and the country by taking office."

from which ministers never recovered. The victory indoors was that of mere skeleton figures—the usual ministerial procession of placemen and boroughmongers. There was no soul beneath those numerical ribs. Even Pitt, from this time forth, began to distrust, and finally to oppose the administration. This was all that was wanted, at any moment, to bring it down crumbling to the dust. So that, though long deferred, Canning had his triumph in full at last.

The issue of sundry blind diplomacies on both sides, was that Pitt and Addington met; but whether the meeting was originally sought by Addington or by Pitt, or whether it was official or private, cannot be determined, as the only two persons who were competent to decide, could not agree upon those points. The substance, however, of what passed at the interviews was mutually admitted. Addington wanted to get Pitt *into* the ministry; for, it seems, he had stiffened latterly towards Pitt, and wrought himself into a notion that he could keep the control of the cabinet, with Pitt working under him! Pitt, on the other hand, would have nothing to do with the ministry unless he were the *head* of it;[*] and not even on that condition unless he were directly commissioned by the king. They differed no less widely upon the elements of which the new government was to be composed. Addington insisted upon the old system, and the old hands, Bragge, "Brother Hiley," and the rest of his troop. Pitt demanded a broader basis, a larger constituency of opinion, a wider compass of parties and talents. At Pitt's own desire, for the purpose of preventing misconception, the articles were set down and submitted to the king; but his

[*] Pitt had made a resolution from the beginning of his public life never to join any administration, except as chief. He stood out for his full market-value at once.

majesty received at the same time, such an account of Pitt's exorbitant demands, that he was more displeased with him than ever. "He carries his removals," said his majesty, "so far and so high, that he will turn *me* out at last." And thus the negotiation ended.

But the Addington sands were run. Even if the chief had not himself resigned, every other member of the Cabinet must have gone out, from the sheer impossibility of keeping the timbers of the wreck together. Matters having clearly come to this pass, Addington submitted with the best grace he could; but not without a little ill-temper. He quarrelled with Lord Hawkesbury before he gave up, and put the king out of humour by talking of personal bickerings, which his majesty very properly told him he had nothing to do with. Addington was no sooner gone than the king sent Lord Eldon to Pitt, with a friendly message. Pitt, who had all this time kept aloof from the king's presence, waiting with austerity to be summoned, drew up at Lord Eldon's request, a paper containing the heads of what he should require from the king, laying down the plan of an administration on a scale so comprehensive as to embrace persons of the highest ability, of all parties. This paper gave great offence to his majesty, who wrote back an answer to Lord Eldon, in which he spoke of Pitt in such terms that the letter could not be shown to him. The consequence was that the negotiation halted for a week, and Parliament was kept in a condition of suspended animation. Addington unable to go on, and nobody knowing what was to happen next.

By some means, however Pitt and the king were brought together. This was on the 7th of May, 1804. Pitt, unmoved by the disturbance that was going on in the frame of royalty, proposed his broad administration, *including Fox*.

The king's hatred of Fox was a passion. Lord Eldon was accused of having taken advantage of the weak state of his majesty's mind, to prejudice him against Fox, and prevent his admission into the cabinet. The accusation was made by Lord Grey and Lord Grenville. The Chancellor denied it. Who could tell what had taken place with a crazy old man in the sanctuary of the royal closet? But there is no doubt that the Chancellor had as profound an aversion to Fox as the king himself, for he admitted that he threatened to resign if Fox were brought in.[*] All the old court bigotry was concentrated upon this point; but had Pitt kept his ground, the king must have given way, as he was compelled to do only two years afterwards. Unfortunately, he again sacrificed the country to the superstitions of the sovereign. This was Pitt's infirmity. He could not resist the tender melancholy of the king—he who was like a bleak rock, amidst the roaring surge of popular discontent.

As soon as he withdrew from the king he sent for Canning. Their confidence in each other had never suffered flaw. His impetuous young friend was the first person he thought of, the moment he accepted office. Canning was despatched to Lord Grenville, and Granville Leveson to Fox, to acquaint them with what had passed. Fox *knew he was proscribed*, and although Pitt made a distinct overture to him, he declined office. All his friends refused to go in without him. Grenville, Windham, Spencer, would have nothing to do with the administration, unless it were based upon the comprehensive

---

[*] "Life of Lord Eldon," ii., 17.

principle, which the exclusion of Fox rendered impossible. Pitt stood alone. In vain he negotiated with Grenville; and he was so indignant at the rejection of his offers, that he said he would " teach that proud man he could do without him, if it cost him his life."* He kept his word too well. It *did* cost him his life.

In this dilemma he had nothing left but to patch up an administration from the wretched *débris* of the Addington Cabinet; and was even obliged in a few months to call in Addington himself. But this connection did not last, although the minister tried to cement it with a peerage.† Addington resigned in a pet, because Pitt would not all at once appoint Bond Hopkins and other joints of his tail to lucrative places.‡ Personally, this was no great loss; but Lord Buckingham resigned at the same time, and poor old Dundas, now Lord Melville, so long the indefatigable coadjutor of Pitt, was impeached for appropriating certain balances of the public money to his own use. These domestic disasters came heavily upon a ministry, already suffering severely from external failures.

Canning's opinion of Pitt's position was made up even before his attempts at coalition failed. He saw that Pitt could not form a strong government; that the opportunity was lost for that union of parties, which recent circumstances had so singularly conspired to favour; and that a cabinet constructed upon any other principle must inevitably fail. He communicated his impressions to Pitt, before a single appointment was made out, assuring him, at the same time, that for his own part, he would rather not take office, but that he was quite ready, if he could be of use, to do any thing Pitt desired; that the cabinet

---

* "Life of Lord Eldon," i., 449.
† It was on this occasion Addington was created Viscount Sidmouth.
‡ "Diaries of Lord Malmesbury," iv., 338.

was out of the question, as he did not yet consider himself qualified, and that there were only two offices which seemed to come to him in the regular course of promotion—those of the Treasurer of the Navy and the Secretary at War. Pitt received this communication with his usual caution; went into the country, and in a day or two, wrote to Canning, offering him his choice of the two offices he had pointed out. He selected the former.

There was, probably, a little reserve on both sides. Pitt had miscalculated his resources; and Canning had all along pertinaciously warned him of his danger. Neither of them could have been very well satisfied with the result, which was not the less mortifying to the minister, because it had been foreseen by the more active sagacity of his friend.

The last effort of the Pitt cabinet, after struggling through two uncomfortable sessions, was the defence of Lord Melville, in which Mr. Canning, not less from his official connexion with the subject, than from old associations, bore a conspicuous share. The feeling against Lord Melville was perfectly savage. It was not the shout of partisans that rang in his ears, when the articles of impeachment were carried against him, but the yell of bloodhounds. He was no sooner condemned, than the House of Commons burst out with a growl; and one Sir Thomas Mostyn is said to have given a *view hollo!* and to have exclaimed: " We have killed the Fox !"

Mr. Whitbread moved the articles of impeachment. His speech was clear and able; but some passages struck Mr. Canning's acute sense of the ridiculous so forcibly, that he scribbled a parody on them, while Mr. Whitbread was yet speaking. The following is the impromptu—now printed for the first time:

FRAGMENT OF AN ORATION.

Part of Mr. Whitbread's Speech, on the Trial of Lord Melville, put into verse by Mr. Canning, at the time it was delivered.

I'm like Archimedes for science and skill,
I'm like a young prince going straight up a hill;
I'm like (with respect to the fair be it said),
I'm like a young lady just bringing to bed.
If you ask why the 11th of June I remember,
Much better than April, or May, or November,
On that day, my lords, with truth I assure ye,
My sainted progenitor set up his brewery;
On that day, in the morn, he began brewing beer;
On that day, too, commenced his connubial career;
On that day he received and he issued his bills;
On that day he cleared out all the cash from his tills;
On that day he died, having finished his summing,
And the angels all cried, 'Here's old Whitbread a-coming!'
So that day still I hail with a smile and a sigh,
For his beer with an E, and his bier with an I;
And still on that day, in the hottest of weather,
The whole Whitbread family dine altogether.—
So long as the beams of this house shall support
The roof which o'ershades this respectable court,
When Hastings was tried for oppressing the Hindoos;
So long as that sun shall shine in at those windows,
My name shall shine bright as my ancestor's shines,
Mine recorded in journals, *his* blazoned on signs!

The issue of this trial, by which Lord Melville lost his office at the Admiralty, was erased from the list of the Privy Council, and fell into total disgrace, seriously affected Pitt's spirits. His health was already giving way under the undue anxieties that devolved upon him; and he was so oppressed by the difficulties of his progress, that he re-opened the negotiations with the Grenvilles towards the close of 1805. But they would not move without Fox; and all that remained was to strengthen his administration from his own stock. With this view he made arrangements to bring Canning and Charles Yorke into the cabinet, on the opening of the following session. Events on the continent were beginning to favour him. The victory of Trafalgar, darkened only by the loss of Nelson, had been received throughout the country with joy, and the hopes of the people were beginning to revive. But in the midst of their hopes, Pitt was dying. Extraordinary mental exertions, embittered in the end by the failure of all his plans, had done upon him the heavy work of time in the very flower of his manhood. The battle of Austerlitz finally crushed him. He died of *old age*, at forty-six.*

No man was more misunderstood on some points than Pitt. No minister was ever so strangely praised for the worst parts of his policy, or so slighted for the best. No man ever got credit so largely for opinions he did not hold. These curiosities of fame are illustrated with wonderful success in that famous epitaph upon him in the Guildhall, written by Mr. Canning.

Leaving the Sinking Fund and the War to the admiration of the Pitt club, let us linger a moment over a trait or two of Pitt's character, which are not so well known as they ought to be. This icy man, who was the cause of so much bloodshed and misery, was tenderly attached to Lady Eleanor Eden, and it nearly broke his heart to give her up; which he did from a conviction that the demands made upon his time by public affairs were incompatible with the attentions due to such a woman. She is said to have been of a lofty style of beauty; quite dazzling from the grandeur of her forehead. Lord Malmesbury

---

* "Sir William Farquhar told me that he preserved his faculties till within twelve or fourteen hours of his death, which came on *rapidly*, and that Pitt died of *old age* at forty-six, as much as if he had been ninety."—" Diaries of Lord Malmesbury," iv., 346.

tells us that there was a report that he was going to be married to her, his attachment had so far betrayed itself in society. He was gracious in all companies to women, and possessed an instinctive taste in matters of costume—he who was himself so plain and careless. Wraxall speaks of his "inclination" for one of the Duke of Richmond's daughters; and Lady Hester Stanhope says there was a young lady he admired so much that he drank out of her shoe. Then he was fond of round games with young people, and used to play at speculation with the eagerness of a child. His private intercourse was full of little humanities, which nobody dreams of who regards him only as a statue mounted on a pedestal, with some hard state-paper rolled up and clutched in his hand. His manner was partly constitutional, and had something to do with the integrity of his mind, which did not deal in professions. All travellers in the highest regions of the Alps have observed that it is the property of the purest snow to be the coldest to the touch.

Whatever this proud minister may have appeared to strangers, he certainly had the power of attracting the affections of people immediately about him. Canning was devoted to him. It was not attachment—it was *allegiance*. During Pitt's life-time he followed him with reverence—after his death he declared himself his disciple.* "To one man, while he lived," said he, "I was devoted with all my heart, and all my soul. Since the death of Mr. Pitt, I acknowledge no leader; my political allegiance lies buried in his grave."†

There was a closer resemblance between them, than between Pitt and any other English statesman. In Canning, the points of similarity were more graceful and

* Speech at Lisbon in 1816. † Speech at Liverpool in 1812.

refined—in Pitt, more original and vigorous. They both possessed that faculty called *genius;* but Pitt's genius was more practical and diffusive. He was nearer to the people, and understood them better. Canning had less sympathy with them, treated them rather *en prince*, and dealt with popular topics more rhetorically. Pitt could afford to do things out of the openness of his intellect, which Canning was obliged to approach dexterously. Pitt gave you the impression of a man who stood clearly on his purpose, and was too much in earnest to be conscious of any ambition beyond it. Canning always had the classical air about him of an orator who felt he was addressing posterity.

The death of Pitt was an irretrievable calamity to his party, and no attempt was made to keep the Cabinet together. The king was once more alone in the royal closet. Even Lord Eldon could not comfort him.

VIII.

ALL THE TALENTS. THE SLAVE-TRADE.

IT was the beginning of the year 1806, and the opening of parliament was at hand. Time pressed; an administration was to be formed on a sudden that should be able to conquer the difficulties that killed Pitt. But cabinet makers cannot make cabinets without materials; and they were not to be found on that side to which the king was accustomed to look for help, and to which his heart, palpitating under the weight of the coronation oath, now yearned more beseechingly than ever.

In this extremity Lord Hawkesbury was sent for—the young gentleman whom the king himself used to say had no head. Great must have been the royal need when this headless nobleman was to be put at the head of the government. His lordship, however, feeling that his head was not quite strong enough for the responsibility, very wisely showed his heels; and there was no alternative left but Fox and the Grenvilles.

This might have been seized upon as a signal triumph over kingly prejudices, to see such a man as Fox borne into office on the shoulders of the people, against the will of the monarch. But Fox had too fine a nature, too large, and liberal, and benevolent a spirit to exhibit or permit any exultation in such circumstances. His majesty had always been haunted by a notion that Fox was a ferocious republican, and that he would behave like a sort of wild Orson if he got into the Cabinet. But his majesty lived to alter his opinion, and he often afterwards declared that Fox acted towards him with the utmost personal deference, and never like a minister who had been forced upon him.

The new government, with Lord Grenville at its head, and Fox as Foreign Secretary, presented a powerful array, no less remarkable for ability than for a strong Whig aristocratical leaven fermenting through the mass. This was the ministry that was designated *All the Talents* —a title which Mr. Fox, in an admirable rebuke to Mr. Canning, gently repudiated by saying, that it was impossible they could arrogate such a description to themselves, when they saw *him* on the opposite side of the House.

There was one rueful mistake in the structure of the ministry—the admission of Lord Sidmouth. It brought, as usual, a train of evils with it, for Lord Sidmouth was a noun of multiude, and when he was appointed, it was necessary also to appoint his friends. On this occasion he stipulated that the chief justice, Lord Ellenborough, should have a seat in the Cabinet. Lord Ellenborough was a man of unquestionable merit; but the union of the judicial and executive functions in one person, was a bad precedent, and furnished the Opposition with a legitimate topic of complaint. The arrangement is said to have been effected through the agency of Sheridan, at the express desire of the Prince of Wales, which gives it rather a worse complexion. His royal highness was beginning to turn before his time. It was not long since he had attempted to interfere, through the same channel, to prevent the presentation of the Catholic petition. The change in the prince's politics, was at least premature. Decomposition had begun to set in too soon upon his royal highness's principles. His father still "sat crowned and sceptered."

Mr. Canning took his stand upon this appointment at once, and set up the ensign of hostility, which he never lowered until the administration was dissolved. He did not become simply a member of the Opposition, but its influencing spirit and vital principle. He now presents himself for the first time as a bold and able party leader, seizing every opportunity for improving the prospects of his own side, and for surprising and damaging the enemy. In this new character he discovered unexpected practical talent in the business of debate, and was recognised without hesitation as the head of the movement. There was nobody else qualified to succeed to the great vacancy, nobody else in whose capacity his party placed sufficient reliance, or who was known to have so entirely possessed the confidence, or inherited the opinions of Pitt.

That opposition was one of the most determined ever witnessed in Parliament. It spared no means or materials by which the administration could be effectually assailed. Amongst other weapons to which it resorted, was the "No Popery" cry. Mr. Canning can scarcely have had any thing to do with this war-whoop. He was himself an advocate for emancipation; and although at this period he had never voted on the subject but once, and that against the measure—or, more technically, against the expediency of its introduction—in 1804, he cannot be suspected of having had any share in getting up a senseless clamour, which the entire tendency of his conduct proves him to have held in odium and contempt.

But this cry, dishonest as it was, materially assisted the aims of the Opposition, who were not loth to avail themselves of it to the full extent of all the mischief it might produce. As upon former occasions, the aid of ridicule was drawn in, to strengthen out of doors the labours of the restless malcontents within; and Mr. Canning's reputation was again put into requisition as sponsor for certain verses that appeared at this time in the public journals.

The best of these is a piece called " Elijah's Mantle," which contains, amongst other scraps of pleasant malice, the following passage on Lord Henry Petty (the present Marquis of Landsown), who held the office of chancellor of the exchequer, in the new Cabinet.

> "Illustrious Roscius of the State!
> New breeched and harnessed for debate,
> Thou wonder of thy age!
> Petty or Betty art thou hight?
> By Granta sent to strut thy night
> On Stephens' bustling stage.
>
> Pitt's 'Chequer robe 'tis thine to wear;
> Take of his mantle, too, a share,
> 'Twill aid thy Ways and Means;
> And should Fat Jack and his Cabal,
> Cry ' Rob us the Exchequer, Hal!'
> 'Twill charm away the fiends."

Another piece, called "Blue and Buff," is less in the manner of Canning, although attributed to him with equal confidence. Whether such squibs were really written by the brilliant leader of the Opposition, was of little consequence, so long as they were received as his, and obtained influence and circulation under the sanction of his name; and as Mr. Canning himself never interfered to claim or disavow them, the members of his party could scarcely be expected to repudiate a deception so serviceable to their interests.

One of Mr. Canning's most effective speeches, was in reply to a motion made by Windham for the repeal of the Additional Force Bill. In this, as in other motions brought forward by the administration, especially the United Service Bill, the new ministers developed a military system which differed materially from that of Pitt, which proceeded upon opposite and more popular principles, proposing to mitigate the severities of compulsory enlistment, and to introduce periodical terms of service, at the end of which the soldier would be at liberty to demand his discharge. All these measures were opposed, ineffectually, by Mr. Canning. He maintained the superior efficacy of Mr. Pitt's iron rule, which converted a soldier into a shooting machine, and was convinced, should it ever be relaxed, that there would be no resource left but the conscription. His speeches on these questions are amongst the most successful he ever delivered, as party speeches; rapid in argumentation, crowded with the happiest images, splendid in retort, and satirical to a height of bitterness, which would have been intolerable, but for the wit which lighted up and carried off the invective.

This bitterness, unfortunately, lay at the bottom of the hostility with which the administration was uniformly assailed from first to last. It was not ordinary party warfare. It was a contest of extermination—war to the knife, and no quarter. Windham was especially the object of vituperation, because he had been Pitt's colleague for eight years, had invariably supported his continental system, and was now to be found in the ranks of his opponents. Mr.

Canning endeavoured to provoke disunion between Windham and his new allies, by showing how widely they differed on some essential points. One of these was the total separation of the civil and the military character which Windham maintained was indispensable to the discipline of the army. The soldier, he asserted, should be cut off from the rest of the population, shut up in his own world, and never permitted to approximate towards the immunities of the citizen. Yet all the principal whigs set up the opposite doctrine, and espoused Mr. Windham's military measures, on grounds the very reverse of those on which Mr. Windham introduced them.

"He has heard it asserted," exclaimed Mr. Canning, "as the main principle and chief praise of his measure, that it promotes and secures this contaminating union; and, to my astonishment, he has accepted in silence the panegyrics which his feelings must have disavowed. I can excuse him for having disdained to answer the attacks of his opponents, but I am surprised that he should not have vindicated himself from the support of his friends."

The key-note of the opposition was, the disproportion between the professions and the performances of ministers.

"A story," said Mr. Canning, "has been related by one of his majesty's ministers of an old Roman moralist, who wished to build his house in such a style of architecture that every person could see into it. Like this man's house, the transactions of the present ministry are to be; but I am inclined to believe that the architecture of the house is not Roman, but Gothic; and that it is only remarkable for its huge windows that exclude the light, and its narrow passages that lead to nothing."

The taunt was uncandid. But we must not look for candour from an angry opposition. The embarrassments by which ministers were impeded on all sides were not of their own making. They found them ready made; and, before they could take any decisive steps in advance, it was necessary to relieve their feet of the meshes in which their predecessors had entangled them.

Were it possible to have obtained a solid peace with France, Fox alone could have negotiated it with success. He was personally known to Buonaparte,* and idolised by the French people, on account of the noble stand he had made against the European confederacy in the time of the Revolution. His opinions on that subject were well understood and appreciated on the continent, and wilfully misrepresented at home. Burke once said, that the Revolution had shaken Fox's heart into the wrong place. Fox, more wise and generous, speaking of Burke's book on the Revolution, said, " Burke is right after all ; but Burke is often right—only *he is right too soon.*" This was the real difference between them.

If any English minister had a chance of being received in a cordial spirit by the French government, it was unquestionably Fox. But he failed in his object—an object very near to his heart in taking office. Why did he fail? Because he had all the Pitt disputes to clear up first; and it was not easy to restore a good understanding, where Pitt had been embroiling the negotiation beforehand. For of all men in the world, Pitt was the fondest of troubled waters; perhaps on account of his extraordinary skill in fishing in them.

For this failure, Mr. Canning ungenerously attempted to cast a slur on Mr. Fox's memory; and, in an amendment on the address in December (read but not moved), he deliberately censured one of the noblest acts of that

* Mr. Fox took advantage of the short peace of Amiens to consult the archives at Paris for materials connected with his history, and, in common with the rest of the English, waited upon the First Consul at the Tuileries.

o

minister's life—the intimation Fox conveyed to M. Talleyrand, of a plot which had been communicated to him, for the assassination of the First Consul. Mr. Canning's conduct towards Mr. Fox, upon all occasions after the death of Pitt, was irreconcileable with the general tenor of his parliamentary life—it was irascible and vindictive, and not always ingenuous. Some allowance, perhaps, ought to be made for the heats of political controversy—although it is hard to find any excuse for temporising with justice. But every public man discloses his human frailty in leaving us something to forgive:—so let these faults of Mr. Canning's—and serious faults they were—be consigned to oblivion, along with the multitudes of fugitive political errors, which have their origin in temporary excitements, and expire with the occasion that gave them birth.

If Fox failed in exacting a peace to satisfy Mr. Canning, he had the higher glory of bringing forward measures for the abolition of the slave trade—for which his name will be held in veneration by the latest posterity. " The ardent wishes of his mind," said Lord Howick, speaking of him with deep emotion, shortly after his death, " were to consummate, before he died, two great works on which he had set his heart; and these were the restoration of a solid and honourable peace, and the abolition of the slave trade." His last effort was upon this question, when he made that memorable declaration, that if, during the forty years he had sat in Parliament, he had accomplished nothing else, he should think he had done enough!

How strange it is to look back upon the odd fancies people formerly entertained on this question of the Abolition. They had no clear conception of its bearings. The agitation of it seemed to disturb all fixed ideas. When it was first started it had much the same sort of effect as a proposal for unloosening the settlements of landed property, or annihilating the Funds. People looked upon it in vague dismay, as a movement against vested rights and long established privileges. They had got confused notions into their heads about the slave trade and slavery; they confounded them at first, scarcely knew there was any difference between them or what it was, and so fell into a state of crude, moping superstition, very difficult to be dealt with by the vulgar processes of reasoning.

Wilberforce was the parliamentary apostle of Abolition. He worked at it day and night, and prayed for it with his daily bread. Honour to him for that, in spite of all his crotchetty little ways and eccentricities! But he was a sad bore to Pitt, always popping in his fears and misgivings at the most inopportune moments; a sort of philanthropic Paul Pry, perpetually forgetting his umbrella, and hoping he didn't intrude. Nobody ever had such an inobtrusive way of obtruding his advice upon every body. No matter what the question was, or who the person, or how slight the acquaintance, Wilberforce was sure to find some excuse for a hint or a warning, with such excellent intentions, that it was impossible to give vent to the vexation he occasioned. He had no suspicion of the possibility of doing mischief; but went blundering on with the most amiable sincerity of purpose, good-naturedly setting all his friends right, and knocking his head against every body's business with a simplicity of character upon which experience was wasted in vain.

The dull integrity of Wilberforce was always for going forward, in and out of season; all he looked to was the truth and justice of the matter, and *that,* he thought would carry it against all obstacles; he had no idea of the low struggle of passions and interests which renders the cunning use of means even more essential to success than the purity of the end; he never could be brought to understand the value of *timing* and economising his efforts; and, like an unpractised rower, he expended a hundredfold more strength upon the oar than, skilfully employed, was necessary to propel the boat.

To Pitt, when he was in office, all this was quite fearful; for Wilberforce had not the remotest notion of ministerial machinery, of parliamentary tact, or the necessity of management, and he used to be struck with amazement at Pitt's sagacity and cleverness in that way, which seemed to him like an inspiration. Whenever he saw any thing wrong, or what he supposed to be wrong, he could no more help himself from just pointing it out, than faithful watch-dogs can help their instinct in barking at footsteps in the night. He would make the most awkward motions out of sheer benevolence and good-heartedness, to the indescribable embarrassment of government or the total discomfiture of his own friends; and once was on the point of making a motion which would have broken up the administration—a result as far from his intention as the destruction of the monarchy itself—and was only prevented by a private entreaty from Pitt. But what was to be done with this charitable, unwise man—this gentle, impracticable being? To oppose him openly was out of the question, for there was really no gainsaying him on principle: he was propriety itself carried to a fault; it would be like opposing one of the decencies of life, although every body must feel how inconvenient it is to have even the decencies themselves thrust under one's eyes, and rung in one's ears every hour in the day.

But those very qualities which rendered Wilberforce so unsafe, and so tantalising on all other questions, made him the fittest man in the world for the slave trade. It required all his perseverance, all his enthusiasm, all that faculty of resistance to the petty harassing difficulties which eternally rose up against him, increasing as he advanced; that happy constitution of mind which kept him still fresh and sanguine in the midst of disappointments; that fortunate blindness of zeal, which enabled him *not* to see impediments of a kind which would have seriously interfered with the *amour propre* of other men; that enduring faith which sustained him through good and evil; and that vanity—for vanity he had, supreme and towering—which carried him like a butterfly to the end. Wilberforce was the only man who could have worked on in Parliament for the Abolition, with the requisite one-idead energy. He was not a man for a crisis, but a man for a continuance; a great man for a committee—a great sitter—a great sifter of small facts—a man not to be put down by fatigue, so long as it bore upon his own paramount object—a man who had always a quantity of papers and correspondence in his pocket, about cruelties and atrocities, which he whipped out and read at every opportunity—who never met you in the street, but he had a new fact to tell you about the horrors of slavery—who contrived to insinuate that one subject into every company, and every topic of conversation—and who grew so completely identified with it, that whenever he made his appearance, or wherever you fell in with his name, he at once brought the question to your mind, and set you thinking about the poor blacks. All this made Wilberforce, personally, very troublesome; and, in spite of the toleration which the amenity of his manners secured for him, people often tried to keep clear of him, as well as they could without offence. *But this was the only way in which the Abolition could have been carried.* It was this that diffused the feeling of indignation throughout the upper classes, and brought them to a familiar knowledge of the crimes which their humanity, thus perpetually urged, prohibited at last. But even this constancy of Wilberforce's could not have achieved its object, had it not been seconded by the moral influence of his character. No weight of personal authority alone could have effected it; and mere perseverance, without high character, would have gone for nothing. Wilberforce happily united both.

The noblest eloquence was long expended upon this subject in vain. What could eloquence do against the phalanx of prejudice and selfishness by which it was opposed? Slavery was looked upon as a right—*one of the rights of property.* The slave trade was, of course, essential to its maintenance. At first all the country gentlemen rose *en masse* against any interference with it. The commercial body fought for it as if it were a balance of exchanges in perpetuity. The lawyers defended it as they would an entail. The army and navy stood up for it as they would for the honour of the British flag. Lord Eldon flatly denied the doctrine that the principle of slavery was incompatible with our constitution—in fact, he seemed to think that the Constitution couldn't get on without it; and General Gascoigne—brave General Gascoigne!—declared that, so far from abolishing the slave trade, it ought to be increased ; and that if slavery had never before existed in the world, it ought to be begun now ! All the strong old monopolies and superstitions were up against the Abolition ; headed by the giant West India Interest, and followed by all the other ogre-monopolies, none knowing whose turn might come next. And then there were many strictly Christian people, who, like ants, made it a solemn law to themselves to follow in the track over which the burden of their faith was first carried, and who, holding the same belief that was held before the Flood, were convinced, and not to be put out of their conviction by any human means, that the slave trade (or slavery, for it was all one to them) was an old Scriptural institution; and these faithful people would as soon have thought of knocking down the parish churches, or putting the Archbishop of Canterbury on short commons, or any other imaginable sacrilege, as of preventing a free-trade in the blood, bones, and muscles of the blacks, or black-a-moors, as some of the funny members of the Opposition used to call them. The friends of Abolition had to contend against these fierce and motley cohorts, who were themselves the bitterest opponents on general questions, but united in total blindness upon this; like enemies who met in the dark and kept close together for mutual protection.

In spite of this extensive conspiracy, Mr. Fox's resolution was agreed to in the Commons, by a majority of 114 to 15, then sent up to the Lords and carried. Lord Castlereagh voted against it. That was faction. Mr. Canning declared that it was impossible for the ingenuity of man to devise a form of words for the repeal of the slave trade in which he should not concur: but he censured ministers for not bringing the subject more fully before Parliament. It was necessary to find some objection; and it is hardly to be regretted that the objection which he did find was so little to the purpose.

Under the malignant spell of party spirit, he carped at every proposition that came from the opposite side. He was an uncompromising champion, nevertheless, in this great cause. His speech in 1799 demolished most of the dogmas upon which the defenders of the slave trade relied. A glance at one or two passages will show how thoroughly he had entered into the subject.

One of the points set up was that of the *right*—an unfortunate assumption at a time when the French had brought rights of all kinds into disrepute.

" The right ! I have learned, indeed, by painful experience of what has of late years passed in the world, to associate the word *right*, with ideas very different from those which, in old times, it was calculated to convey. I have learnt to regard the mention of rights as prefatory to bloody, destructive, and desolating doctrines, hostile to the happiness and to the freedom of mankind. Such has been the lesson which I have learnt from the rights of man. But never, even in the practical application of that detested and pernicious doctrine, never, I believe, has the word *right* been so shamefully affixed to murder, to devastation, to the invasion of public independence, to the pollution and destruction of private happiness, to gross and unpalliated injustice, to the spreading of misery and mourning over the earth, to the massacre of innocent individuals, and to the extermination of unoffending nations ; never before was the word *right* so prostituted and misapplied, as when the right to trade in man's blood was asserted by the enlightened government of a civilised country. It is not wonderful that the slavery of Africa should be described by a term consecrated to French freedom."

Another argument was, that the slave trade was the means of rescuing the negroes from a worse fate, because they were all either convicts or prisoners of war at home, and if not sold for slaves would be put to death. The legislature of Jamaica, with this general assertion on their lips, had just passed an act to prohibit the importation of slaves *above* twenty-five years old. Mr. Canning treated this act with scorn and derision. How were the custom-house officers to distinguish the contraband importation? How was the age to be known? By what parish register? By what testimony? By mark of mouth?

"All this has been gravely argued. But mark, how the Assembly of Jamaica has put it down. They will take nothing above twenty-five years old. How is this? Have they found some secret by which they can prevent any African from being guilty of a crime, any African from being made a prisoner of war, after he was five-and-twenty? Or did they mean to consign all those who were above that age, and were yet, in spite of this salutary regulation which precluded them from all escape from their country, so headstrong as to become convicts and captives, to consign them unpityingly to their fate? The women too— they were not to be more than twenty-five. Their crime the House had often been told (as they could not be prisoners of war) was witchcraft. What secret had the Assembly of Jamaica found, by which the practice of that dark act (which I am far from meaning to defend), could be confined within the limits of five-and-twenty? Or, were they determined to rescue none but the young witches, and to leave the old ones to their fate? I am ashamed to appear to treat with levity, a subject at which I cannot look without horror and disgust. But when the most absurd and unreasonable pretences are set up in defence of the most abominable practices, it is impossible not to feel the attempt to impose on one's understanding, as an aggravation of the outrage to one's feelings."

Now that the slave trade and its ghastly horrors, and its train of shattered fallacies and impudent pretences, have all vanished, the attempts that used to be made in Parliament to prop up the iniquity, appear nearly incredible. One gentleman—be his name immortal!—Sir W. Young, defended slavery on the ground that it had produced some of the greatest men amongst the ancients. "If," said he, "gentlemen would look into their 'Macrobius,' they would find that half the ancient philosophers had been slaves." Another gentleman, in the same debate, objected to a fact stated by Mr. Wilberforce, that there were parts of Africa where civilisation was making such progress, that books were not uncommon amongst the inhabitants. " Books!" exclaimed Mr. Dent, in the utmost alarm; " books! the black-a-moor have books! and this given, too, as a reason why they should not be exported as slaves! What produced the French Revolution? Books! He hoped, whatever the House did, it would not be induced to stop the slave trade, in order that the inhabitants of Africa might stay at home to be corrupted by books!" " Now, I must complain," said Mr. Canning, " of a little unfairness in the arguments of the honourable baronet and the honourable gentleman, thus contrasted with each other. ' Export the natives of Africa,' said the honourable gentleman, ' lest they become literati at home.' ' Bring them away,' said the honourable baronet, ' that they may become philosophers in the West Indies.' I much doubt whether the remedy or the disease be the worse for the patient; but, undoubtedly, it does seem a little hard, that no means could be found to prevent the dangers of African literature, except in the practical philosophy of the West Indies."

The greatest stress of all was laid upon the antiquity of slavery. This was a difficulty which paralysed many persons of tender conscience. They felt with you, that slavery was cruel, that it blighted human beings, crushed the godlike part of them, and reduced them to the condition of the lower animals. But it was a sacred institution—it had flourished in the earliest ages—it had a divine origin—and was *tabooed* by the consecrating hand of time. Mr. Canning did not forget to deal with this hoary superstition. It is one of the happiest passages in the speech.

" Little, indeed, did I expect to hear the remote origin and long duration of the slave trade brought forward with triumph; to hear the advocates of the slave trade put in their claim for the venerableness of age, and the sacredness of prescription. What are the principles upon which we allow a certain claim to our respect, to belong to any institution which has subsisted from remote time? What is the reason, why, when any such institutions had, by the change of circumstances or manners, become useless, we still tolerated them, nay cherished them with something of affectionate regard, and even when they became burdensome, did not remove them without regret? What? but because in such institutions, for the most part, we saw the shadow of departed worth or usefulness, the monument and memorial of what had, in its origin, or during its vigour, been of service or of credit to mankind? Was this the case with the slave trade? Was the slave trade originally begun upon some principle of public justice or national honour, which the lapse of time, which the mutations of the world have alone impaired and done away? Has it to plead former merits, services, and glories, in behalf of its present foulness and disgrace? Was its infancy lovely, or its manhood useful, though in its age it is become thus loathsome and perverse? No. Its infant lips were stained with blood. Its whole existence has been a series of rapacity, cruelty, and murder. It rests with the House to decide, whether it will allow to such a life the honours of old age, or endeavour to extend its duration."

If Mr. Canning did not lend the aid of his eloquence to assist the triumph of Mr. Fox's abolition resolution, it was because he believed that the necessity of getting rid of the new administration was paramount to every other consideration. But he could not withdraw the influence of his opinion, which was explicitly announced in a declaration that he was " decidedly in favour of the speedy extinction of that disgraceful traffic."

That there were some grounds for Mr. Canning's sleepless hostility against these ministers must, of course, be conceded. No administration is perfect. The Grenville administration contained elements which were extremely difficult of combination. Windham was theoretical, hasty, and sometimes impracticable. Grenville kept in check the tendency of his colleagues towards one class of domestic improvements, and Sidmouth suppressed another. There were balances to be consulted and poised before any measure could be agreed upon; and this led to delays in some instances, and to an imperfect utterance of the real designs of the cabinet in others. Nor were these the only personal impediments that acted as a drag upon the progress of the government. Sheridan had latterly grown careless, and had fallen into the Prince's interest, and given so little support to Fox, that an estrangement gradually grew up between them.* Differences of temper, too, became apparent between Fox, whose composure was never ruffled even by the attacks of Canning, and Grenville, whose haughty conduct throughout the war was not well calculated to promote the happy issue of the negotiations with France. Yet, notwithstanding all this, the spirit of the administration was comprehensive and enlightened; and the proceedings of the Opposition were factious, harassing, and vindictive.

Mr. Pitt would never have carried on an opposition with so little candour and so much bitterness. He had a higher sense of what was due to Mr. Fox, and to himself. Mr. Canning in this single instance sacrificed every thing to his attachment to Mr. Pitt's memory. He went beyond Mr. Pitt in his defence of Mr. Pitt's principles. It could not have been more ably done—it might have been done more fairly. Justice had greater claims upon him than Pitt.†

---

* Sheridan called on Fox during his illness, when the latter requested Lord Grey to remain in the room, in order to prevent any private conversation. The interview was cold and short.

† Mr. Canning's numerous speeches during this period, must be traced

The effect of this incessant warfare upon the enfeebled frame of Fox, already sinking under a severe illness, was fatal in the end. He struggled as long as he could; attended the House night after night to answer Canning; but his opponent was too young and elastic for him; and at last he was missed from his accustomed seat. These debates had broken him down. He wished to breathe the air of St. Anne's Hill, but the journey, short as it is, was impossible in his state; and the Duke of Devonshire proposed that he should break it, by resting on the way at the duke's villa, at Chiswick. He was removed to Chiswick, where he lingered a few days, and died. What solemn thoughts must have pressed themselves upon Mr. Canning's mind; could he have looked onward and foreseen an event which was to happen within a few years in the same chamber, produced in a great degree by very similar causes. But it is wisely ordained that the practical admonitions of life shall be gathered from the experiences of the past, and not from the terrors of the future.

The death of Mr. Fox, following so soon upon the death of Pitt, broke up the close masses known as the two great parties in this country. They were no longer to be distinguished by the same marks—they were no longer bound together by the same obligations. Hitherto people were, not to say Tories or Whigs, but Pittites or Foxites. It was not that they believed in this or that set of principles, but that they believed in Pitt or Fox. It was the ruling mind that led them. Now they were to be guided by other means, and the means were yet to be devised.

Lord Howick succeeded Fox at the Foreign Office, and discharged his trust with great ability. To his hands was

through the regular parliamentary records. They are not preserved in any other collection.

committed the introduction of a bill in the Commons for securing to all his majesty's subjects in common the privilege of serving in the army or navy. By the Irish Act of 1793, Catholics were already qualified to serve in Ireland; but the provisions of that act applied only to Ireland. This incongruity consequently arose, that should an Irish regiment be called into England (to which contingency all Irish regiments were liable under the Union), the Catholics would be compelled to leave the service, the English law not permitting Catholics to carry arms in defence of the country! The new bill proposed to extend the Irish Act to England. It also proposed to allow Catholics and Dissenters to attain the highest ranks in both services. Upon the latter provision his majesty quarrelled with his ministers.

Lord Grenville declared in his place in the House, that the bill had been, in the first instance, submitted to his majesty, and approved of by him. Lord Sidmouth declared that his majesty did not understand it, and that he was under the impression that it did nothing more than extend the Irish law to England. Mr. Perceval, who was beginning just about this time to make himself very conspicuous on all subjects relating to religious tests, asserted, that the question at issue really was, whether the legislature should give up Protestant ascendency or not!

His majesty's distress on the slightest allusion to a Catholic concession must be referred to the state of his nerves. He was kindly hearted and benevolent on other subjects. But the mention of a Catholic produced upon him much the same sort of effect which Gulliver tells us is produced upon English ladies by the sight of a toad. This one settled abhorrence was for ever agitating his mind. Something of the same sort seems to have danced in the blood of a few of his ancestors; and in this respect he particularly resembled his grandfather, who is said to have had a horror of vampires.

Ministers withdrew the bill. They could not force the royal conscience, but they were resolved to vindicate their own. Lord Grenville and Lord Howick expressed their desire to reserve, in the minutes of the cabinet, a right to declare their opinions on this measure, and to renew it at any time they thought proper. The king was terrified, and demanded a written pledge that they would never agitate the subject again. The demand was refused. After this it was impossible the king, who would not be advised, and his advisers, who would not be coerced, could keep together. Mr. Perceval sprang the rattle of Church in Danger! and to use Mr. Windham's phrase, the old intolerant party, after having abdicated their claims for two successive parliaments, " stole into power under the despicable cry of ' No Popery!'"

On the 24th of March, 1807, the retiring ministers delivered up the seals of office, and had the satisfaction of closing their labours by obtaining the king's assent, in their last interview with him, to the bill for abolishing the slave trade.

This able administration was driven out by clamour, and through the insidious power exerted over the poor old king by men as bigoted as himself, but more capable and cunning. Lord Eldon and Lord Hawkesbury enjoy the historical honour of being considered as his majesty's chief instigators on this occasion. Mr. Canning stands clear of it: indeed, so far from having participated in the *underhand* means that were employed to procure the dismissal of ministers, he no sooner learned that such a result was likely to take place than he communicated it, with what delicacy he might, to that section of the government with whom he happened to be on terms of private friendship, urging them to the necessity of adopting some course to avert his majesty's displeasure. His enmity, however it is to be lamented on other grounds, was at least open, loud, and public. Nor did it die with its object, if the following lines, which may be described as the epitaph of the Grenville administration, written by its bitterest opponent, were justly ascribed to him.

ALL THE TALENTS.

When the broad-bottom'd junta, with reason at strife,
Resign'd, with a sigh, its political life;
When converted to Rome, and of honesty tired,
They gave back to the devil the soul he inspired;

The demon of faction that over them hung,
In accents of horror their epitaph sung;
While Pride and Venality join'd in the stave,
And canting Democracy wept at the grave.

" Here lies in the tomb that we hollowed for Pitt,
Consistence of Grenville, of Temple the wit;
Of Sidmouth the firmness, the temper of Grey,
And Treasurer Sheridan's promise to pay.

" Here Petty's finance, from the evils to come,
With Fitzpatrick's sobriety creeps to the tomb;
And Chancellor Ego,* now left in the lurch,
Neither dines with the Jordan,† nor whines for the Church.

" Then huzza for the party that here is at rest,
By the fools of a faction regretted and blest;
Though they sleep with the devil, yet their's is the hope,
On the downfall of Britain to rise with the Pope."

Other stinging satires on the same subject were also

* Lord Erskine.   † Mrs. Jordan.

attributed to him, but without much apparent justification.*

In the strife of parties, as in love, all things are considered fair. But if the verses above cited were really written by Mr. Canning, they are not creditable to him. It is bad enough to make war upon the dead; but it is worse to employ weapons which would have been despised in the lifetime of the adversary. In these rabid lines the "No Popery" cry is revived, and shouted with frantic exultation over the grave of the Whig cabinet. We can fancy it all to belong to Mr. Canning—except the use which is made of that most unworthy expedient.

The great crime of the Grenville ministry was, that it took office at a wrong moment. It was impossible, under the influence of the then existing circumstances, to complete any of their objects, or even to open them with any reasonable chance of making an impression. The transition from Pitt, to a government of peace and liberal amelioration, was too sudden. Fox and his party assumed the government too soon for their own glory, and the permanent good of the country. Their failure may be ascribed to the single fact, that they allowed themselves to be placed in a *false position*.

* The well-known satire, called "All the Talents," published during the existence of the ministry, was attributed to various people. The secret of the authorship was well kept, while this poem was passing rapidly through several editions. Stockdale himself, who published it, is said not to have known from whence the MS. came. The author was Eaton Stannard Barrett, who wrote the "Heroine," "Woman," and other works.

IX.

THE DUKE OF PORTLAND'S ADMINISTRATION. MR. CANNING APPOINTED SECRETARY OF STATE FOR FOREIGN AFFAIRS. THE DUEL.

THERE was some difficulty in getting up a new administration. The "Church in Danger" and the "No Popery" cry had already determined which way it was to march; but recruits were wanted. The parts were settled, but it was necessary to find actors to fill them.

Fifteen years before, the difficulty would have been insuperable; but ever since the Duke of Portland's coalition with Pitt, the intermixture of parties afforded a convenient escape from the embarrassment of choice. The sacrifice of opinion on some points for the sake of strength upon others, began now to be considered legitimate in the formation of an efficient government. This easy virtue of public men was very lucky for the king; for if his majesty had been thrown upon the Church and State party exclusively, he could not have constructed a cabinet that would have lasted a week.

The Duke of Portland was selected as the nominal head—a highly respectable nobleman in bad health, who never made his appearance in Parliament, and sustained himself by opiates and laudanum through the fatigues of forming a government, which he was unable to control.

The duke was an indolent man, and possessed in an eminent degree the talent of dead silence. He was afflicted with the stone, and this physical agony, added to the mental anxiety of office, ultimately broke him down. He used to drop asleep in his chair over his state papers from exhaustion and infirmity. And this was so visible from the first, that Lord Chatham (out of pretended respect to the memory of Pitt) was actually associated with him by the king's desire, in the formation of the ministry. He suffered this without remonstrance, and tacitly allowed Lords Eldon and Hawkesbury to go between him and the king at a moment when the whole responsibility of the government was about to be devolved upon him. It was not surprising that his colleagues soon began to disavow his authority and set up for themselves in their own departments; so that, although Burlington House continued to be resorted to by the adherents of the administration, it was to all intents and purposes nothing more than the ministerial rendezvous.

The real head of the government was Mr. Perceval, a gentleman expressly engaged to do the hard work. The only recommendation he possessed was his profound intolerance, the depths of which even his majesty's plummet could not sound. Mr. Perceval was a practising barrister, and it was not to be expected that he would give up business without a consideration. His majesty accordingly offered him the Chancellorship of the Duchy of Lancaster for life, if he would take the Chancellorship of the Exchequer for as long as he could manage to keep it. The Commons of England thought this too high a price to pay for the services of " a second-rate lawyer," and voted an address to his majesty, praying that neither the said office, nor any other not usually held for life, should be granted for any other term than during pleasure. His majesty wisely submitted to this unequivocal expression of opinion, and the new ministry opened with a defeat.* This was a more inauspicious beginning than the elevation of Lord Ellenborough to the cabinet, which, although indefensible in principle, was at least sanctioned without a division by the Upper House, and carried in the Lower by an overwhelming majority.

The Cabinet was finally made up before the close of March, 1807. Lord Eldon succeeded Lord Erskine on the woolsack; Mr. Canning was appointed Foreign Secretary, Lord Hawkesbury Home Secretary, and Lord Castlereagh Secretary at War. In other places were to be found Lords Camden, Mulgrave, and Chatham, and Mr. George Rose. The Duke of Richmond—the most agreeable of boon companions!—with Sir Arthur Wellesley, (now Duke of Wellington) as secretary, undertook the government of Ireland, at a crisis which demanded the greatest sagacity, discretion, and fortitude. The hazardous honour had been previously declined by the Dukes of Rutland and Beaufort, and Lord Powis.

Mr. Canning is said to have coquetted for office with the Grenville party, just on the eve of their dismissal, and then, finding the case hopeless, to have surrendered himself to the Tories.† This assertion impudently put

* There is a strange mistake upon this subject in Lord Malmesbury's Diaries. It is there stated in a note [vol. iv., p. 376] that the motion was made by Mr. Martin, and *lost* by a majority of 93. The motion was made by Mr. Bankes, and *carried* by a majority of 113. This was on the 25th of March, and on the 8th of April his majesty forwarded an answer to the House, to the effect that he had granted the office "only during his royal pleasure."

† "This political Killigrew just before the breaking up of the last administration, was in actual treaty with them for a place; and if they had survived four-and-twenty hours longer, he would have been now declaiming against the cry of 'No Popery!' instead of inflaming it."— "Peter Plymley's Letters."

forth at the time, is not only false but the very reverse of the fact. Instead of coquetting with the Grenville ministry, he firmly resisted the temptations they held out to him. In the November of 1806, there was a general election ; and Lord Grenville, desirous of strengthening his government by the addition of some of Pitt's followers, made splendid offers to Canning, with *carte blanche* for any three or four friends he would name. The negotiation was intrusted to Lord Wellesley, who conducted it with skill and delicacy ; but Canning peremptorily refused to join the administration upon any terms.*

It was a more serious charge against him, that he joined this Perceval-Portland Ministry, from which the Catholic question must have been excluded by a pledge, either actually given or clearly understood.

To this charge there is no answer to be made but that Mr. Canning strictly followed the example of Mr. Pitt. He knew that during the king's lifetime that question could not be carried, and he bowed to the necessity. He could not reconcile it with his sense of duty to decline office because his majesty's determination was fixed on that subject ; or, having taken office, to make a useless resistance to his majesty's convictions. This is all the defence or palliation that need be offered for his connexion with this Ultra-Protestant Ascendency Administration. Like Pitt he resigned, because he could not effect the emancipation of the Catholics ;—like Pitt he took office again, knowing that such a measure could not even be proposed.

It must be remembered also that Mr. Canning, like Pitt, considered emancipation as a question of *expediency*, and not of *right;* never to be insisted upon against the

* "Diaries of Lord Malmesbury," iv., 354.

free will of the people, the monarch, and the Parliament; and to be promoted only as the development of opinion and opportunity became favourable to its success. This view of the question may have been wrong ; but Mr. Canning's conduct must be tried by his own opinions and not by the opinions of others.

If the precedent of antagonist elements in former cabinets could be admitted as an excuse, he had an ample apology. Even the ministry which had been just displaced, exhibited the most discordant materials. Sheridan, the knight-errant of annual parliaments—Grenville, the inflexible enemy of all reform ; Fox, the consistent advocate of peace—Windham, who had abandoned his own party to support the war ; Grey, the ardent friend of religious freedom—Sidmouth, the representative of the king's zealotry, and, heretofore, the object of the unlimited ridicule and contempt of all those with whom he was now associated. If Mr. Canning had waited until a ministry perfectly agreeing on all points could have been formed, he might have waited till doomsday.

The new ministry had to contend against several adverse circumstances.

They had to meet a Parliament convoked by their opponents only in the preceding December.

They laboured under the imputation of having got into office by a discreditable intrigue, and they had to face its consequences in the fury of their adversaries. The imputation was true. The Duke of Portland had no sooner heard of the Catholic Bill, than he protested against it in a private letter to his majesty, offering his services, at the same time, in the formation of a new administration, should such an alternative become necessary. A clearer case of factious intrigue never was made out—although the proofs of its existence did not transpire until many years after the chief actors in it had gone to their graves.

They were also accused of allowing themselves to be fettered with pledges which rendered them the slaves, not the advisers, of the crown. The fact was self-evident. The new ministers avowedly went into office on the pledge which had been constitutionally rejected by their predecessors.

These disadvantages were enhanced by their want of personal weight. None of them possessed enough of the public confidence to qualify them for the high and responsible offices to which they were called. They all wanted reputation; and some of them—Hawkesbury and Castlereagh in particular—also wanted ability. Canning was dreaded for his sarcasm, his ready powers of debate, his unflinching courage, and the extraordinary tact he possessed in justifying his conduct; but even Canning, although hated, feared, and envied quite enough to make him of importance to any administration, was not yet considered to have attained the full rank of a statesman. " He is unquestionably," observes Lord Malmesbury, " very clever, and very essential to government; but he is *hardly yet a statesman*, and his dangerous habit of *quizzing* (which he cannot restrain) would be most unpopular in any department which required pliancy, tact, and conciliatory behaviour. He is honourable and honest, with a dash of the Irishman; and all his plans and ideas of governing would partake of this, and might be as dangerous in practice, as he makes them appear plausible by the eloquent way in which he expresses them."*
This was written immediately before the government was organised. During the progress of its formation, the

* "Diaries," iv., 367.

Duke of Portland offered Canning his choice of the Foreign Office or the Admiralty. Canning went immediately to consult his friend, Lord Malmesbury; and it is a curious commentary on his lordship's opinion, as to his fitness for a department requiring pliancy, tact, and conciliatory behaviour, that he instantly recommended him to take the Foreign Office, where these qualities are indispensable. Canning had never before had an opportunity of acting upon his own responsibility; and Lord Malmesbury, judging of him in moments of excitement and suspense, feared rather than anticipated that his spirits would carry him away. But Canning was scarcely established in the Foreign Office, when his able diplomatic friend had occasion to bear testimony to his judgment, coolness, and promptitude under new and singularly trying circumstances.

When Parliament met, in April, ministers were simultaneously attacked in both Houses; and separate motions were made, to the effect, that it was unconstitutional in the confidential servants of the crown to fetter themselves by pledges to the sovereign. Mr. Canning, in reply, turned the argument against the late ministers, who had insisted upon the right of proposing a measure which they knew the king would never allow to pass into law.

"What was required in the stipulations claimed by the late ministers? That they should be allowed to recommend one policy, whilst they pursued another. The terms upon which they wished to hold their offices, were that they should be allowed to propose measures, that they might afterwards abandon them. The yearly moving of this question would have the effect of making an unfair division of the popularity and odium. The odium would be great, and all fall upon the crown: the benefit would be small, and that the Catholics might have; but the whole of the popularity the ministers were to have."

Having thus made it appear that his colleagues, instead of coming in upon a pledge, had rescued his majesty from a plot, he concluded by threatening an appeal to the country, a threat which frightened the Cabinet a great deal more than the Opposition. Even Lord Malmesbury was alarmed. "Canning," says he, "was too imperious last night about the threat of dissolution." But events proved that Canning was right. Parliament was dissolved before the end of the month. The extremity was forced upon them. And what was the result? Scarcely a single member of the Opposition was returned for the place he had previously filled. In the division which had tested the strength of ministers in the preceding Parliament, they mustered with difficulty a surplus of 32. In the new Parliament they commanded an easy majority of 195.

The state of Europe when Mr. Canning undertook the office of Foreign Secretary, was more precarious than it had been at any previous period. The power of Napoleon was supreme, and that supremacy was crowned by the peace of Tilsit, nominally entered into between France, Russia, and Prussia; but really between Napoleon and Alexander. The poor Queen of Prussia was invited to attend. But it was only that she might be the more effectually cheated. Napoleon asked her to dinner, then suddenly pretended to be so fascinated by her naive and charming coquetry, that he desired Talleyrand to get the treaty signed after dinner without her knowledge, lest her bewitching beauty might tempt him to give up too much!

By that treaty, signed on the 8th of July, 1807, Europe was divided between the two potentates. The whole of the south was surrendered to Napoleon, already master of Italy, and arbiter of Germany, and pushing his advanced posts as far as the Vistula. And the crowns of Naples, Holland, and Westphalia were conferred on his three brothers.

While the emperors were thus partitioning Christendom on a raft on the Niemen, Mr. Canning was forming a plan for the protection of England against the imperial conspiracy. The first intimation the world had of his design, was the sudden appearance, in the month of August, of an English fleet in the Sound, the bombardment of Copenhagen, and the capture of the whole navy of Denmark.

Intelligence of this event had scarcely arrived, when it was followed by the gallant victors conveying the Danish fleet into the harbour of Portsmouth. This extraordinary and apparently unprovoked aggression upon a neutral power who had at that moment, peacefully floating in our waters, merchantmen with their rich cargoes, to the value of upwards of 2,000,000*l.* sterling, naturally enough provoked much astonishment and indignation.

Upon the opening of the session the speech from the throne announced that, no sooner had the peace of Tilsit confirmed the control of France over the powers of the continent, than his majesty *was apprised of the intentions of the enemy to combine those powers in one general confederacy* against England, and that, for that purpose, it was intended to force the neutral states into hostility against his majesty, so as to bring to bear upon England the whole naval force of Europe, and *specifically the fleets of Portugal and Denmark.* It became, therefore, the indispensable duty of his majesty to place those fleets out of the reach of such a confederacy.

Such was the ministerial explanation. The fleet of Portugal would have been seized also, but for the promptitude of Napoleon, who intercepted the intentions of ministers by detaining the Portuguese shipping in the ports of France. The issue of the affairs of Portugal is well known. The unfortuate Prince Regent, unable to resist the tyranny of Napoleon, transported himself and the members of his family to Brazil.

The Opposition denounced the conduct of government in unmeasured language, and called upon ministers to show the grounds upon which they had committed so flagrant a violation of the law of nations. Ministers contented themselves with stating that the measure had not been adopted without notice to the Prince Royal of Denmark, who was duly warned that if he did not avow himself an ally, or guarantee his neutrality by placing his fleet in the hands of the English government, to be delivered up at the close of the war, England must protect herself by seizing upon his navy.

To all this, it was objected, that ministers had no justification for adopting such a course. Mr. Ponsonby declared that, "no writer on the law of nations, or on any other law, had ever maintained that one power could be justified in taking from another power what belonged to it, unless a third power meant, and was able to take the same thing : the justification therefore rested on the necessity." But this was exactly Mr. Canning's case. He maintained that it *was* an act of necessity ; and that if England had not seized upon the Danish navy, France would have seized upon it (which she was notoriously able to do), and would have used it against England.

But where, demanded the opposition, was the proof that such an intention existed? Ministers stated, in reply, that they had received private information that there were *secret* articles in the treaty of Tilsit, sanctioning Buonaparte's plan for combining the navies of Europe to crush the maritime power of Great Britain. This astounding statement was met on all sides by explicit and circumstantial contradictions. France denied it—Russia denied it*—the Opposition discredited it, and covering the government with opprobrium, succeeded in carrying along with them a strong and angry feeling out of doors. "Ministers," exclaimed Lord Grenville, "have asserted that there are secret articles in the treaty of Tilsit affecting the interests of this country; and the French government have asserted that there are none. Here then is a challenge, and it is incumbent upon ministers to prove their assertion." But ministers could not prove their assertion without v olating their honour.

In this exigency Mr. Canning relied upon the general necessity of the case. He bore the taunts of his opponents, now grown insolent in their attacks on his public character, with calmness and dignity; and to every renewed demand for the production of his information, he replied by repeating his determination never to reveal it. "Though the conduct of his majesty's ministers," he said, "might be held up in a few speeches in that House to the execration of the country, they would run that risk, and incur that penalty, rather than *suffer the secret to be torn from their bosoms.*" At length Mr. Adam made a specific motion, the purport of which was, that the Foreign Secretary had violated his trust to the crown, in reference to the communications of government with their accredited ministers abroad. Mr. Canning answered him and withdrew, stating that as a high criminal charge was preferred against

* When our ambassador at St. Petersburg, acting under the instructions of Mr. Canning (which, says Lord Malmesbury, were "incomparable,") demanded of the Russian minister to be shown the secret articles, the minister, after being much pressed, declared that none of them were injurious to the interests of England.

him, he should retire and throw himself upon the judgment of the House. The judgment of the House vindicated him by a sweeping majority of 168 to 67.

There were many persons who firmly believed that there were no secret articles; that the government had never received any secret information; that ministers had committed the outrage in a paroxysm of fear. Time passed away, and the obloquy still hung suspended over their heads.

Seventeen years afterwards—in 1824—a book was published in Paris, a sort of confession of the life of a man who had been much mixed up in the political intrigues of his day; and this book, to the astonishment of every person who had taken any interest in the matter, and who yet survived to learn its solution, contained the following revelation. It is the famous Fouché who speaks:

" About this time it was that we learned the success of the attack upon Copenhagen by the English, which was *the first derangement of the secret stipulations of Tilsit, by virtue of which the Danish fleet was to be placed at the disposal of France!* Since the death of Paul I., I never saw Napoleon give himself up to such violent transports of passion. That which astounded him most in that vigorous stroke (*vigoureux coup de main*) was the promptitude with which the English ministry took their resolution. He began to suspect some new treachery in the Cabinet, and gave me orders to ascertain if it had nothing to do with the ill-will created by a late removal, —that of Talleyrand from the office of Foreign Secretary."

The suspicion was unjust to Talleyrand; and a comparison of dates ought to have satisfied the emperor that the resentment of his minister could have had nothing to do with the attack upon Copenhagen. Talleyrand was

* "Memoirs of Fouché."

removed on the 8th of August,* at which time the English fleet must have been under-weigh for Zealand.

This passage confirmed the statement of ministers, by the evidence of a most unexpected witness; but it still left the source of their information in impenetrable darkness. The mystery, however, has been subsequently cleared up, so that we are now enabled, putting these discoveries together, to show, not only the correctness of the intelligence, but the pressure of the necessity upon which the government acted.

Government, it appears, was in possession of Napoleon's designs, nearly two months before the treaty was signed. The most singular incident in the transaction is, that the first intimation on the subject was communicated to the Duke of Portland, by the Prince of Wales, in an audience at Carlton House, in the month of May. Ministers learned through this channel, that a plan was formed by Napoleon for surprising the Danish fleet, with the assistance of which he intended to invade the north-east coast of England; and that he also meant to avail himself of the Portuguese fleet for the same purpose. The proposal had in fact been made to Denmark, to include her in the continental system of blockading England; and she accepted it, either from cowardice or ill-will, although she afterwards denied that she had ever assented. The same proposal was made to the Regent of Portugal, who rejected it, and at once communicated the notable project to the Prince of Wales.†

Such was the nature of the disclosures which were made to the British government, and such the channel

* "Life of Prince Talleyrand," iv., 121.
† "Diaries of Lord Malmesbury," iv., 391.

through which they were received. The confidence reposed by the Regent in the honour of an English minister was safe. Mr. Canning left his vindication to time, which has already rendered full justice to the secrecy, foresight, and sagacity he displayed on an occasion, when the existence of England depended upon the celerity and success with which the project was executed.

The seizure of the Danish navy was an act of imperative necessity; one of those master-strokes of policy, which instead of being justified, which hints a doubt, ought to be commemorated in columns and statues. The Danes were in this position, that they could not remain neutral. They refused to become our allies, and must have become our enemies. We deprived them of the means of hostility, in mere self-defence. The question was, not whether it was justifiable to take their ships, but whether we or Napoleon should take them—a question of a few hours, which Napoleon would have solved, had we delayed. It was not a moment for an English minister to turn doctor-in-law. His business was to save the country first, and find arguments for it afterwards.

The affairs of Spain next occupied attention. The French had crossed the Pyrenees, expelled the authorities, and taken possession of all the strong-holds. The king and the royal family had been first cajoled, then kidnapped; the coffers of the state had been plundered; the towns given up to rapine and the brutal lusts of the soldiery; the government was usurped; and the whole country was in a state of insurrection. In this deplorable extremity, the provincial juntas sent over delegates to England, for the purpose of soliciting aid. The enterprise was one of great danger, certain to be accompanied by great losses, and, worse than all, exceedingly doubtful in its results. But Mr. Canning felt that the necessity of resisting the encroachments of Napoleon was paramount over all other considerations; that it was the peculiar duty of England to protect the aggrieved; and that our interests, as well as our honour, justified the sacrifices we were now called upon to make. He not only, therefore, encouraged the spirit of resistance in Spain by every assurance of sympathy and support, but proceeded to collect a force for the purpose of acting against the French, wherever its services might be most available. At the head of this force, he placed Sir Arthur Wellesley, whose great military talents he was the first minister to recognise, employ, and reward.* These proceedings, and the noble stand he made on behalf of the dethroned sovereigns and outraged nations of Europe led him into a protracted course of diplomatic negotiation

* "It was Mr. Canning," says Mr. Stapleton, "who discerned the great military talents of Sir Arthur Wellesley, and insisted upon their employment in the Peninsula."—"Political Life of the Right Honourable George Canning, from 1822 to 1827." i. 291. It is unnecessary to fortify by additional evidence a fact obvious enough from Mr. Canning's position in the government; but it is desirable to correct a strange misstatement in the "Military Life of the Duke of Wellington," written by Major Jackson and Captain Scott, in which it is asserted that the command of the army on this occasion was given to Sir Arthur Wellesley "at the instance of Lord Castlereagh." The gallant authors took up this notion apparently from a mistake they had fallen into about his lordship, as the next sentence implies. Sir Arthur's "extraordinary military talents," they inform us, had not been sufficiently appreciated by the nation, or by the most exalted personages in the realm, but fortunately were not "overlooked by the talented nobleman above-named, who, at the time of which we write (1808) *held the office of Secretary of State for Foreign Affairs*," and then they run on into a panegyric upon his "immovable firmness," which has nothing to do with this part of the subject. ("Military Life of the Duke of Wellington," i. 296.) It is clear that these gentlemen assigned to Lord Castlereagh the merit of having first recognised Sir Arthur's talents, under the supposition that his lordship was then Secretary for Foreign Affairs. The passage would be set right at once by transferring the inference to the minister who did fill that office.

with France and Russia, arising out of the joint application of the two emperors to England to put an end to the horrors of the war. Throughout the whole of the correspondence he persisted in refusing to negotiate a peace, unless the rights of Spain were fully admitted ; and he displayed such ability, high principle, and firmness in the conduct of these transactions as to wring from the most reluctant of his adversaries repeated testimonies of admiration.

Our active interference on behalf of Spain fortunately united the suffrage of all parties in Parliament; and if the bitterness occasioned by the aggression on Denmark had been allowed to pass away, a closer union of public men for the common defence of the country might have been effected at this juncture. Mr. Canning showed his desire to cultivate this amicable disposition during the discussions which arose on the state of Spain ; but the Opposition, rankling under the severity of his wit, refused his advances. The widest political differences may be compromised—heresies may be reconciled—but scathing personalities, which wound men's self-love and vanity, are never to be forgiven! They looked upon him as a man who spared nobody—which was true; and they were determined, opportunely and inopportunely, never to spare him.

This was a harassing session with him. He was not wholly with the ultra-Tory party, which was now in the ascendant in the government: there were many minor points on which he differed from them. On the other hand, there were some questions on which he agreed with the Opposition. His spirit was clearly on that side of the House, and he would have been there himself, could he have controlled its excesses and governed Whig tendencies with a Tory judgment. As it was, although the station he occupied afforded him the means of carrying out his views to a certain extent, it also forced him into an occasional struggle between his private convictions and the necessity for defending the general policy of the government. Dr. Duigenan was appointed a privy-councillor—a new insult to the Irish Catholics; and Mr. Canning, who had nothing to do with the appointment, was obliged to endure his share of the obloquy and disgrace. The Catholic petition was introduced by Mr. Grattan, and it was necessary that Mr. Canning should deprecate discussion, at the risk of being misunderstood and misrepresented. He was called upon, also, to vindicate the Duke of York in the matter of his low amours, and to draw the parliamentary distinction between the virtues of the commander-in-chief and the miserable depravities of Mrs. Clarke's paramour. It became his duty, also, to oppose Mr. Whitbread's motion for the exclusion from Parliament of all placemen and pensioners; Mr. Canning contending, as a minister of the crown, that it was necessary for the good of the country that public men who were pensioned off out of office, but who looked to office again, should continue to enjoy the advantage of assisting in the labour of legislation. Through the mire of topics such as these he was condemned to drag his eloquence, which did double duty in the arduous position in which he was placed, of answering not only for his own acts and opinions, but for the bigotry and blunders of his colleagues.

Unfortunately, the greatest blunderer of them all—Lord Castlereagh—was thrown, by his situation as Secretary at War, into such close relations with the Foreign department as to make his errors and his incapacity a source of constant irritation to Mr. Canning. The feelings of the latter towards a minister whom he considered to be inadequate to the grave responsibilities of his office, were not much improved by two charges of corruption which were brought forward against his lordship in the House of Commons. One of them was for being party to the sale of a seat in Parliament, and then requiring the gentleman who had purchased it either to vote for the government on the inquiry respecting the Duke of York, or to resign.* The other was for attempting to traffic for a borough.

Mr. Canning opposed the former motion, because it was avowed to be a first step towards parliamentary reform. But in voting on the latter question he took care to protect himself against being suspected of sheltering Lord Castlereagh's misconduct under his approbation; observing that, " while he would vote for the order of the day, he would by no means be understood to pronounce the case as not of very serious importance." This expression of opinion had more weight with the House than the vote which accompanied it, and the order of the day was negatived. Mr. Canning hastened to repair this unlucky *mésaventure* by moving that, under all circumstances, the House saw no necessity for a criminating resolution, which was carried. This was on the 25th of April, 1809; and it betrayed that uneasiness in his own position, and that entire want of confidence in the

---

* The members of the Grenville administration joined the government in resisting this motion against Lord Castlereagh. It seems that such things were done by all administrations, and they were consequently bound to protect each other. Sir Samuel Romilly observes, that, considered merely with reference to their own interest, it was impolitic. "Nothing that can be proved against them," says that upright man, " will do them more injury in public opinion than this screening of political offences, through fear of recrimination. It will do more towards disposing the nation in favour of parliamentary reform, than all the speeches that have been, or ever will be made, in any popular assemblies." —" Memoirs of Sir Samuel Romilly," ii., 287.

discretion of his colleague, which shortly afterwards led to more serious results.

If the glory—lingering as it was—of Copenhagen belonged to Mr. Canning, the ignominy of Walcheren attaches almost exclusively to Lord Castlereagh. That unfortunate expedition, indeed, involved the whole administration in disgrace; but, chiefly the minister who presided over its execution.

Several months had been occupied in secret preparations, and at length, towards the close of July, 1809, one of the most formidable armaments that ever left the shores of England—consisting of an army of 40,000 men and a fleet of seventy-nine ships of the line, thirty-six frigates, and numerous small craft, amounting altogether to between 400 and 500 pendants, set sail for the Low Countries. The objects were the reduction of Flushing, the capture of the French ships of war in the Scheldt, and the destruction of their arsenals and dock-yards. Lord Chatham (who was wholly unknown as a soldier and had no reputation as a civilian), commanded the army, and Sir Richard Strachan the fleet. Flushing surrendered, and the troops took possession of the island of Walcheren. From this moment a paralysis appears to have descended upon the councils of ministers, and to have stricken both commanders. Nothing more was done. No attempt was made to proceed up the river. Antwerp, the emporium, was abandoned to the enemy; Flushing, a plague-town in a swamp, was held fast. Autumn set in, and brought with it the usual epidemic. Still the commanders stirred not, although the pestilence had already commenced its havoc, and the men were dropping by scores and by hundreds into the grave. The possession of Flushing for any conceivable purpose, offensive or defensive, was so utterly useless that it was impossible to comprehend why it was not evacuated. Some threw the blame upon the military commander—others, upon the admiral; the public, more just than the partisans of either, condemned both in the well-known epigram:

> Lord Chatham with his sword undrawn,
> Stood waiting for Sir Richard Strachan;
> Sir Richard, longing to be at 'em,
> Stood waiting for the Earl of Chatham.

In December the troops returned home—or all that was left alive of them, escaping an inglorious death, only to linger on in hopeless decrepitude. Between the 1st of January and the 1st of June, 1810, including relapses, there were admitted into the hospitals, from the corps which had served in Walcheren, 35,000 patients!

There are some considerations connected with this expedition which are indispensable to the formation of a correct estimate of the sagacity of the minister who was charged with its management.

The same expedition had been suggested during the war, to three different administrations, and rejected as impracticable by each. The opinions of several experienced military men were taken upon its policy and practicability, and they were all against it. Yet Lord Castlereagh, cognizant of these facts, issued orders for the embarkation of an enormous army, which he placed under the command of a nobleman, who was entirely ignorant of the service; and, as if his lordship were resolved that nothing should be omitted to render the failure conspicuous and complete, the expedition was despatched just as the sickly season was setting in, and recalled just as it ended.

It was notorious that Walcheren was one of the most

unhealthy spots in the world, yet not one medical authority was consulted on the subject, and no unusual precautions were adopted. One hospital ship was provided; the Surgeon-General implored Lord Castlereagh to furnish two more, and was refused. Walcheren was taken on the 15th of August. On the 29th, Lord Chatham wrote home that the progress of the army was at an end. The men were taking the infection at the rate of 200 a day: it appeared further, that if Walcheren was to be retained, it would become necessary to build defences, and to feed the inhabitants, 37,000 in number. His lordship, finding that the government would do nothing, returned home on the 14th of September, and left the army to its fate. His successors wrote again and again to entreat for a decision, but it was not until the middle of November, that the first order for evacuation was issued, and it was not until the 28th of December it was carried into effect. The results of this memorable expedition may be thus summed up: loss in lives, eight or nine thousand men, in money between two and three millions sterling;—gain, a poor Flemish town, which we were only too glad to give back again to its famished population.*

It was impossible that Mr. Canning could regard with indifference the danger of committing the country to a project which Mr. Pitt had long before rejected, unless it was carried out with foresight and energy at least equal to the risk. It was one of those hazardous undertakings, the success or failure of which depend mainly on the skill, decision, and vigilance with which they are conducted.

* All the documents and evidence concerning the expedition were laid before Parliament and published. See also " Observations, &c. on the Subject of the late Expedition to the Scheldt," 1810.

Influenced by such impressions, Mr. Canning was placed in a painful situation: as Foreign Secretary, administering the external affairs of the kingdom, he was brought into constant intercourse with Lord Castlereagh. His plans in fact, were at the mercy of the executive genius of the war department; a state of things to which Mr. Canning in justice to himself, felt it impossible to submit. He accordingly signified to the Duke of Portland the absolute necessity of making a change in the war department, tendering his own resignation as the alternative. No circumstance can more distinctly mark Mr. Canning's objection to the expedition, and his sense of Lord Castlereagh's unfitness to conduct it, than the fact that this announcement was made early in April, three months before it sailed.

The duke required a little delay. It was desirable to wait, at all events until the charge against Lord Castlereagh for trafficking for a seat in Parliament should be disposed of; to which Mr. Canning consented. The matter was then broken to Lord Camden, Lord Castlereagh's uncle, through whose influence his lordship had been hitherto promoted to and sustained in his various offices. Lord Camden admitted that such a change was necessary. In May the whole subject was laid before the king, and his majesty agreed to the necessity of a new distribution of the business of the war department, by which the political correspondence would be transferred to the Foreign Office. But this arrangement, which would still have left in Lord Castlereagh's hands the superintendence of the expedition, was not effected. New arrangements were proposed from time to time; fresh delays were created; the members of the cabinet being fully aware of Mr. Canning's feelings on the subject, and Lord Castlereagh being all this time allowed to suppose that he carried into his official duties the entire confidence of his colleagues. Finding that no communication had been made to Lord Castlereagh, and objecting alike to the concealment and the delay, Mr. Canning obtained an interview with his majesty in June, and tendered his resignation. But the moment was inconvenient and he was assured that the communication would be made to Lord Castlereagh as soon as the expedition had sailed. Further delays took place, and at length Mr. Canning was prevailed upon against his judgment, but in deference to the scruples and anxieties of others to let the matter lie over until after the result of the expedition should be known, it being then distinctly understood that the Marquis Wellesley was to be appointed to the war department. The moment the intelligence of the surrender of Flushing reached England, Mr. Canning reminded the Duke of Portland that the time was now come for putting the new arrangement into execution; and he then discovered that no intimation whatever had been conveyed to Lord Castlereagh of the intended change, and that the consequence of persisting in it would be to break up the administration. Under these unexpected circumstances Mr. Canning reverted at once to his original alternative, and, declining to attend the cabinet, informed his grace that he held office only till his successor was appointed. The facts were *now* communicated to Lord Castlereagh for the *first* time, although his uncle and other personal friends had been in possession of them for months. His lordship immediately sent in his resignation.

That Lord Castlereagh was ill-treated all throughout, is quite certain; but not by Mr. Canning. That his lordship had good reason to complain of the secrecy and insincerity that were practised towards him, cannot be denied; but Mr. Canning, instead of being a consenting party to the deceit, protested against it over and over again, and in vain pressed his resignation as the only alternative left. The excuse was the critical state of public affairs, and the danger of a disruption in the ministry.*

All the members of the cabinet, or all who were consulted, agreed in their opinion of Lord Castlereagh's incapacity; yet they suffered him to originate† and conduct this important expedition, and then, when it failed, they announced to him that he had been all along distrusted by his colleagues. This was not a pleasant discovery to make at a moment when his ostentatious plans had just terminated in disgrace and humiliation. Irritated at the treatment he had received, his chivalrous logic resolved it into a personal quarrel, and in a long letter, abounding in "misapprehensions," he sent a message to Mr. Canning.

Lord Castlereagh's method of dealing with the subject, was curiously characteristic. He admitted Mr. Canning's right to demand his removal; and objected only to the

* The poor Duke of Portland seems to have been frightened all throughout by the two imperious gentlemen he had to deal with, and the fear of losing Canning. When Canning originally announced his determination to resign unless the conduct of the war was taken out of the hands of Lord Castlereagh, the duke wrote privately to Lord Eldon, saying, "If it cannot be prevented, I see nothing but ruin to the country, and to Europe, and so I told him plainly and distinctly "—" Life of Lord Eldon," ii., 80. The king expressed the same opinion. The source of all the evil that followed, was timidity, and indecision, and delay on the part of the duke, in which he was encouraged by the Chancellor, to whom procrastination was the breath of life. He should either have accepted Mr. Canning's resignation at once, or at once have complied with his demand. Lord Eldon, who disliked Canning, threw the whole blame upon the vanity of the Foreign Secretary.

† We have Lord Castlereagh's own authority for the assertion that he "originated" the Walcheren Expedition. In his letter to Mr. Canning, he observes, "You allowed me to *originate* and proceed in the execution of a new enterprise," &c.

mode in which it was proposed to be carried out. His words are these:

"I have no right, as a public man, to resent your demanding upon public grounds, my removal from the particular office I have held, or even from the administration, as a condition of your continuing a member of the government. But I have a distinct right to expect that a proposition, justifiable in itself, shall not be executed in an unjustifiable manner, and at the expense of my honour and reputation."

It is clear that it was the mode of executing the proposition, and not the proposition itself, which Lord Castlereagh professed to consider objectionable. He admitted that the original proposition was that which he had no right to resent, but contended that the mode of executing it afforded just ground of offence; and he visited this offence, not on the persons who committed it, but on the author of the proposition, which he had disclaimed the right of resenting. It is a pity, if duels must be resorted to for the vindication of personal honour, that personal honour should not be a little more exact in fixing the responsibility. So far as Lord Castlereagh's honour was concerned, it stood in the same predicament after the duel as before, seeing that he obtained no satisfaction whatever, except from the only person concerned in the transaction, who, on his own showing, stood clear of the imputed offence.

Mr. Canning had nothing to do with the execution of the proposition, which Lord Castlereagh admitted he had a right to make. The mode of putting that proposition into effect rested with others, who alone were responsible for it. Mr. Canning might have declined Lord Castlereagh's hostile invitation on this very obvious ground. But he thought that the terms of Lord Castlereagh's letter precluded explanation; and he surrendered his judgment to a very foolish custom, which proved nothing either way.*

The parties met on the 21st of September, near the Telegraph on Putney Heath, Lord Castlereagh attended by Lord Yarmouth (afterwards Marquis of Hertford), and Mr. Canning by Mr. Charles Ellis (afterwards Lord Seaford). Having taken their ground (in sight of the windows of the house where Pitt died!) they fired by signal, and missed. The seconds endeavoured to effect an accommodation, but failed, and they then declared that, after a second shot, they would retire from the field. The principals again fired, and Lord Castlereagh's ball entered Mr. Canning's thigh, on the outer side of the bone. According to some accounts of the meeting they were placed to fire again, when the seconds, seeing the blood streaming from Mr. Canning's wound, interfered, and so the affair ended.† Mr. Canning afterwards published an account of the whole transaction, which was rendered necessary by certain statements published by Lord Camden. Lord Castlereagh's secretary also issued

* Contemporary opinion ran strongly against Lord Castlereagh. Wilberforce blames him for having sent the challenge, not on the impulse of the first angry feelings, but after chewing the cud of his resentment for twelve days.—"Life," iii., 431. In another place, he ascribes the challenge to his lordship's "Irish education and habits,"—p. 427. These censures are inconsistent. The Irish habit is more hasty and hot-blooded. If Lord Castlereagh did deliberate for twelve days, it must have been because his quick nature had undergone a sea-change. Sir Samuel Romilly blamed both parties. He says that Lord Castlereagh's "honour" was in no way impeached by what had happened, and that Mr. Canning deserved censure for accepting a challenge upon such grounds.—"Memoirs," ii., 300. The leading Tory publications took the same view of the false conclusion drawn by Lord Castlereagh from his own premises.

† Wilberforce tells us that two pistols, thrown away by the combatants, were found upon the ground, and that Lord ——— picked up one of them and carried it off, his gardener securing the other.

a " detail," as he described it, " of the original cause of the animosity," which was answered by a " statement" from Mr. Canning.

Mr. Canning's wound was fortunately slight, and after a short confinement at his house, Gloucester Lodge, in Brompton, he was sufficiently recovered to attend the Levee on the 11th of October, and resign the seals of the Foreign Office into the hands of his majesty. Mr. Huskisson resigned with him, nobly sacrificing his ambition to his friendship.* The infirm Duke of Portland, shattered and wrecked by these disasters, went into retirement and died. The administration was at an end.

* "Speeches of the Rt. Hon. W. Huskisson," p. 51. There never was a more disinterested proof of attachment, for Mr. Huskisson's office (under Secretary to the Treasury) was in no way involved in the quarrel, and Mr. Perceval in vain entreated him to remain. Mr. Sturges Bourne gave a similar testimony of his friendship by resigning at the same time.

X.

GLOUCESTER LODGE. MEMORABILIA.

RANELAGH was in its meridian glory, about the middle of the eighteenth century. The crowds of people it drew westward, steaming along the roads on horseback and afoot, suggested to some enterprising spectator the manifest want of a place of half-way entertainment, that might tempt the tired pleasure-hunter to rest awhile on his way home, or, perhaps, entice him from the prosecution of his remoter expedition on his way out. The spot was well-chosen for the execution of this sinister design. It lay between Brompton and Kensington, just far enough from town to make it a pleasant resting point for the pedestrian, and near enough to Ranelagh to make it a formidable rival. Sometimes of a summer's evening there might be heard the voices of brass instruments, coming singing in the wind over the heads of the gay groups that were flaunting on the high-road, or, through the fields on their excursion to Ranelagh; and, sometimes, decoyed by the sound, they would follow it, thinking they had mistaken the path, and never discover their mistake until they found themselves in the bosky recesses of Florida Gardens.

Florida Gardens, laid out in the manner of Ranelagh,

and Vauxhall, and the Mulberry Garden of old, flourished about sixty years ago: after that time, the place fell into waste and neglect, although the site was agreeable and even picturesque in its arrangements. It was bought by the Duchess of Gloucester, who built a handsome residence upon it, which being in the Italian style, was at first called Villa Maria; but subsequently, in consequence of the duchess making the house her constant resort in the summer months, became generally known by the name of Gloucester Lodge. Her Royal Highness died here in 1807, and Mr. Canning purchased her interest in the estate from her daughter the Princess Sophia.

It was in this charming retreat—profoundly still,
> With over-arching elms.
> And violet banks where sweet dreams brood—

that Mr. Canning, during the long interval which now elapsed before he returned to office, passed the greater part of his leisure. We avail ourselves of this interval of repose to group together, with a disregard for chronological unity, which we hope the reader will not be disinclined to tolerate, a few waifs and strays of personal and domestic interest, otherwise inadmissible to an audience without risk of intrusion. There are parentheses of idle fancy and memory-gossip in every man's life— wet days when he turns over old letters at the fire-side— or indolent sunny days, when he can do nothing but bask in the golden mists and run the round of his youth over again in his imagination. Such lazy hours may be fairly represented by a few indulgent pages of disjointed memorabilia.

The grounds of Gloucester Lodge were shut in by trees. All was seclusion the moment the gates closed. "The drawing-room," says Mr. Rush, "opened on a portico from which you walked out upon one of those smoothly-shaven lawns which Johnson, speaking of Pope's poetry, likens to velvet." Here Mr. Canning received the most distinguished persons of his time, Gloucester Lodge acquiring, under the influence of his accomplished taste, the highest celebrity for its intellectual re-unions. His own feelings always led him to prefer home parties, and, as has already been noticed, he rarely went abroad, except amongst close friends or on occasions of ceremony. His private life was not merely blameless, but quite admirable; he was idolised by his family; and yet, says a noble contemporary, such was the ignorance or malevolence of the paragraph writers, that he was described as a "diner-out."*

The wit which sparkled at these entertainments was of the highest order: but there was something even better than wit—a spirit of enjoyment, gay, genial, and playful. Mr. Rush gives us an amusing account of a scene which took place at a dinner at Gloucester Lodge, immediately after the breaking up of Parliament. Several members of the diplomatic corps were present. Canning, Huskisson, and Robinson, were like birds let out of a cage. There was a great deal of sprightly small talk, and after sitting a long time at table, Canning proposed that they should play at "Twenty Questions." They had never heard of this game, which consisted in putting twenty questions to find out the object of your thoughts, something to be selected within certain prescribed limits. It was arranged that Mr. Canning, assisted by the Chancellor of the Exchequer, was to ask the questions, and Mr. Rush, assisted by Lord Grenville, was to give the answers—the representatives of, probably, nearly all the monarchs of

* "Historical Sketches," &c. By Lord Brougham.

Europe, and the principal ministers of England, watching the result in absolute suspense. The secret was hunted through a variety of dexterous shifts and evasions, until Canning had at last exhausted his twenty questions. " He sat silent for a minute or two," says Mr. Rush ; "then, rolling his rich eye about, and with his countenance a little anxious, and in an accent by no means over-confident, he exclaimed, ' I think it must be the wand of the lord high-steward !'" And it was even so. A burst of approbation followed his success, and the diplomatic people pleasantly observed that they must not let him ask them too many questions at the Foreign Office, lest he might find out every secret they had !

But Mr. Canning was not always in such glorious moods after dinner. His animal spirits sometimes sank under the weight of his public responsibilities. Rush was dining with him one day, when he held the seals of the Foreign Office, and the conversation happening to turn upon Swift, he desired Mr. Planta to take down " Gulliver's Travels," and read the account of the storm on the passage to Brobdignag, so remarkable for its nautical accuracy. It describes the sailors, when " the sea broke strange and dangerous, hauling off the lanniard of the whip-staff, and *helping the man at the helm.*" Canning sat silent for a few moments, and then in a reverie repeated several times: " And helped the man at the helm—and helped the man at the helm!"

On another occasion Mr. Rush takes us after dinner into the drawing-room, where " some of the company found pastime in turning over the leaves of caricatures bound in large volumes. They went back to the French revolutionary period. Kings, princes, cabinet ministers, members of parliament, every body figured in them. It was a kind of history of England in caricature for five-and-twenty years. Need I add that our accomplished host was on many a page. He stood by. Now and then, he threw in a word, giving new point to the scenes."* Mr. Rush does not appear to have been aware that these volumes of caricatures contained the works of the famous Gilray, an artist of coarse mind, but of rapid invention, great humour, and original genius. Gilray helped very materially to sustain Mr. Canning's popularity, if he did not actually extend and improve it. Mr. Canning frequently gave him valuable suggestions, which he worked out with unfailing tact and whimsicality, making it a point of honour, as well as of gratitude and admiration, to give Mr. Canning in return, on all occasions, an advantageous position in his designs. The importance of having the great caricaturist of the day on his side, is nearly as great to a public man, especially to one assailed by envy and detraction, as that ascribed by Swift to the ballads of a nation. Gilray always turned the laugh against Mr. Canning's opponents, and never forgot to display his friend and patron in an attitude that carried off the applause of the spectators. In one of his sketches he represents Mr. Canning aloft in the chariot of Anti-Jacobinism, radiant with glory, driving the sansculotte mob before him; nor did Mr. Canning, on the other hand, omit any opportunity of drawing Mr. Gilray into favourable notice. In the satire upon Addington, called " The Grand Consultation," Gilray's caricature of " Dramatic Royalty; or, the Patriotic Courage of Sherry Andrew," is particularly alluded to in the following verse:

" And instead of the jack-pudding bluster of Sherry,
And his 'dagger of lath,' and his speeches so merry!

* " Residence at the Court of London, First Series." pp. 233-4.

>   Let us bring to the field—every foe to appal—
>   Aldini's galvanic *deceptions*—and all
>   The *sleight of hand tricks* of Conjuror Val."

Canning's passion for literature entered into all his pursuits. It coloured his whole life. Every moment of leisure was given up to books. He and Pitt were passionately fond of the classics; and we find them together of an evening, after a dinner at Pitt's, poring over some old Grecian in a corner of the drawing-room, while the rest of the company are dispersed in conversation.[*] Fox had a similar love of classical literature, but his wider sympathies embraced a class of works in which Pitt never appears to have exhibited any interest. Fox was a devourer of novels; and into this region Mr. Canning entered with gusto. In English writings his judgment was pure and strict; and no man was a more perfect master of all the varieties of composition. He was the first English minister who banished the French language from our diplomatic correspondence, and vindicated before Europe the copiousness and dignity of our native tongue.[†] He had a high zest for the early vigorous models, in all styles, and held in less estimation the more ornate and refined. Writing to Scott about the "Lady of the Lake," he says, that on a repeated perusal he is more and more delighted with it; but that he wishes he could induce him to try the effect of "a more full and sweeping style"—to present himself "in a Drydenic habit."[‡] His admiration of Dryden, whom he pronounced to be "the perfection of harmony,"[§] and his preference of that poet of gigantic mould over the melodists of the French school, may be suggested as an evidence of the soundness and strength of his judgment.

---

[*] "Life of Wilberforce," ii. 34. [†] "Quarterly Review," 1827.
[‡] "Life of Scott," iii. 265-6. [§] Ib., iii. 321.

Yet, it is remarkable, that with this broad sense of great faculties in others, he was himself fastidious to excess about the slightest turns of expression. He would correct his speeches, and amend their verbal graces, till he nearly polished out the original spirit. He was not singular in this. Burke, whom he is said to have closely studied, did the same. Sheridan always prepared his speeches; the highly-wrought passages in the speech on Hasting's impeachment were written before-hand and committed to memory; and the differences were so marked, that the audience could readily distinguish between the extemporaneous passages and those that were premeditated. Mr. Canning's alterations were frequently so minute and extensive, that the printers found it easier to re-compose the matter afresh in type than to correct it. This difficulty of choice in diction sometimes springs from *l'embarras des richesses*, but oftener from poverty of resources, and generally indicates a class of intellect which is more occupied with costume than ideas. But here are three instances which set all popular notions on this question of verbal fastidiousness by the ears; for certainly Burke, Canning, and Sheridan were men of capacious talents; and two of them, at least, present extraordinary examples of imagination and practical judgment, running together neck and neck in the race of life to the very goal.

Mr. Canning's opinions on the subject of public speaking afford a useful commentary upon his practice. He used to say, that speaking in the House of Commons must take *conversation* for its basis; that a studious treatment of topics was out of place. The House of Commons is a working body, jealous and suspicious of embellishments in debate, which, if used at all, ought to be spontaneous and unpremeditated. Method is indispensable. Topics ought to be clearly distributed and arranged; but this arrangement should be felt in the effect, and not betrayed in the manner. But above all things, first and last, he maintained that reasoning was the one essential element. Oratory in the House of Lords was totally different; it was addressed to a different atmosphere—a different class of intellects—more elevated, more conventional. It was necessary to be more ambitious and elaborate, although some of the chief speakers had been formed in the Commons. He thought the average speaking in the Peers better than that in the Lower House; one reason for which was, perhaps, that the House was less miscellaneous, and better stocked with thoroughly educated men.

His own speeches can never be cited in illustration of the system he recommended for the popular branch of the legislature. Yet although his eloquence was elevated far above the average imagination and acquirements of his audience, it never perplexed their understandings. The argument was always clear; he kept that to the level of their practical intelligence, and all the rest only went to raise their enthusiasm, or to provoke their passions. Wilberforce, who was at least unprejudiced, says, that Canning " never drew you to him in spite of yourself," as Pitt and Fox used to do; yet, that he was a more finished orator than either. As far as this goes, it is quite just. Canning had less earnestness than Pitt or Fox; there was less *abandon* in his speeches, less real emotion: but he was a greater master of his art, and commanded remoter and more various resources. His wit transcended all comparison with any orator of his time. His humour was irresistible. Wilberforce went home crying with laughter, after his account of Lord Nugent's journey to lend *the succour of his person* (Lord Nugent being, as every body knows, not a very light weight) to constitutional Spain. The light horseman's uniform—the heavy Falmouth coach—threw the House into convulsions, just as if it had been an assembly of pantomimic imps, lighted up with laughing gas. The passage will stand by itself, without introduction, as a capital specimen of the best humoured political raillery. There is not a particle of ill-nature in it; and it had no other effect on Lord Nugent (whose own nature was incapable of a small resentment) than that of increasing his high opinion of Mr. Canning's great powers. Lord Nugent was long afterwards one of Mr. Canning's warmest supporters.

"It was about the middle of last July, that the heavy Falmouth coach—(loud and long-continued laughter)—that the heavy Falmouth coach—(laughter)—was observed travelling to its destination through the roads of Cornwall with more than its usual gravity. (Very loud laughter.) There were, according to the best advices, two inside passengers—(laughter)—one a lady of no considerable dimensions—(laughter)—and a gentleman, who, as it had been since ascertained, was conveying the succour of his person to Spain. (Cheers and laughter.) I am informed, and having no reason to doubt my informant, I firmly believe it, that in the van belonging to the coach—(gentlemen must know the nature and uses of that auxiliary to the regular stage-coaches)—was a box, more bulky than ordinary, and of most portentous contents—it was observed, that after their arrival, this box and the passenger before-mentioned became inseparable. The box was known to have contained the Uniform of a Spanish General of cavalry—(much laughter)—and it was said of the helmet, which was beyond the usual size, that it exceeded all other helmets spoken of in history, not excepting the celebrated helmet in the 'Castle of Otranto.' (Cheers and laughter.) The idea of going to the relief of a fortress blockaded by sea, and besieged by land, with the uniform of a light cavalry officer, was new, to say the least of it. About this time the force offered by the hon. gentleman, which had never existed, but on paper, was in all probability expected—I will not stay to determine whether it was to have consisted of 10,000 or 5000 men. No doubt, upon the arrival of the General and his uniform, the Cortes must have rubbed their hands with satisfaction, and concluded that now the promised force was come, they would have little more to fear. (Laughter.) It did come, as much of it as ever would have been seen by the Cortes or the King; but it came in that sense and no other, which was described by a witty nobleman, George, Duke of Buckingham, whom the Noble Lord opposite (Lord Nugent) reckoned among his lineal ancestors. In the play of the *Rehearsal*, there was a scene occupied with the designs of two usurpers, to whom one of their party, entering says—

'Sirs,
' The army at the door, but in disguise,
' Entreats a word of both your Majesties.'

(Very loud and continued laughter.) Such must have been the effect of the arrival of the Noble Lord. How he was received, or what effect he operated on the councils and affairs of the Cortes by his arrival, I do not know. Things were at that juncture, moving too rapidly to their final issue. How far the Noble Lord conduced to the termination *by plumping his weight into the sinking scale of the Cortes*, is too nice a question for me just now to settle." (Loud cheers and laughter.)

"Canning's drollery of voice and manner," says Wilberforce, "were inimitable. There is a lighting up of his features, and a comic play about the mouth, when the full force of the approaching witticism strikes his own mind, which prepares you for the burst which is to follow."* This quality of humour was not within the range of Pitt or Fox.

In descriptive power, and in the higher uses of imagination, Canning certainly excelled all his contemporaries, except Burke; and it is doubtful whether he was not more judicious even than Burke, in his choice of the occasion. The following well-known passage from his speech at Plymouth, in 1823, may be cited as perfect in its kind:

" Our present repose is no more a proof of inability to act,

* "Life of Wilberforce," v. 217.

than the state of inertness and inactivity in which I have seen those mighty masses that float in the waters above your town, is a proof they are devoid of strength, and incapable of being fitted out for action. You well know, gentlemen, how soon one of those stupendous masses, now reposing in their shadows, in perfect stillness—how soon, upon any call of patriotism or necessity, it would assume the likeness of an animated being, instinct with life and motion—how soon it would ruffle, as it were, its swelling plumage—how quickly it would put forth all its beauty and its bravery, collect its scattered elements of strength, and awaken its dormant thunder—such is one of those magnificent machines, when, springing from inaction into a display of its might—such is England herself, while apparently passive and motionless, she silently concentrates the power to be put forth on an adequate occasion."

The facility with which Canning could bring his fancy to bear upon the driest subjects, without suffering them to lose a jot of their importance, is marvellously illustrated in his speech on the Report of the Bullion Committee. "Of his powers of argumentation," observes Lord Brougham, "his capacity for the pursuits of abstract science, his genius for adorning the least attractive subjects, there remains an imperishable record in his celebrated speeches on the Currency, of all his efforts the most brilliant and the most happy."* Mackintosh said of him, that he incorporated in his mind all the eloquence and wisdom of ancient literature. He thought Canning and Plunkett the finest orators of their time; and that Canning, especially, excelled in language.

Had he cultivated the bar, his great talents for speaking to evidence, and for dissecting the circumstantial bearings of a case—developed so successfully in his speech on Colonel Wardle's motion respecting the Duke of York—must have carried him to the highest eminence. But he never liked the profession, although he struggled hard in

* "Historical Sketches." Art. Canning, p. 278.

his youth to devote himself to it, and to overcome his early *passion* for the House of Commons. In a private letter written to a college friend,* while he was at Oxford (Sept. 1st, 1788), he fully confesses this besetting desire, and his resolution to wrestle with its influence. The glimpse of character we get in the following passage from this letter is striking:

" I am already, God knows, too much inclined both by my own sanguine wishes, and the connexion with whom I am most intimate, and whom I, above all others, revere, to aim at the House of Commons as the only path to the only desirable thing in this world—the gratification of ambition; while at the same time every tie of common sense, of fortune, and of duty, draws me to the study of a profession. The former propensity, I hope, reflection, necessity, and the friendly advice and very marked attention of the dean,† will enable me to overcome; and to the law I look as the profession which, in this country, holds out every enticement that can nerve the exertions, and give vigour to the power of a young man. The way, indeed, is long, toilsome, and rugged; but it leads to honours, solid and lasting; to Independence, without which no blessings of fortune, however profuse, no distinctions of station, however splendid, can afford a liberal mind true satisfaction; to Power, for which no task can be too hard, no labours too trying."

The serious aims of eighteen, expressed in so didactic and formal a style, are characteristic. With what concentrated power and perseverance the writer followed up his purpose, we have seen; and had it not been for the unfortunate difference with Lord Castlereagh, and for that irascible and haughty temper which kept Mr. Canning so long aloof from the government, while Lord Castlereagh's more ductile disposition speedily accommodated

---

* Mr. John Frank Newton.

† The gentleman here alluded to was Dr. Cyril Jackson, Dean of Christ Church, who entertained the highest opinion of Mr. Canning's talents, and looked forward confidently to the high destiny which awaited him.

itself to every change, he would have attained the summit of his ambition much earlier, and with less cost of suffering and resentment.

At this time Mr. Canning, strange to say, was ignorant of French. He had frequently resolved to set about it, but never could find the right moment to begin. In this letter to his friend, he expresses his determination to carry into effect a plan he had formerly laid down for accomplishing his purpose. Mr. Newton (to whom the letter was addressed) had invited his correspondent to accompany him on his return to the West Indies, where Mr. Newton's family lived. The object of the invitation was to give Mr. Canning, who had taken a great interest in the slave question while he was at Oxford, the opportunity of personally investigating the condition of the negro.

"The return you mention to me with you is a pleasing, fairy scheme, but which, then at least, will not be put in execution. My plans for next summer are fixed, and I think will be improving and agreeable. You may know that I am shamefully ignorant of French, and though I have fifty times formed the intention of learning it, I never yet have brought my intention to the maturity of practical application. By this time twelvemonth I intend to procure a smattering sufficient to call a coach or swear at a waiter; and then to put into execution a plan formed long ago, in happier days, of going abroad with my three fellow-scribes, the Microcosmopolitans. Our idea is not that of scampering through France and ranting in Paris, but a sober sort of thing—to go and settle for two months in some provincial town, remarkable for the salubrity of its climate, the respectability of its inhabitants, and the purity of its language; there to improve our constitutions by the first; to extend our acquaintance with men and manners by the second; and to qualify ourselves for a further extension of it by perfecting ourselves in the third."

This sensible design, so very much in the spirit of the "Microcosm" itself, Mr. Canning is said to have fulfilled.*

* "New Monthly Magazine," 1828. A writer in this publication says that Mr. Canning carried the project into effect, and mentions Mr.

Be that as may, he was a perfect master of French long before he made his way into the Foreign Office under Lord Grenville.

The letter runs on in the same gossipping confidential vein, giving us a glimpse of some of his contemporaries, and of that college weariness which grows out of the departure of familiar faces.

"This scheme I have always looked forward to with delight, and do so now more than ever, on account of the dull avenue of four Oxford terms through which I have to approach its execution. To say the truth, Oxford is so completely uncongenial with my wishes and habits of mind and body, that I dread, even at this distance, my return to it. There are literally not five faces there which I have any very ardent desire ever to behold again. Wallace is gone, Western is gone, Newton is gone; and why am not I gone? I expect, however, at my return a small cargo of Etonians, who will in some measure comfort me for the utter emptiness and unamiableness of the generality of the good folks whom Christ Church can boast. I have also

R. Smith, Mr. Frere, and Mr. George Ellis, as the three Microcosmopolitans who accompanied him. There must be some mistake in this statement. Mr. George Ellis was not a Microcosmopolitan. He was educated at Westminster School and Trinity College, Cambridge, and although a close intimacy afterwards existed between him and Mr. Canning, there is no evidence to show that they ever met until after both had left college. Mr. Ellis was one of the wits of the "Rolliad," and afterwards, on the other side, of the "Anti-Jacobin." There is an anecdote related of him and Pitt, that at their first interview Canning made some amusing allusions to the "Rolliad," which embarrassed Ellis, as they were probably intended to do, when Pitt very good-humouredly turned round, and said—
"Immo age et à primâ dic hospes origine nobis."
Mr. Ellis, however, is remembered by more permanent contributions to our literature—his "Specimens" of the early English Poets and of the early Prose Romances. Of his labours in these works, it has been judiciously remarked, that "others dug deeper for materials; but he alone gave vivacity to antiquities, and diffused those graces of literature and society, which were peculiarly his own, over the rudest remains of barbarism." Mr. Ellis was known to have been engaged for some time on a Life of Windham, but ill-health appears to have interrupted its completion. The latter part of his life was embittered by severe maladies, and his sick chamber was often cheered by the presence of his friend Canning. He died in 1815 at the age of seventy.

taken it into my head that I shall receive * * * into favour again. The truth about him is, that he is not without good points; his heart has some worth, his abilities very considerable eminence. . . . His character is far above that most nauseous of all things—insipidity, and negative good or evil. As a competitor, he was troublesome and worth crushing; but that once done, and I can assure you it cost me some pains to accomplish it, 'his good now blazes: all his bad is in the grave,' as Zanga says. W. S. has again left Oxford, and I fancy for ever. He is, I hear, gone abroad; but whither, I know not. Pity, that abilities so great should be rendered useless to himself and to society, by such an eccentricity of temper, and unaccountableness of behaviour, as characterises him." *

The letter from which these extracts have been taken presents another feature of interest—an account of the fate of a little debating club which was formed at Christ Church, and to which allusion has been already made.† Mr. Newton, who was one of the members, tells us, that it was established in 1787, and consisted of Jenkinson, Canning, Lord Henry Spencer, Drummond (afterwards Sir William, and some time British Ambassador at Constantinople), Charles Goddard,‡ and himself. It was in fact a "Speaking Society," and came to be called a club by courtesy.

"This club," says Mr. Newton, "in which were heard the first speeches ever composed or delivered by Lord Liverpool and Mr. Canning, met every Thursday evening at the rooms of the members, who were at its first establishment limited to the number of six. Before our separation at night, or frequently at one

---

* The W. S. was, no doubt, William Spencer, the Devonshire House poet, who was a member of Christ Church. Mr. Wallace was afterwards raised to the Peerage, with the title of Baron Wallace. He was a son of a former Attorney-General. Western (the only son of Mr. Western of Cokethorpe Hall, Oxfordshire) distinguished himself at Eton, and was one of Canning's most intimate associates. He died early.

† Ante, p. 59.

‡ Goddard became private secretary to Lord Grenville, at whose house in St. James's-square his college friends used to visit him. He was afterwards Archdeacon of Lincoln.

or two o'clock in the morning, we voted and recorded the question which we were to debate on the ensuing Thursday."*

Mr. Newton is, probably, correct in assigning to Christ Church the honour of Lord Liverpool's first speeches; but Canning had appeared as an orator at a still earlier period in the Debating Society at Eton. This Oxford Club was a close secret. Its members adopted an uniform —a brown coat of a singular shade, with velvet cuffs and collar, and buttons bearing the initials of Demosthenes, Cicero, Pitt and Fox! The members used to dine sometimes in their club costume, in the hall, to pique the curiosity of their fellow students. The mystery was well kept for a time; but it seems from the following narrative that it was betrayed at last.

The whole passage possesses a peculiar value. It shows clearly and unequivocally Mr. Canning's college politics; establishes his connexion with the party in opposition to that with which Jenkinson was associated; and goes even so far as to make a distinct " profession" of principles. Canning and Jenkinson were, in fact, looked upon at Christ Church as the representatives of tory and whig opinions; and were " pitted" against each other accordingly, with all the amicable rivalry and emulation natural to such youthful struggles. The parliamentary tact with which Canning acted in this matter of the club must strike the reader as the foreshadowing of his spirit, looking out into its future career. Had the interests of Europe been at stake, he could not have conducted himself with more diplomatic caution.

" You will be a good deal surprised at the answer which your

* " Early Days of the Right Honourable George Canning. By John Frank Newton, Esq." 1828.

questions relative to the club will receive. That club, Newton, is no more. 'And what dread event? what sacrilegious hand?' you will exclaim. Newton, mine. My reasons I never gave to any of the members, but I will open them to you. What my reasons for first becoming a part of the institution were, I protest I cannot at present call to mind. Perhaps I was inflamed by the novelty of the plan, perhaps influenced by your example; perhaps I was not quite without an idea of trying my strength with Jenkinson. Connected with men of avowed enmity in the political world, professing opposite principles, and looking forward to some distant period when we might be ranged against each other on a larger field, we were, perhaps, neither of us without the vanity of wishing to obtain an early ascendency over the other.

* * * *

So long as the purport and usage of the club were a secret, I was very well contented to be of it; but when it became notoriously known; when the Dean to me (and to me only) in private recommended some reasons against its propriety to my serious consideration—(for had he presumed to interpose authoritatively, that single circumstance, 'albeit considerations infinite did make against it,' would have been sufficient to determine me upon its continuance)—when he represented it to me in a very strong light, as being almost an absolute avowal of parliamentary views—to a professional man an avowal the most dangerous—this representation made me resolve to abandon an undertaking which I saw evidently would neither promise eventual advantage, nor maintain a temporary respectability. Thus resolved, at my return after the Easter vacation, without any previous confidential communication of my reasons, or my intentions, I sent my resignation by Lord Henry on the first night of their meeting. William Spencer was now come, and was that night to take his seat. The message which Lord Henry brought occasioned, as it were, *a combustion;* which ended in the moving of some very violent resolutions. Among others, I was summoned to the bar; of course, refused to obey the summons. A deputation was then sent to interrogate me respecting the causes of my resignation, which of course I refused to reveal; and they were at last satisfied by my declaring, that the reason of my resignation did not affect them collectively or individually. I of course was anxious that every body should know that I was no longer a member of the club; and, therefore, whenever it was a subject of conversation, disavowed my connexion with it. Lord Henry I with much difficulty prevented from resigning at the same time that I did. He, however, attended but two more debates, and then formally 'accepted the Chiltern Hundreds,' to use a parliamentary phrase. They now all unanimously gave out that there had been a complete dissoluton, and that the Thing was no longer in existence; altered their times and modes of meeting; abolished the uniform, and suspended their assemblies for a time. This, it seems, was intended to punish me, by carrying the face of a common, and not a particular secession. It was not long, however, before the truth came out, and their mighty debates are again renewed, not undiscovered; but with less pomp, regularity, numbers, and vociferation. This, then, is a full and true account of the decline and fall, and of the revival also, of the society. I do not think you can blame my conduct, when you recollect that the imputation of parliamentary prospects, already too much fixed upon me, is what, of all others, a person in my situation ought to avoid."

Mr. Canning's humour was incessantly exploding in *bon-mots* and repartees. He could talk epigrams. He was so prolific a producer of " good things," that if he had not been pre-eminently distinguished as an orator and statesman, he might have descended to us with a more dazzling social reputation than Buckingham or Waller. The lines on Mr. Whitbread's speech, thrown off like flashes of light, show how rapidly and successfully he could cast his jest into any shape he pleased. Here are two more trifles redeemed from manuscript, and preserved in this place, not for their merit, but their flavour; as certain common herbs are dropped into the daintiest *potage*, merely to impart to it a *soupçon* of their aroma.

The subject of this epigram was a Mr. Douglas, son of the Bishop of Salisbury, a man six feet two inches in height, and of enormous bulk. This immense gentleman was one of the greatest gourmands of his day, and used to move onward, not walk, like a mountain. The little boys at Oxford always gathered about him when he went into the streets, to gaze upwards at his towering bulk; when he would cry out, characteristically enough, "Get out of my way, you little scamps, *or I will roll upon you.*"

I.
"That the stones of our chapel are both black and white,
　Is most undeniably true,
But as Douglas walks over them morning and night,
　It's a wonder they're not black and blue."

II.
"There's a difference between
　A Bishop and a Dean,
And I'll tell you the reason why,
　A Dean cannot dish up
　A dinner like a Bishop,
Or breed such a fat son as I."

Mr. Canning's political occupations absorbed too much time, to permit him to indulge his literary ambition in any extensive undertaking; but he always manifested a zealous interest in the advancement of letters. The "Quarterly Review" received its first impulse from his hand. The plan was submitted to him, and having received his approval, was carried out under his sanction, assisted by the Ellises, Malthus, Mathias, Gifford, and Heber. Mr. Canning himself was one of its most distinguished contributors.

He was one of the forty members of the Literary Club founded by Reynolds and Johnson; but he did not content himself with the holiday processions and festivals of literature. The Royal Institution of Liverpool was largely assisted by his active exertions; and he was a liberal patron of the Literary Fund, which reckons amongst its white days an anniversary at which Canning and Chateaubriand met. It was on this occasion that the latter, at that time the representative of his sovereign in this country, publicly stated, with a frankness no less honourable to himself than to the admirable institution he addressed, that when he had formerly been an exile in England, without friends or resources, he was indebted to the prompt sympathy of the Literary Fund for the most efficient assistance, without which timely aid, he said, he should never have lived to enjoy the honours which afterwards awaited him at home. There was a strong sentiment of personal regard between Chateaubriand and Mr. Canning, generated by mutual tastes and accomplishments. During a part of the time when Canning was Foreign Secretary, Chateaubriand held a similar office in France; and the correspondence of the two secretaries was conducted throughout this period with extraordinary care. Canning used to sit up till two or three o'clock in the morning over his despatches, to give them a more elaborate finish than usual, from his high sense of the literary character of his correspondent. To this feeling of emulation we owe some of the noblest state documents in our national archives.

He never suffered an opportunity to escape, of promoting the welfare of literary men, or their connexions. Soon after Sir Walter Scott had become involved in pecuniary troubles, Mr. Canning, understanding that he was to meet him at dinner at Mr. Croker's, wrote privately to Sir William Knighton, for the purpose of interesting his majesty, beforehand, on behalf of Sir Walter's son. "I shall be glad," he said, " to have the protection of the king's commands in doing an act of kindness by Malachi Malagrowther." On another occasion, James Mill, the historian of India, a conspicuous Radical, a man of distinguished intellectual power, the friend of Bentham, and the most prominent writer in the " Westminster Review" (items not very recommendatory to the government of the day) was one of the candidates for the examinership in the civil service of the East India Company; a situation of 2500*l.* per annum. The Tories besought Canning to use all his influence against him. Canning refused. He could not see why Mill's radicalism should prevent him from being the best of all possible examiners. These are slight facts, but they disclose fine traits of character; as fragments of ore on the surface indicate the rich veins that lie below.

The concern he felt in the interests of persons who possessed any claims to be considered as connected with literature, exposed him occasionally to some misrepresentations. He was charged by his political enemies with exercising a closer influence over particular newspapers than was consistent with his position. Lady Hester Stanhope tells us that Pitt used to complain of him for repeating his conversations to people who published them in the "Oracle." But Lady Hester's anecdotes must be taken with due allowance for her constitutional volubility, and her tumultuous memory, which always seemed at full flood, carrying down every thing that fell into it with velocity and confusion. It is a curious set-off to this story that Lord Grenville made the same complaint of Pitt, and actually took measures in the cabinet to put a stop to his talking. Mr. Canning at that time was young, and may have committed himself (although it is very unlikely) to some indiscreet confidences; but he had high examples before him. If he admitted some of the journalists to his acquaintance, with any view to create or preserve a salutary influence in the press, he acted upon a policy which had been practised by some of his most distinguished predecessors—especially Sir Robert Walpole—to a much greater extent.

There is one feature in Mr. Canning's life which ought not to be forgotten in these desultory recollections—his habitual observance of religious duties. In this matter, his character contrasts strongly with that of Mr. Pitt, who was indifferent even to the forms of religion. Mr. Canning was perfectly sincere and unostentatious in his Christianity; maintaining its ordinances in his household, without a tincture of austerity or display. Wilberforce confesses that he was surprised at Mr. Canning's devotional sensibility. It happened in 1817, that he went with Canning, Huskisson, Lord Binning, and others, to hear Dr. Chalmers preach at the Scotch Church, London Wall; and he observed Canning so deeply affected at times as to shed tears. Wilberforce, who had a habit of thinking (like too many very pious people) that religious emotion and divine grace are special monopolies, was astonished, and could hardly believe his eyes. "I should have thought," he exclaimed, "that Canning had been too much hardened in debate to show such signs of feeling!"*

Mr. Canning's temper was irritable and anxious, but wholly free from pettiness or malice. He held no ill-will, he concealed no rancour. The real fault was less in what he felt, than in the heat and arrogance of his manner and expressions. He was the most open, but the most unsparing adversary. He treated his opponents with haughtiness, amounting sometimes almost to scorn. They could have found some escape for their spleen from every species of offence except this. Carried on too fast by his genius, too proudly by his prosperity, and by the homage that fluttered round his steps wherever he moved, it was not much to wonder at, that he should have insensibly acquired a tone of confidence and superiority, which occasionally betrayed him into disdainful excesses in debate. It was thus

* "Life of Wilberforce," iv. 325.

when Mr. Brougham accused him of gross tergiversation, that he started to his feet, and in a voice of thunder, with fire flashing from his eyes, exclaimed, " It is false !" But the provocation was heavy, and unexpected, and unwarranted ; and no milder answer could have met the full measure of the wrong.

Another instance was his encounter with Mr. Hobhouse. But here there was a suppositious ground of injury, which drew that fierce rejoinder from Mr. Canning, in which he heaped scorn upon scorn on " the honourable baronet and his man," and said that " in six months the demagogue, admitted to this assembly, finds his level and shrinks to his proper dimensions." The cause of this explosion was a violent pamphlet grossly falsifying a speech of Mr. Canning's, and denouncing the utterer of it with the most furious invectives.* When Mr. Canning read this philippic he wrote a letter to the anonymous author, through the medium of the publisher, telling him " that he was a liar and a slanderer, and wanted courage only to be an assassin;" that no man knew of his writing to him, and that he would wait for an answer till the following night. Of course no answer was ever returned. This pamphlet was generally ascribed to Mr. Hobhouse, and acting upon that impression, Mr. Canning did not omit to deal summarily with the supposed offender. Mr. Hobhouse took

* The speech was in reference to the case of a person named William Ogden, who had been imprisoned during the suspension of the Habeas Corpus Act. Great pains were taken to make it appear that this Ogden had endured the most monstrous cruelty from his gaolers, that he was seventy-four years of age, had seventeen children, and was labouring under a painful malady which the injuries he had suffered had greatly aggravated. There was not a syllable of truth in the whole statement, and Mr. Canning was accused of trifling with human suffering, because he exposed the impudent attempt to impose this audacious fabrication on the credulity of Parliament.

his revenge in his own way, by drawing a sketch of Mr. Canning, in which it would not be very easy to discover the likeness.

"A smart, six-form boy, the little hero of a little world, matures his precocious parts at college, and sends before him his fame to the metropolis: a Minister, or some borough-holder of the day, thinks him worth saving from his democratic associates, and from the unprofitable principles which the thoughtless enthusiasm of youth may have inclined him hitherto to adopt. The hopeless youth yields at once, and placed in the true line of promotion, he takes his place with the more veteran prostitutes of Parliament. There he minds his periods; there he balances his antitheses; there he adjusts his alliterations; and, filling-up the interstices of his piebald patch-work rhetoric with froth and foam, this master of pompous nothings becomes first favourite of the Great Council of the nation."

Mr. Hobhouse, very innocently and intending something very different, betrayed the real secret of all the spleen and jealousy Mr. Canning had to resist through life. It was because he *was* the "first favourite of the Great Council of the Nation," that men of false pretensions and selfish natures shed their spite upon his path. They could not endure his brightness—they could not bear to hear Aristides called the Just. All this is very intelligible. Leading minds at all times have paid this penalty for being in advance, and must be content to take their risk of being shot at from behind.

From the moment he obtained a clear opportunity for carrying out his principles, (unfortunately for England, too near the close of his career), he rose to a height of popularity, never reached before by any member of his party. Fancy the rage of the "mighty hunters," to see themselves distanced by his swifter blood. The Many, everywhere, placed implicit confidence in his character and the universality of his influence. If England entered into a war, in defence of Portugal, he promised her that she would find arrayed under her banners, " all the discontented and restless spirit of the age—all those who, whether justly or unjustly, were dissatisfied with the state of their own countries." These classes all over the earth were his " clients." His eloquence was indentified with their cause; his name was the watchword of deliverance,

" Where Andes, giants of the western-star,
With meteor standard to the winds unfurled,
Looks from his throne of clouds o'er half the world."

The gallantry of his bearing, his personal grace and manliness, and the classical beauty and refinement with which he was ideally associated in the general imagination, secured for him the suffrages of an influential section at home—a section rarely interested in political affairs, but intimately concerned in shaping and colouring public opinion. The women of England were with him with their whole hearts, as they are with every generous champion of human freedom. It was a part of his influence, this charm he exercised over the gentle and trustful; and not the least important. He was sometimes taunted with it—half in jest and half in earnest. Every body who was capable of being jealous of his fame, was most jealous of it for taking that direction, as if it had conquered so much neutral ground! This was the strangest of all the littlenesses to which he was exposed. Even Hazlitt (a very bigoted hater of bigotry in others), found something supercilious and egotistical to suggest about it, and talks of Canning and the love-locks of the constitution!

XI.

THE PERCEVAL ADMINISTRATION. DEATH OF PERCEVAL. THE LIVERPOOL CABINET. THE LISBON EMBASSY. GEORGE IV.

UPON the retirement of the Duke of Portland, Mr. Perceval undertook to replenish the cabinet. He first applied to Lords Grey and Grenville, who indignantly rejected his proposal as involving a dereliction of public principle. He protested he could not see it ; Lord Liverpool could not see it. They could see nothing but office straight before them, with the door shut upon the Papists.

He was more successful with the Marquis of Wellesley, who had just returned from Spain, and who accepted the Foreign Office, to the astonishment of every body. Mr. Perceval himself absorbed the premiership, in addition to the Exchequer.

It was under the auspices of this administration that Mr. (now Sir Robert) Peel commenced his parliamentary career. He was selected by Mr. Perceval to second the Address, which was moved by Lord Barnard, and before the close of the year was appointed Under-Secretary in the Colonial Department. Mr. Canning took very little part in the proceedings of the first session. The principal matter which interested him was the grant of an annuity to the Duke of Wellington, which he energetically supported, and was mainly instrumental in obtaining.

Parliament met in the following November (1810) under novel circumstances. The king was insane. There was no speech for the Houses—no commission to meet them—no authority to prorogue them. It was impossible to proceed to business in the usual way. Without the customary sanction and formalities, this gathering of peers and knights of the shire was, technically, not the parliament, but a convention of the estates. But parliament is too expert in the invention of technical difficulties, not to know how to escape from them. Nothing is impossible to parliament. Nothing *can* be impossible to parliament, after the vote on the Septennial Bill, in 1716, by which it re-elected itself for four years, without thinking it necessary to trouble its constituents.

Parliament resolved itself into a committee on the state of the nation ; and Mr. Perceval moved several resolutions, the object of which was to settle the means of acting in this emergency. These resolutions determined the question so vehemently disputed in 1788 and 1789, that parliament alone had the disposal of the Regency; and that the heir-apparent had no more authority, without the sanction of Parliament, than any private gentleman in the kingdom. Having decided upon the right of Parliament to nominate the Regency, it was next proposed to confer the powers of the crown on the Prince of Wales, *with restrictions*.

This question presented one of considerable embarrassment to Mr. Canning. Consistency demanded that he should follow the course which had been formerly taken by Mr. Pitt, who contended for the right of Parliament to appoint the Regent, and also for the policy of binding him within strict limitations. But Mr. Canning, agreeing in the right, was resolved to resist the restrictions. The difficulty was to steer between these rocks—a task which he performed with the most wary dexterity.

"The right of the two Houses," he observed, "was proclaimed and maintained by Mr. Pitt. This is the point on which his authority is truly valuable. * * * The principles upon which this right was affirmed and exercised, if true at all, are true universally, for all times and on all occasions. If they were the principles of the constitution in 1788, they are equally so in 1811. The lapse of twenty-two years has not impaired—the lapse of centuries cannot impair them. But the mode in which the right so asserted should be exercised, the precise provisions to be framed for the temporary substitution of the executive power — these were necessarily then, as they must be now, matters not of eternal and invariable principle, but of prudence and expediency. In regard to these, therefore, the authority of the opinions of any individual, however great and wise, and venerable, can be taken only with reference to the circumstances of the time in which he had to act, and are not to be applied without change or modification to other times and circumstances."

While the shade of Pitt was appeased by this ample recognition of the abstract principle, the living prince was apostrophised by the management of its application. The policy of this proceeding may readily be discerned, although it was also inspired by a higher motive. His Royal Highness had not attempted to conceal his chagrin at the proposed abridgement of the regal functions ; and the next most likely event would be a new ministry. An exclusive cabinet was no longer probable. The Whigs were the natural successors to power, but they could not succeed alone. These distant signs on the horizon may have influenced Mr. Canning's views ; but it is only fair to add that every consideration which could be urged for the public welfare lay on that side also.

If ever the hands of the sovereign, instead of being fettered, required additional strength, it was at this moment, when the whole force of Europe, concentrated in one mighty arm, was raised aloft in the air, threatening to descend upon us. Mr. Perceval had not a single reasonable pretext for the restrictions, but that when his Majesty should have recovered from the paralysis with which it had pleased God to afflict his understanding, it would be a great comfort to him to find all things in his realm exactly as he had left them; as if they too had been stricken, —more particularly his ministry. This was the second time, within half a century, that the theory of monarchy was practically insulted by a high Tory minister.

But Mr. Perceval had good grounds for what he did. He knew that the Prince held him in no great affection, and, therefore, he endeavoured to make it appear that his majesty's illness was only transitory, and that, under the expectation of his early restoration, it would be indecorous to make any violent changes. This was very sly. It nearly failed, nevertheless; for the Regency bill was no sooner passed than the Prince confided to some of his personal friends his determination to get rid of Mr. Perceval and his satellites. A private communication was made to Mr. Huskisson, through the individual supposed to have been charged with the formation of the new ministry. Mr. Huskisson replied that he could not entertain any proposal of that kind, which did not include those with whom he was personally and politically connected; but that he should have no difficulty in considering such a proposal with the person through whom alone, in that case, it could be made.* That person was Mr. Canning. It happened, however, that Mr. Canning had expressed too

* See Biography of Mr. Huskisson, introductory to his Speeches.

much interest in the case of the unfortunate Princess of Wales, to be personally acceptable to the Regent ; and so the negotiation fell to the ground.

Throughout 1810 and 1811, Mr. Canning seldom appeared in Parliament. When he did, he generally supported the policy of ministers. On one important question, however, he was entirely opposed to them.

It was upon this occasion that he delivered his great speech on the report of the Bullion Committee ;—a speech which for beauty of illustration, mastery of principles and details, and sound reasoning, has never been surpassed at any period in any language. This wonderful effort of intellect, would have been in itself enough for his fame. It renders not only easy and simple, but attractive and fascinating in the highest degree, a subject invariably found to be obscure, difficult, and repulsive in all other hands. Such is the plastic and creative power of genius that the topic grows alluring under his treatment, charming us like some wondrous allegory, and we follow it to the close with so eager an interest in the argument that we come away fairly marvelling how it had been with us all our lives, that we should not have regarded this question of currency, and exchanges, and fictitious values, and Bank restriction, as one of the most captivating that could be presented to the human imagination! *

The subject was new to Mr. Canning, and lay out of

---

* It would be impossible within the narrow compass of this biography to afford the reader even a glimpse of the varieties of Mr. Canning's eloquence. It may be as well to say at once, that such an intention has not been contemplated in this little volume. But it is a great pleasure to the author to refer for full satisfaction on that point to Mr. Therry's very careful edition of Mr. Canning's speeches, the greater portion of which had the advantage of Mr. Canning's personal revision. Old friends, separated by long years and wide oceans, must not converse through books, or something might be added here concerning Mr. Therry's high qualifications for a task which he has executed so ably.

his province. But it was here that Pitt established his fame; and to that circumstance, we are, probably, indebted for this luminous display of financial knowledge. When Mr. Canning brought his mind to bear upon an unfamiliar question, he always exhausted it, and in his first speech developed its fundamental principles so fully, as to leave nothing upon the abstract theory to be added, or misrepresented, by any subsequent speaker. His first speech on Catholic Emancipation was of this description, embracing the whole elements of the subject. His speech on the currency was another and still more remarkable instance. It contains every thing that ever can be said on the bullion side, embellished with an eloquence which, for the first and only time in the records of parliament, rendered the dreary argument intelligible or entertaining.

Mr. Vansittart (afterwards Lord Bexley) moved some counter-resolutions, which, for impudent absurdity, can scarcely be paralleled in the history of the world. One of these proposed to affirm, that it was the " opinion" of Parliament, that a bank note was at that time " held in public estimation," to be of equal value with the current coin, and that it was " generally accepted as such in all pecuniary transactions." At this very time, the bank itself would not give twenty shillings for a one pound note; and such was the greediness with which the metallic currency was absorbed, that it had been found necessary to pass a law to prevent people from giving more than twenty-one shillings for a guinea; notwithstanding which, guineas were rapidly disappearing, while crown pieces were legally raised in value to five-shillings and sixpence, in order to prevent them from disappearing also!

Another attempt was made by the Prince Regent,

when the restrictions were about to expire in 1812, to draw round him some of the friends of his youth; and the Duke of York, at his Royal Highness's request, opened a negotiation with Lords Grey and Grenville, but they again declined; the differences between them and ministers were too great to admit of a junction. Perceval was safe for a little while longer, greatly to the joy of Lord Eldon, to whom he had written privately on the subject, and who declared, that he could not consent to join an administration with which the whig lords were to be associated.

It was expected, after the debate on the restrictions, which were highly offensive to every member of the royal family, that the opposition must have immediately succeeded to office. This result was prevented by divisions amongst themselves. The two leading whigs were requested by the Prince, to draw up an answer to the address; but their antagonist views neutralised each other, and the result was so weak and unsatisfactory as to give the Prince great displeasure. Sheridan, who happened to be present, and who had piques of his own to avenge against the Greys and Grenvilles, supplied a new answer. This affront was not to be pardoned, and the noble lords transmitted a dignified remonstrance to the Prince, complaining bitterly of Sheridan's " interference," in a matter which had been originally confided solely to their judgment. The Prince was alarmed, and sought a reconciliation through the agency of Lord Holland, who then resided in Pall Mall. A private meeting was brought about at his lordship's house, whither the Prince went in the dusk of the evening on foot, muffled up in a cloak. It was stated at the time, amongst the gossip of the day, that at that very moment

Mr. Peel was sauntering through Pall Mall, when he saw this disguised figure issue from the gate of Carlton House, and fancying that he detected the *incognito*, followed him to Holland House. The next day the town was full of rumours—the least of which was, that Lord Holland was carrying on a sinister design for supplanting Lord Grey in the Prince's favour.

The issue of the meeting was the offer of the government to the offended lords. But Mr. Perceval contrived that the king's physician should be of opinion at this critical juncture, that his majesty was likely to recover in a few weeks; and that, if he found his ministers changed, he would be certain to relapse. Of course, under such a responsibility, their lordships again declined office, and Perceval was still secure. The Prince was enraged. He said he would never see the ministers he was forced to keep. " I will come and dine with you, on such a day," he used to say to his friends, " and you on such another day; but as to those fellows, I will never enter their houses. Votes! They shall have no votes from me— by—— !"

While these ministerial negotiations were going forward, Mr. Canning kept aloof from all interference. But the moment the Regency was settled, he felt himself at liberty to vindicate his opinions on the Catholic Question. The great obstacle was removed, and he seized the opportunity of Lord Morpeth's motion, on the 3rd of February, 1812, to deliver a speech, which may be described as a complete exposition of the principles upon which he espoused the cause of the Catholics. It was the Pitt view of emancipation, urged with greater precision than Pitt would have considered necessary, or perhaps, desirable.

The session had not proceeded very far—had scarcely passed through a debate upon a motion for an address to the Regent, beseeching him to form an efficient administration—when both the Cabinet and the Parliament were thrown into temporary confusion, by the assassination of Mr. Perceval, who was slain by the hand of a madman in the lobby of the House of Commons.

Sir Samuel Romilly, the most honest of public men, had formerly been intimate with Mr. Perceval, but had latterly avoided his society. "I could not endure the idea," he observes, "of living privately in intimacy with a man whose public conduct I in the highest degree disapproved, and whom, as a minister, I was constantly opposing. I cannot, indeed, reconcile to my way of thinking, that distinction between private and public virtues which it is so much the fashion to adopt. It may be called liberality, or gentlemanly feeling, or by any other such vague and indefinite term; but it is not suited to any one who is really in earnest and sincere in his politics."* The avowal is courageous. The cant that assigns to vicious ministers, and tyrants, and bigots in high places, all the virtues of private life is false and wicked. Yet it has grown into such an established fashion that the worst political character is only a convertible description of the most amiable domestic man in the world. Was there ever a bad public man who was not a miracle of every private virtue under the sun? Was there ever a Russian autocrat who was not the most perfect father of a family?

Mr. Perceval's death shocked every body. The House voted 4000*l.* a year to his widow, "with the evident intention," says a modern writer, "of her applying this

* "Memoirs of Sir S. Romilly," iii. 38.

munificent provision to the support of her children." But it seems the House was baffled in its object, for the same writer goes on to say that, "to the surprise of the country, the lady, thus amply dowered, solaced herself, without loss of time, in a second marriage, and gave a lesson to the House for their future dealings with the wearers of weeds."*

The death of Mr. Perceval threw open the government once more. Satisfied from past experience of the great difficulty of forming a strong coalition, the Regent expressed a desire to obtain the secret opinions of each member of the cabinet upon two points—whether, should he select one of them as a head, the rest would be disposed to act under him? and whether, supposing that neither Grey nor Grenville, nor Wellesley nor Canning, should be brought in, they could themselves carry on the business of the country? The answers were, upon the whole, doubtful and wavering, but favourable to the policy of making an offer of negotiation, let it turn out how it might.† Lord Liverpool was accordingly desired to treat with Canning and Lord Wellesley. While this was going on, Lord Eldon was in a state of the most ludicrous nervous anxiety, insisting upon making it appear that unless they came in upon a strict understanding that Lord Liverpool should be the head of the administration, and Lord Castlereagh the leader in the Commons, they should not be *let in*. He was sure they would take it—they had been so long out of office. He was mistaken. They refused to join any government constructed on the principle of resistance to the Catholic claims.

Under these circumstances the Regent considered it

* " Life and Times of George IV.," by the Rev. G. Croly, p. 385.
† " Life of Lord Eldon."

advisable to leave things as they were. But the House of Commons insisted upon a change, and agreed to an address, praying for a strong and efficient government. Thus urged, his Royal Highness had recourse to Lord Wellesley, who, through Mr. Canning, tried Lord Liverpool and the existing ministers, and, failing there, made a last appeal to the Whigs, where he failed also. In this extremity Lord Moira was directed to consult with Lords Grey and Grenville, and had nearly effected his purpose, when the negotiations went off upon a difference respecting the appointments in the household. Sir Samuel Romilly supposes that it was never intended they should come in; and that Lord Eldon was the obstacle.* The Regent was, consequently, obliged to put up with the old set, and the Sidmouths; the office of Prime Minister devolving upon Lord Liverpool, who held it for fifteen years.

These negotiations were not carried on without some personal perplexities. When the Whigs made a difficulty about the household, the members of the household offered to resign, for the purpose of removing the obstacle; and Sheridan was requested to communicate their intention to the two Whig lords. But he never did. He went further—he offered to bet five hundred guineas that no such step was in contemplation! † The treachery was discovered when it was too late.

Lord Moira, having failed with Lords Grey and Grenville (little aware of how near he had been to success), attempted to get up a ministry on a scheme of his own, to the exclusion of the great leaders on both sides. He was to be Prime Minister himself, and Mr. Canning had already

* " Memoirs of Sir S. Romilly," iii. 42.
† See Moore's " Life of Sheridan."

accepted office as Secretary for Foreign Affairs, and a meeting was appointed at Carlton House, to kiss hands. Mr. Canning arrived first, and was shown into an anteroom, while Lord Moira was closeted with the Regent. He had not waited very long when Lord Liverpool suddenly appeared, coming from the Regent's apartment, to which Mr. Canning was momentarily expecting to be called. The *equivoque* was perfect. Mr. Canning had been led to believe that he was about to join an administration from which Lord Liverpool was to be excluded upon principle; and Lord Liverpool believed that he was invited to join an administration of which Mr. Canning was wholly ignorant! It is scarcely necessary to add, that this project was brought to a sudden close by the discovery in the anteroom.

The new government found themselves immersed in embarrassments. The manufacturing districts were in a state of unprecedented turbulence and distress; and these responsibilities pressed so severely upon ministers, that after the close of their first session they made splendid overtures to Mr. Canning. They offered him the Foreign Secretaryship (then held by Lord Castlereagh,) and appointments for his political friends; all of which he declined. This refusal did not proceed upon any objections arising out of the Catholic Question; because he afterwards (May, 1819) stated that in the formation of that ministry, every member entered into office with the *express stipulation* that he should be free to maintain his opinions on the subject of the Catholic claims. The real obstacle was Lord Castlereagh. It was proposed that Lord Castlereagh should retain the lead in the House of Commons, to which Mr. Canning would not consent. This was a point of honour with him—and something more. Mr. Stapleton says, that Mr. Canning himself did not consider the lead in the Commons an impediment, but that his friends did, and that the question was referred to three experienced members of the House, who decided for the rejection of the offer.* But this statement hardly agrees with Mr. Canning's own explanation of the circumstance, in his speech at Liverpool in the following October, in which he says, that the seals of the office of Secretary of State had been tendered to him *twice* during the previous six months, but that he had declined them. " I declined office, gentlemen," he adds, " because it was tendered to me on terms not consistent, *as I thought*, and as my immediate friends *agreed* in thinking, with my personal honour ; because, if accepted on such terms, it would not have enabled me to serve the public with efficiency." There is, indeed, very little room to doubt that Mr. Canning was strongly convinced that he ought not to go into the House of Commons as Secretary of State, without also holding the position of ministerial leader. The Regent himself tried to persuade him out of this conviction by arguing that the leadership must, in effect, be vested in him, although nominally in Lord Castlereagh. The fallacy, however, was too apparent ; and Mr. Canning, in a private letter to Wilberforce, discloses the full force of his personal objections, by showing that he could not have accepted office without maintaining Lord Castlereagh in his station :

" And yet," he says, " I will venture to affirm that no effort on my part to reject for myself, and to preserve to Lord C. the station of command, would have prevented him from saying in three weeks, that I was studiously labouring to deprive him of it. Pray, therefore, be not led astray (nor let others, where you can help it), by the notion that I have been squabbling about a trifle."

* " Political Life," i. 68.

And he concludes by observing:

"If I could have placed this power fairly *in medio*, I would have conquered, or endeavoured to conquer, *all my other feelings of reluctance*. But to place it, and to engage to maintain it in his hands, in whose it now is, and then to place myself under it, would have been not only a sacrifice of pride, but an extinction of utility."*

The refusal clearly proceeded upon personal grounds. He felt that his "efficiency" would have been destroyed in such a position; besides all the other risks to the public service which might be run by being placed in so equivocal a relationship with Lord Castlereagh. No man certainly was so ready to sacrifice office upon the suggestions of honour or the public good. In a subsequent speech at Liverpool, he stated that of more than twenty years he had been in Parliament, upwards of one half were passed out of office. "I have oftener," he said, "had occasion to justify my resignation or refusal, than my acceptance of official situation."

Unfortunately his refusal on this occasion was not the wisest course he could have adopted, either in reference to the country or himself; and we find him many years afterwards alluding to it in terms of ill-suppressed regret, and declaring that two years of office in the then circumstances of Europe, would have been worth ten years of life. Yet he sacrificed that great ambition, and left Lord Castlereagh to glean the harvest of which he had sown the seed. But repentance followed quickly upon the rejection of office; and, notwithstanding his personal objections to taking office *with* Lord Castlereagh as leader of the Commons, a very short interval had elapsed when he accepted the Lisbon embassy *under* Lord Castlereagh, as Secretary of State for Foreign Affairs.

* "Life of Wilberforce," iv. 40.

This transaction certainly admits of explanation; but no explanation can diminish its inconsistency.

Mr. Stapleton says that Mr. Canning was going to Lisbon, on account of the illness of his son, and that the cabinet happening to want an ambassador to Portugal at the time, thought it a good opportunity to avail themselves of his services;—one of those transparent excuses which never can be employed without suspicion. It is quite true that Mr. Canning was going to Lisbon on account of the illness of his son, and it is very probable that he would have gone there without any reference to the ambassadorship; but all that has nothing to do with the question of accepting an appointment in 1814, under a ministry with whom he refused to co-operate in 1812.

It is stated by Mr. Stapleton, that Mr. Canning was induced to accept the embassy to Lisbon " because the government made it the condition of enrolling in its ranks those of his personal friends, who had attached themselves to his political fortunes."* The author of a biography of Mr. Huskisson, subsequently published, denies this statement; at least so far as Mr. Huskisson is concerned; and says, that long before the Lisbon appointment, Mr. Canning had released his adherents from all political allegiance, and, as Whitbread sarcastically said, desired them " to shift for themselves."†

Lord Brougham condemns Mr. Canning severely, and says that it was the love of power which led him to the imprudent step of serving under a successful rival on a foreign mission of an unimportant cast.‡ This lust of dominion is not quite so base as the lust of money; but Lord Brougham might as well have accused him of the

* " Political Life," i. 70.   † " Speeches of Mr. Huskisson," i. 65.
‡ " Historical Sketches." Art. Can. 287.

one as the other. If the passion for office was so predominant, how did it happen that Mr. Canning had so often and so recently refused much higher and more influential stations?

Controversies respecting motives are never very satisfactory. People always differ about them, and shape them according to their own prejudices. But in this instance, any graver or meaner aspersion than that of misjudgment would be unwarrantable. All that can be said is, that Mr. Canning committed a *mistake* in accepting this appointment. It placed him under the necessity of vindicating his conduct, which, right or wrong, is always injurious to a public man. The world is sure to distrust the prudence of the politician, or the soldier, who allows himself to be placed at a disadvantage.

The facts, as they were brought before Parliament, had certainly a very suspicious aspect. Appearances were altogether against Mr. Canning.

The embassy was stated to have been appointed, for the purpose of meeting the Prince Regent of Portugal on his return to Europe:—the Prince never returned. Mr. Sydenham, our minister at Lisbon, only just appointed, was strictly limited in July to an allowance of 5200*l.* per annum, on the score of economy:—he was shortly afterwards superseded, and Mr. Canning nominated to his place at an annual expenditure of 14,200*l.* These facts were insisted upon by Mr. Lambton (afterwards Lord Durham) in a speech of excellent temper, but clear and uncompromising, on the 6th of May, 1817: after Mr. Canning's return. Sir Francis Burdett was the only person who spoke in support of Mr. Lambton's resolutions. Mr. Canning's reply was victorious.

He proved, by the correspondence of ministers with our ambassador at Rio de Janeiro, that the Prince Regent had frequently expressed his desire to revisit Europe, and that the appointment was not determined upon until the arrangements for that event were finally settled. The failure of the Regent's visit was a matter for which neither he nor the government could be held responsible. He showed that he was going to Lisbon with his family, when the embassy was proposed to him, and that his own preparations had advanced so far, that when he arrived there, he found a private house provided for his use, which he could not occupy in his official character.

The question of cost was even more triumphantly disposed of. Mr. Canning went to Lisbon in quality of ambassador, and not in that of simple minister, which he could hardly have accepted, after having presided over the whole diplomacy of the country; besides which, the appointment of an ambassador, was an old promise to the Regent. There were two classes of ambassadors—two salaries attached to the rank: Mr. Canning selected the lower. Had he even availed himself of the scale which had been recently fixed by a Committee of the House of Commons, he would have been entitled to 14,236*l.* per annum—exactly 36*l.* more than he actually drew. With respect to Mr. Sydenham's expenses, he showed that Mr. Sydenham's *salary* had been unfairly contrasted with the *whole* expense of his own mission, including extraordinaries. Upon an investigation of the items, it appeared that Mr. Sydenham (who had not been superseded by Mr. Canning, but who, after a residence of only *three weeks* in Lisbon, was obliged to return in consequence of ill-health) received six months' salary (besides outfit, &c.) and an additional sum of 2000*l.* for loss on the relinquishment of office; and that Mr. Casamajor, who had been for a short interval *chargé d'affaires*, and who could not contrive to live quietly in lodgings, without any of the " pride, pomp, or circumstance" of a diplomatic establishment, under 100*l.* a week, received 2500*l.* more; so that the six months preceding Mr. Canning's appointment (a service in reality of only three weeks) cost 7100*l*; or, with outfit, &c., added, 9700*l.*! The two years preceding presented a still more extraordinary contrast; for in those two years, during the mission of Sir Charles Stuart, the expences were for the first, 32,007*l.*, for the second, 31,206*l.*

The defence was complete at all points—even on the most doubtful of all, his union with the administration. He asserted his right to think and act for himself, and repudiated the doctrine by which any party attempted to arrogate an exclusive control. This passage contains one of those remarkable assertions of the right of private judgment which nobody in the ranks of the old tory party, except Mr. Canning, ever dared to utter.

" To this exclusive doctrine I have never subscribed. To these pretensions I have never listened with submission. I have never deemed it reasonable that any confederacy of great names should monopolise to themselves the whole patronage and authority of the state: should constitute themselves as it were, into a corporation, a bank for circulating the favours of the House and the suffrages of the people, and distributing them only to their own adherents. I cannot consent that the administration of the government of this free and enlightened country, shall be considered as rightfully belonging to any peculiar circle of public men, however powerful, or of families, however preponderant; and, though I cannot stand lower in the estimation of the honourable baronet than I do in my own, as to my own pretensions, I will (to use the language of a statesman,* so eminent that I cannot presume to quote his words without an apology), I will, as long as I have the faculty to think and act for myself, '*look those proud combinations in the face.*'"

By this principle Mr. Canning regulated his conduct. He owed no political allegiance to any party—he denied the divine right of aristocratic combinations. He joined the administration, because he agreed with the administration; and in the exercise of the same unfettered discretion, he would have left them if he differed from them;—he did leave them when the point of difference arose. The freedom, candour, and *novelty*, of this course of action, offended both whigs and tories—especially the latter, whose anger was inappeasable, that he should thus come between the wind and their nobility. But out of these elements of discord there was gradually rising-up a Middle Party, which Mr. Canning called into life, with " No Reform " inscribed on one side of its banner, and " Free Trade and Catholic Emancipation " on the other. The importance of the functions assigned to this party in the tremulous state of transition through which the country was now passing, cannot be exaggerated. This party formed the only creditable retreat from obsolete doctrines which could neither be maintained with success, nor abandoned without humiliation. It flung a bridge across the chasm that divided the old times from the new, over which the legislature, pressed onwards by the people, was glad enough at last to make its escape.

Mr. Canning's defence was considered conclusive by the House, and Mr. Lambton's motion was thrown out by a majority of 174. He was so well satisfied with the result himself that he went up to Mr. Lambton, after

* Mr. Burke.

the debate, and thanked him warmly for the open and manly spirit in which he had brought the question to issue.

The term of his residence in Lisbon occupied altogether seventeen months, during six of which he held no official position, for he sent in his resignation the moment he learned that the Regent had relinquished his intention of visiting Europe. During that interval great events had occurred on the Continent. Buonaparte had broken bounds at Elba, revived the martial spirit once more in France, dispersed the Bourbons, and, after some wondrous efforts, had finally sunk at Waterloo. Mr. Canning took no part in these excitements, but kept his private station undisturbed by political influences, dispensing social hospitality to his countrymen, and receiving distinguished marks of their admiration and respect. Amongst other proofs of their feelings towards him, the British residents at Lisbon entertained him at a public dinner, when he delivered that speech in which he described himself as a disciple of Mr. Pitt. On his return to England he touched at Bordeaux, and was there detained to receive a similar testimony from the merchants of that city, who invited him to a public entertainment on a scale of unusual magnificence.

Shortly after his return, a vacancy occurred in the office of President of the Board of Control, occasioned by the death of the Earl of Buckinghamshire; and Mr. Canning accepted the office on the especial invitation of the Prince Regent.

The times were full of danger, and the government was placed at home and abroad in a situation that demanded the exercise of the highest qualities of statesmanship. The war was now over,, and there was leisure to estimate the policy of such a fearful expenditure by its results. The grand aim of the war was the deliverance of Europe. Had that end been accomplished? A comparison of the map of Europe in 1815, with the map of Europe before the war, offered the best answer. If it were true of Napoleon that he shifted and pulled down the ancient barriers of independent kingdoms like hurdles, to accommodate the greater or lesser droves he thought fit to hunt into or out of them, it was no less true that his conquerors swept away the old landmarks with as little compunction, but with a deliberate affectation of justice to which Napoleon never pretended any title. Their crimes against the rights of nations were as palpable as his, with the greater crime of hypocrisy superadded to all the rest. The settlement of 1815 was in fact a new dismemberment. Norway had been already struck down by a perfidious treaty, which Mr. Canning declared in the face of Europe had " filled him with shame, regret, and indignation." Venice and Genoa were annihilated; Prussia was suffered to inflict upon Saxony territorial wrongs as flagrant as those which she had herself suffered from the hands of France; Holland was never restored to her ancient republican liberties, but was paralysed by monarchical trammels repugnant alike to her spirit and her traditions; and still farther oppressed and weakened by the addition of a discordant and insurrectionary population. Spain alone was replaced in her original integrity. She was restored with the most scrupulous honour. She even got back the Inquisition.

At home the prospect was no less gloomy. The people were dissatisfied with the fruits of victory. The taxes were rising upon them like the inevitable tide upon some doomed wretch who, in ignorance or defiance, has ventured too far out upon the strand. The instantaneous transition to peace increased the calamity. It suddenly withdrew the stimulus by which the population had hitherto been sustained, and reduced them at once to a state of destitution. Trade had to explore new channels—industry to make to itself new resources; but these things were impossible. Stagnation and distress were rapidly spreading over the face of the country; discontent had set in amongst the industrial classes; large and tumultuous meetings were held in the principal towns, and even in the outlying agricultural districts; and the issue of all this uneasiness was a loud and universal cry for Parliamentary Reform.

It might have been hoped that the example of Mr. Pitt's conduct in a similar crisis would have operated as a warning to the Government. But it had the opposite effect. Instead of avoiding the course which he had taken with such fatal results, they imitated it to the letter. Instead of seeking to remove, or even expressing a desire to investigate the grievances of the people, Ministers opened a new reign of terror at once.

There was no difficulty in getting up a case of insurrection. Conspiracies, incendiarism, republican speeches, and foolish bravadoes in the face of the magistracy, are easily hunted up in times of excitement. The system of coercion fairly begun, there was no lack of the frenzied exhibitions it was so admirably calculated to produce. On the one side a fresh violence was found daily necessary to guard against the consequences of the last; and on the other more desperate outbreaks followed closely upon every new aggression. And so it went on for three years.

The physical sufferings of the people aggravated the wildness with which they caught at the loose theories of property and representation which are set afloat with such facility in times of commotion. They convened public meetings, and spouted social-economy fallacies of that class which have always found favour, in seasons of famine and hardship, with the starving multitude. Lord Castlereagh declared that they contained within themselves a principle of counteraction. It would have been happy for all parties if he had trusted to its influence; but he thought that the argument most likely to reach the understanding of an illogical multitude was a troop of dragoons. This argument was tested with deplorable success on the field of Peterloo.

There were plots in abundance, real and fictitious, from the Cato-street conspiracy, by which a butcher and two shoemakers engaged to cut off the Ministers' heads and put them in a bag, to a formidable plan for storming the Bank, destroying the barracks, blowing up the bridges, and setting fire to every thing, including the Thames itself. The means by which this latter design was to be accomplished were traced to a bundle of pikes and some powder in an old stocking.

To avert such tremendous calamities, the most stringent laws were passed. The right of discussion was abridged; public meetings were allowed to be held only by special grace of the magistracy; correspondence and co-operation, and free action in an infinite variety of small things essential to the comfort and self-respect of individuals, were strictly prohibited; and finally the work of pacification was crowned by the suspension of the Habeas Corpus Act. All this time spies were moving darkly through the country, instigating the crimes which were thus visited with the heaviest punishments.

The judgment of the people upon these proceedings,

was pronounced by one jury after another, in verdicts which might be regarded as accusations against the government. When the executive resorts to extraordinary powers, and then seeks to vindicate them by appealing to the tribunals of the country, it in effect puts itself upon its trial before the people. In all such cases it is to the decision of the juries, the guardians of order and justice, that we must look for the condemnation or acquittal of the government.

Mr. Canning was eager in the defence of ministers. He vindicated every one of their acts; and never displayed greater felicity of expression, wit more dazzling, or argument more cogent and effective than in his speeches on the State of the Nation, on the Seditious Meetings Bill, the Indemnity Bill, the Foreign Enlistment Bill, and the Prince Regent's speech. It is impossible to look back upon his conduct during those years of strife and misery, without a feeling of profound regret. It was deplorable enough, after all that had transpired of personal contempt and distrust towards the Castlereaghs and Sidmouths in former days, to find him associated with them in the cabinet; but worse, still worse, to find him making himself extravagantly prominent in the justification of their misdeeds. Perhaps his excessive zeal on behalf of his colleagues, may be ascribed to the nervous uneasiness of the relation in which he stood to them. Keenly alive to the unpopularity of his position, rendered conspicuous above all the rest by the splendour of his arms, it seems as if this very consciousness only made him the more anxious to assume a confidence in the proceedings of the government, which his judgment must have secretly disowned. To this mental warfare must be attributed the unusual bitterness he manifested towards his opponents throughout the time he held the office of President of Council. He never showed so much excitement or impatience before. The slightest contradiction called him up, and all questions, from the spirit in which they were treated, became more or less personal before they were finally disposed of. He was ill at ease with himself; and dissatisfied with the distorting circumstances by which he was surrounded.

He despised most of the men with whom he acted; and most of the men with whom he acted distrusted him. He who had been the darling of the age of Pitt, was now confided in by no great political party; he was too liberal for one, too arrogant for another, and could not yet see his way to the advent of that Central Party, wiser than either, which was, even at this inauspicious moment, germinating under his influence. Every thing conspired to thwart his ambition—to ruffle his temper—to force him into situations where he was condemned to defend measures he disapproved. He allowed himself to be martyred on points of honour.

The death of George III., towards the close of January 1820, reduced ministers to the necessity of a general election, which they would gladly have avoided. His Majesty had wonderfully spun out a long life, and died at last at a very awkward moment. But he could not keep alive for the sake of his ministers. It was marvellous how he kept alive so long, soliloquising and playing the harpsichord at Windsor. He had not had a lucid interval for nine years. For a great part of the time he was totally blind and almost totally deaf; and had such an objection to be shaved, that his beard had grown to a patriarchal length. There was much unaffected emotion exhibited by all classes when he died. People had got used to him; a generation or two had grown up in his time, and had come into the world lisping their allegiance to him; and everybody felt that a great many years must elapse before they could reconcile themselves to a new version of the nation anthem. There never could be another " great George, our king!"

In the following March, Mr. Canning sustained a severe domestic affliction by the death of his eldest son, George Charles Canning, in the nineteenth year of his age. The epitaph he wrote on this melancholy occasion, inspired by the most tender sorrow tempered with religious resignation, is entitled to a place amongst the noblest productions of that class in our language.

The national excitement consequent upon the general election had scarcely subsided, when an unexpected circumstance threatened to disturb the joyous opening of the new reign. George IV. had scarcely time to adjust the affair of his coronation robes with his tailor, when news arrived that his wife was coming back to England to assert her right to be crowned by his side. Had an avalanche from the summit of the Schreckhorn been announced in the drawing-room at St. James's, it could not have produced greater consternation.

XII.

QUEEN CAROLINE. LORD CASTLEREAGH.

On the 8th of April, 1795, the Prince of Wales was married to the Princess Caroline of Brunswick. In a few days the happy couple, for whom the joy-bells had rung out so lustily on that morning, were perfectly miserable—in a few months they separated. The prince put away his wife. She had committed no crime, but one which it was impossible for a gentleman of the prince's high temperament to pardon—she had outlived his liking.

Never was a poor bride so stunned, as this luckless princess by her first experiences in England. Every thing about her was strange and discouraging. Her education and habits, her tastes and feelings, and the usages she had been reared amongst—all seemed to go wrong in England. She had never seen any thing half so grand, half so cold, as St. James's. The stateliness of the place struck like frost into her blood. Her own family had been so grievously cut up and despoiled, and retained such scanty traces of pomp and ceremony, that their rank was advertised chiefly by the politic friendship of surrounding states. But even this did not avail when Napoleon came upon the scene. That sagacious remodeller of kingdoms and constitutions, laid such stress upon the tiny principality of Brunswick, that he said he would rather cede Belgium than suffer the duke to re-enter his territory. That worthy race of Wolfenbuttle, with milky hearts and warlike moustaches, had a close escape of being superannuated amongst the old Teutonic traditions.

The Princess had been brought up in this little court, which could hardly be called a court. The whole circle was composed of occasional birds of passage, principally military—for resident nobility there were none. Travellers were cheerfully received. The sight of visitors enlivened the quiet palace, and threw all its inmates into motion; just as the appearance of a troop of strolling players calls up out of their sleepy recesses the tranquil population of an English village. This sort of life had something in it of the ease and *abandon* of an out-post. Formal distinctions were out of the question. There was a slight show of state etiquette at first: a matter of mere observance, which restrained one's animal spirits for a quarter of an hour; and then every body was frank and equal, and licensed for gaiety and frolic. They used to play at proverbs, and lively forfeits of all sorts; and sup at little round tables, in merry groups, like people in a fashionable *café*. It was a Palace of Revels, a Court of High Romps.

In this open life the manners of the Princess were formed. To the pure all things are pure; and that which was mere out-spoken joyousness in this little German retreat would have been imprudence, or worse, elsewhere. Had she lived all her life in the same round of hearty diversions she might have gone on to the end with honour, and—which is a part of the source of honour to a woman—with happiness. But she was suddenly carried away to another country, where a different standard of morals and different social institutions prevailed, to marry a man she had never seen, whose reputation for excesses of all kinds—the basest amongst the rest—was enough to terrify and revolt her. It was said, too, that her heart had already admitted feelings which she was required by this sacrificial act to silence for ever. The story was doubted by some who thought her incapable of an attachment, judging by the after-course of a life perverted at the very spring by those upon whom the sacred duty devolved of directing it wisely and kindly. But we cannot speculate upon what she might have been under natural influences, from what she became under the blight of that selfish and most disastrous marriage. Even as it was, she discovered sympathies which struggled out as they might, darkly and miserably for herself. But who shall accuse her under such circumstances? What woman could have remained true to any thing human or to herself, who was at the mercy of the Prince of Wales?

Think of the images of sin, of seduction, of low depravity, of the grossest violations of good faith and common decency, which glared upon her from all sides in this scrupulous Royal Family, upon which she had been engrafted, and which resented with such virtuous indignation the slightest breach of decorum. She had scarcely touched our shores when the timid feelings of the bride were outraged and insulted by finding Lady Jersey already installed, and retained, too, in spite of the express interdict of the Sovereign.* When she was taken to the palace, the Prince came to her after some delay, and

* "The Princess, the moment she saw the Prince and Lady Jersey together, saw her fate—but she married him. 'Oh! mine God,' she used to exclaim in her own earnest way, 'I could be the slave of a man I love, but to one whom I loved not, and who did not love me—impossible—c'est autre chose.' "—" Diary of the Times of George IV.," i., 23.

having received her, turned away and called for a glass of brandy. Water was suggested, but the Prince negatived it with an oath, and left the room.* That was a trivial specimen of brutality. Worse might have been expected from a Prince who, talking of his approaching marriage with a lady he had never seen, called it " buying a pig in a poke;" and who declared to the Lord Chancellor that " he, the Prince, was not the sort of person who would let his hair grow under his wig to please his wife." Worse might have been expected from such a quarter—and worse came. On the night of the wedding, this *exigeant* prince, who looked for so much refinement and courtly etiquette in his wife, reeled drunk into the bridal chamber, and fell under the grate.†

Of the minor trespasses on her feelings—the insults to which she was obliged to submit—the tales that were industriously buzzed in her ears—nothing need be said. Let Perdita pass; and Mrs. Fitzherbert, too, with her recognised respectability, not the less galling to the Princess on that account; and Lady Hertford, who supplanted Mrs. Fitzherbert; ‡ and all the rest. But look around on the

* "Diaries of the Earl of Malmesbury," iii., 218.

† This almost incredible fact is stated on the authority of Lady Charlotte Bury. "Judge," said the Princess, "what it was to have a drunken husband on one's wedding-day, and one who passed the greater part of his bridal-night under the grate where he fell, and where I left him. If any body say to me at dis moment, 'will you pass your life over again, or be killed,' I would choose death."—"Diary of the Times of George IV.", i., 37. And this was in 1810, long before her great troubles came ! The statement is borne out to a certain extent by Lord Malmesbury, who says, that on the evening of the wedding-day, the Prince appeared "unhappy, and as a proof of it, had manifestly had recourse to wine or spirits."—" Diaries," iii., 220.

‡ The decision of the House of Lords, by which Lord and Lady Hertford were appointed guardians to Miss Seymour, "led to that intimacy between the Prince and Lady Hertford, which ended by Mrs. Fitzherbert's dismissal. It had a still more important effect, for it produced that hostility towards the Catholics which the Prince manifested after he became regent."—See " Memoirs of Sir Samuel Romilly," ii., 152.

scions of this royal stock for the revelations, which, year after year, accumulated their baneful influences around the unhappy stranger : the life of Mrs. Jordan, dragged through the gossip of the green-room, forestalled at the playhouse treasury, careering through the splendid misery of Bushy Park, to expiate all in poverty and exile ; the hideous exposures of Mary Ann Clarke; and the darker infamies of other palatial misdeeds, which must never find expression, except in the backward shudder of history. Were these things likely to elevate, refine, and strengthen the resolves of a discarded woman—a woman utterly alone amongst strangers, tempted, spied upon, persecuted, and condemned to suffer the extremity of injustice after her innocence was clearly established by the most searching investigation to which any woman, be her rank or circumstances what they might, has ever been exposed in a country where legal tribunals, or public opinion, are supposed to exist ?

The residence of the Princess at Blackheath, was a sort of court banishment. Montagu House (so called after the Duke of Montagu) was a curious rambling place, described by one who lived in it in the Princess's time, as an incongruous piece of patchwork, which dazzled when it was lighted up at night, but was, in reality, all glitter, and glare, and trick. There was a round tower in the grounds, which used to be a great source of amusement to the Princess ; it was guarded by a nightly watchman, and the lady in attendance slept in it, and one of the foolish jokes got up to while away time was the invention of little dramatic incidents, to give an air of romance to this round tower. And such were the thoughtless trifles which were afterwards interpreted so cruelly to her disadvantage. From the very beginning of her life, this poor wayward, heedless Princess was the victim of erroneous suspicions. Nobody seems to have understood her character.

When she was brought over to England, she appears to have made an indifferent impression upon the new society to which she was introduced. Yet Lord Malmesbury, who was intrusted with this delicate piece of diplomacy, assures us that she had a pretty face, fine eyes, good hands, tolerable teeth; that her expression was not very soft, nor her figure very graceful, that she had a good bust and *des epaules impertinentes*. The portrait is at least womanly, and, with her real good-nature beaming in it, agreeable. But she wanted *tact*, the quality most necessary in her new circumstances. She was not brought up in a knowledge of artificial dignity, and she could not adapt herself to it. Her education had been sadly neglected in matters of costume and externals, which are so highly prized in England; and overwrought in every thing else, to the detriment of her faith and her understanding. It was an education of folly and weakness, of menace, privation, injunction, with the examples of those who inculcated it flying in the face of its precepts. Her father made no disguise about his amours. The duchess told Lord Malmesbury that he was in love with the Duchess of G., Lady O., and Lady D. B., and solaced himself with the private society of an Italian girl all the time. Her mother was a gossip; weak, credulous, capricious, but without any absolute vice. It was not very wonderful that thus descended and nurtured, the Princess should have had an excellent heart and no judgment. The lack of judgment made her heart more capacious than it was quite fitting it should be: she wanted all the people of England to love her (that was the first piece of folly she uttered); and she could not comprehend how such a thing was impossible in this country, and altogether inconsistent with the elevation and remoteness of her position.

If such were her dispositions in the midst of her own circles, where she was known and admired, and free to indulge in her impulses, what could be expected from her at Blackheath, where she was placed in the most dangerous relation towards society that the most subtle malice could devise?

Her mode of life here surprised and perplexed every body. She was regarded, not unkindly, (for people liked her robust good-nature), as a strange person with strange foreign habits. She was free, coarse, vulgar, boisterous; had a gross constitution, used to eat onions and drink ale, which she called *oil;* and sit on the floor, and play forfeits and romps; and talk broad, humourous, scandal to her ladies, for the sake of the fun—not the malice, which never interested her. She hardly knew how to get through her time; used to walk out in the snow in pink boots, and run through the garden at night in a red cloak, a handkerchief tied under her chin, and her slippers down at the heels; picked up an acquaintance with Lady Douglas at her own door, and was glad of any one that came to dinner. Her feelings were warm, eager, liberal; but she had no manners, no delicacy. She used to plan imaginary intrigues for her ladies to fill up the evening, in imitation of the gallant age of De Grammont; just as children play at soldiers or house-building with cards and toys. She would ask gentlemen (there was nobody else she could ask) to dinner and supper. Canning lived in the neighbourhood, and was constantly invited; and one of her strange amusements on such occasions was blindman's buff (a favourite pastime of Napoleon and Charles II.), in which she frequently joined with Sir William Scott, Canning, and others;

and whenever this solitary woman showed any one of these visitors the smallest marks of her good will, she was immediately suspected, or pretended to be suspected.

Unconscious of the watch that was set upon her, she probably grew more and more careless and fantastical, from being permitted to believe that she had her own way. Suddenly, without a word of notice, half her household was swept away to be interrogated. Throughout this terrible crisis, the Princess acted with a dignity worthy of the noblest character. She sent for the Duke of Kent, and made him bear witness that she would not see one of her servants, lest it might be supposed that she desired to tamper with them. *

The investigation was conducted with the utmost severity, and ended in her acquittal,† The king, anxious to atone for the wrong, expressed his intention to receive her at court; but the Prince interposed, and would not suffer it.‡ She was again sent forth to be persecuted. That dangerous tendency of her nature, which yearned for sympathy of some sort, and which might have slumbered or taken a safer direction, under wiser treatment, was thus encouraged, tempted, provoked into vice. Up to this time she was indiscreet, which a better woman

* The Lords who were appointed to enter upon the "delicate" investigation, issued an order to bring before them six of the Princess's most confidential servants from her house at Blackheath. "The order was executed," says Sir Samuel Romilly, "without any previous intimation to the Princess, or to any of her servants."—"Memoirs," ii., 150. The princess said they were welcome to examine all her servants if they thought proper.

† "The result," says Sir Samuel Romilly, "left a perfect conviction on my mind, and I believe on the minds of the four lords, that the boy in question is the son of Sophia Austin."

‡ The king's answer, as written by the Cabinet, after stating that his majesty was satisfied about her innocence, added, that "his majesty sees with 'concern and disapprobation,' &c., certain parts of her conduct. The king struck out with his own hand the word 'disapprobation,' and substituted 'serious concern.' "—"Memoirs," ii., 186.

might have been in such circumstances; but she was innocent. After this, she was lost. Whose was the guilt?

Mr. Canning was one of her earliest and most steadfast friends. Governed by his advice, she had hitherto observed the most judicious conduct, in reference to Parliament and the royal family. When the Prince of Wales's income became the subject of debate, in 1803, Mr. Canning offered to take any step about an increase in her appointments which she might direct; but she begged of him not to interfere, not to mention her name in or out of Parliament; adding, that she relied entirely on the King's goodness, and that she wished to be left undisturbed by publicity in her retirement. This was the course he had all throughout advised her to adopt; and had she continued to follow his injunctions, her just rights would have been fully recognised at last. There were none of her adherents for whom she entertained so strong a regard as Mr. Canning, notwithstanding that she deviated so widely, in the end, from the line he had marked out for her. Lord Eldon, whom she liked at first, and Perceval, who, from party motives, attached himself zealously to her cause, both fell into disgrace with her, because she thought that they had supplanted Mr. Canning with the King.

Perceval was her principal adviser when the four lords drew up their report. He wrote her reply, which was retouched by Plumer;* and then collecting the evidence and all the other documents, which constituted that digest of royal scandal, known by the emphatic title of "The Book," he got it printed. Canning strongly condemned this step, and instantly returned the copy which had been sent to him, saying, that if they printed they published,

* "Memoirs of Sir S. Romilly," ii., 171.

and that, let the disgraceful disclosure come from what quarter it might, he was determined it should not be supposed to come from him. Perceval's real intention was to publish it, for the purpose of bringing odium on the opposite party. But in this, as in all things else, he acted with too hot a resolution. "The Book" was scarcely printed, when a change of administration took place, and it became imperatively necessary to suppress the publication. But some copies had got out surreptitiously, and the difficulty was to recover them. Perceval going out in a hurry (he seems to have been always flushed and excited), left a copy on his table; it was stolen, and it cost him 10,000*l.* to get it back again.* The editor of a Sunday paper, who had by some means obtained another copy, issued a mysterious notice of his intention to publish it, and was stopped by an injunction;† but afterwards assured his friends that he had compromised the matter for 1000*l.* Another copy got into the hands of another person connected with the press, who compromised for the sum of 5000*l.*‡ Such was the anxiety manifested in the endeavour to retrace a false step, which any man of common sense ought to have known the hopelessness of attempting.

It was in 1812, that these matters first came before Parliament; so long as his Majesty was in possession of his senses, it was felt that Parliament had no right to interfere in his family dissensions; but the Regency altered the case. The Queen was about to hold a drawing-room, and Mr. Whitbread demanded of the minister, whether

---

* Lady Hester Stanhope states, that "she *knows* this to a certainty."
—"Memoirs of Lady Hester Stanhope," i., 306.

† "Memoirs of Sir Samuel Romilly." ii., 171.

‡ These two cases of compromise are stated on the authority of the individuals themselves—both of whom are now dead.

the Princess of Wales—so long proscribed from the circles over which she ought to have presided—was to make her appearance on that occasion. " Mr. Perceval," he said, " *ought* to know, for he *had* been her devoted adherent, had written her vindication and published it, which publication had been extensively read, although it was bought up at an enormous expense by the right honourable gentleman's secretary." But the times had changed with Mr. Perceval. He was the Regent's " devoted adherent" now, and the Princess had nothing to expect from his fidelity, because she had no means of rewarding it. Her star was setting; she was urged to leave the country. Once out of England, a surrender in itself to a certain extent of her legitimate rights, the annihilation of all further hope of restitution followed as a matter of course. She went abroad in 1814, contrary to the urgent advice of Mr. Whitbread and Mr. Brougham. She returned on the death of George III., to set up her claim to be crowned with her husband, contrary to the advice of Mr. Canning.

Her proceedings on the continent were the acts of a mad woman—of one made desperate by the total blight of her affections, the entire misdirection of her life, by the sense of friendliness and isolation, the mockery of state through which she moved, and by that terrible contempt of opinion which grows upon systematic injustice. Her folly, combined with the sensuality of her life, exposed her anew to persecution; and she was still watched and dogged as of old, and eyes glared upon her where she least suspected treachery, in her most secret and careless moments. Out of the intelligence thus basely procured, arose the famous Milan Commission. It was not a government measure— it was worse. It originated in this way. A mass of papers, concerning the conduct of the Queen (for she was called queen everywhere except in the Litany) had been put into the hands of Sir John Leach, in his capacity of Chancellor of the Duchy of Lancaster, and, as such, first law adviser to the Prince. He was to examine and report upon these documents; and he did so, to the effect, that competent persons ought to be sent abroad to collect and arrange evidence of the facts, before any ulterior steps should be taken. This was agreed to; he selected the persons himself, and they were sent out, not by the sanction of the Cabinet, but with the concurrence and privacy of Lords Eldon and Liverpool. Sir John Leach got into odium by this transaction, and it was even said that he went over to Italy himself to forward the project. This he denied; but he admitted, that he did happen to go just at that time to Italy, and, by a very odd coincidence, to Milan amongst other places; but he protested that he never communicated with any body all the time, on the subject of the commission which was sitting there, and which he himself had appointed. Be that as it may, it was this Milan Commission by which the evidence was collected, that was brought against the Queen on her trial. The result was a severe blow to the Tory government—an insignificant majority, which compelled them, as a matter of decency, to abandon the bill. The only member of the Cabinet, who stood out to the last against Lord Liverpool's proposal to relinquish the prosecution, was Lord Eldon. But he always stood out to the last, and was rather proud of standing out alone.

Mr. Canning's conduct throughout this affair was misunderstood and studiously misrepresented. He had been on terms of intimacy with the Princess from the beginning, and could not, without doing violence to his feelings, as a gentleman who had been once admitted to the honour of her confidence, take any part in the proceedings against her. *He never did take any part in those proceedings.* In 1814, when he was unconnected with the government, he had had frequent intercourse with her, and he then approved of a separate arrangement, and advised that she should live abroad with her family at Brunswick, or in any society she might prefer, " of which," he declared, " she must be the grace, life, and honour." He defended that advice in 1820. It was founded on the fact of " alienation and hopeless irreconcilement," and because he saw that " faction had marked her for its own." He had foreseen, he said, that with her income and with her fascinating manners, she would become the rallying point of political intrigue.

Had the Princess followed Mr. Canning's advice in her mode of life, her residence abroad would have rescued her from all those dangers by which she was encompassed on her return, and which he, who knew her character well, had predicted so accurately. He could not anticipate the errors into which she fell, and if he could, he might still have tendered the same advice, from a conviction that the farther the scene of such errors was removed from England the better for her own sake and the repose of the country.

On her return, with this dark cloud of accusation impending over her, Mr. Canning was a member of the government. Ministers had a clear duty to perform. But before they pressed on the prosecution, an offer was made to her of 50,000*l.* a year if she would live abroad, under an adopted name. She spurned at this proposal, although it afterwards appeared that it had originally emanated from her own party, and was responded to by the government from a desire to avoid the demoralising exposure. There being no alternative left, Her Majesty was brought to trial. While these proceedings were going forward, Mr. Canning declared in the House of Commons that he would have nothing to do with the prosecution. His disclaimer was remarkable. " So help me God !" he exclaimed, " I will never place myself in the situation of an accuser towards this individual." He added, that if any sacrifices on his part could have prevented the painful discussion, he would have readily made them, and would have withdrawn at once, but that it might occasion suspicion that some injustice was intended by his colleagues.

He remained in office, as long as there lingered the least hope of an amicable adjustment. When that failed he resigned. But the King commanded him to remain in office, and graciously absolved him from all participation in the prosecution. He availed himself of this permission, and left England. He had no share in the Bill of Pains and Penalties: he was out of the country during the whole term of its progress. On his return he found the matter, although brought to an end by the withdrawal of the Bill, yet so mixed up with the general business of the session that it was impossible to avoid the discussion of the subject, unless he were to absent himself altogether, which he could not continue to do consistently with his ministerial responsibility. There was no escape but resignation; and His Majesty, on this occasion, reluctantly yielded to his wishes.

It is not enough merely to exonerate Mr. Canning from censure in these transactions. He deserves credit for the courage and delicacy with which he acted. He had ample justification, had he been disposed to avail himself of it, for assisting at the trial of the Queen. The shame she had brought upon herself by her proceedings abroad, which could not be considered otherwise than as an unpardonable infidelity to her true friends and advocates; and her return against his wishes, released him from all personal obligations. She stood no longer in the same relation to her former adherents. Her case was altered. The old contract was vitiated by the introduction of new circumstances. A solemn accusation, strongly fortified by criminating appearances, was drawn up against her; and he might have justly pleaded his strict duty as a minister of the crown, which demanded the abnegation of private feelings in the discharge of a public responsibility. But he resolved from the first to take no part against her. He never even discussed the subject of the prosecution with his colleagues. He never attended a cabinet meeting on the subject. He tried to protect her against her bad advisers; he used the influence he possessed to promote an honourable arrangement, to prevent a publicity injurious to both parties, and prejudicial to the morals of the country: failing in that, he went out of office. The sacrifice was a large one to him at that moment, but it was due to the unfortunate Princess who, in better times, had bestowed distinguished marks of favour upon him. To the other ministers must be assigned the full glory of the state revenge, which, robbed of its victim in the House of Lords, descended to an idle conflict with her hearse.

Mr. Canning's retirement from the Board of Control, in December, 1820, was no sooner made public than the Court of Directors of the East India Company took an opportunity of expressing to him their deep regret at the circumstance, and the sincere respect by which his conduct, during the five years he had occupied that arduous situation, had impressed them. But still higher marks of their approbation awaited him. In the following March, the Court of Proprietors of East India Stock, at a special meeting convened expressly for the purpose, passed a formal resolution confirming the strong testimony of regard already voted by the Court of Directors, seconded and supported by public men, wholly opposed in politics to Mr. Canning, including Mr. Perry of the " Morning Chronicle," and Mr. Hume; and scarcely another year had elapsed, when the Court of Directors, eager to recall him to the public service, and still more to that service in which they were so deeply interested, offered him the office of Governor-General of India. Mr. Canning accepted the appointment, and, soon after the commencement of the session of 1822, was announced as the successor to Lord Hastings.

In a pecuniary point of view, this appointment was very acceptable to him. His private fortune had been unavoidably straitened, and the noble income of the oriental viceroyship promised to repair it in a short time. But this temptation would not have withdrawn him from the political arena where he had won all his past triumphs, had there existed the least likelihood that office would be thrown open to him at home. There was no chance, however, of such an event. The ministry had recently suffered some reverses; and Lord Sidmouth had resigned the Home Secretaryship. At that moment the public looked anxiously to see Mr. Canning replaced in power, but Mr. Peel was appointed to the vacancy. Lord Liverpool, in fact, could not avail himself of Mr. Canning's services. The King would not suffer it. The old story! Had Mr. Canning helped His Majesty to immolate the Queen—had he not checked the current of royal vengeance by holding aloof from the prosecution—he might have been at the head of every thing.

There being no disguise about the antipathy of the

"highest personage in the realm" towards Mr. Canning, the appointment to India was sanctioned with alacrity. The Ultra-Tories rubbed their hands and chuckled at the prospect of getting rid of him. The lowest grade of Reformers had much the same feeling, because of his Toryism; but it was restrained by admiration of his talents, which the Tories envied, and respect for his liberal opinions, which the Tories abhorred. But the body of the English people regarded his approaching departure with unaffected sorrow. They felt that they were about to lose the greatest of their living statesmen.

Impressed with sentiments of pain and regret at his separation from friends who had long bestowed the most signal confidence upon him, Mr. Canning repaired to Liverpool to take leave of his constituents. His connexion with that place had been a succession of the most gratifying triumphs, each fresh election increasing the number of his supporters, and converting enemies into active partisans. He had been four times elected for Liverpool. At the first election he had four antagonists, the most formidable of whom was Mr. Brougham; on the third election there were three candidates, but as the struggle advanced, fresh names were added to the poll, and new bars were opened, until at last there were no less than twenty-one candidates in the field; a curious piece of electioneering manœuvring which was described by Mr. Canning, in one of his speeches, with exquisite humour. Some of Mr. Canning's noblest orations were delivered at dinners and meetings amongst his constituents, his eloquence rendering the scene of its achievements as renowned as Bristol, represented, instructed, and elevated by Burke.

Mr. Canning's visits to Liverpool were galas to the people. He was received with the most lavish honours;

entertainments were planned for the purpose of rendering homage to his genius; and the " Canning Club" was instituted to commemorate his connexion with the borough. He generally took up his residence at Seaforth House, the residence of his friend Mr. Gladstone (the father of the Right Honourable W. Gladstone), situated on a flat stretching north of the town, and overlooking the sea. The room which he occupied looked out upon the ocean, and here he would sit for hours, gazing on the open expanse, while young Gladstone, who has subsequently obtained such distinction in the councils of his sovereign, used to be playing on the strand below. The house is no longer in the possession of Mr. Gladstone, who let it to Mr. Paulet, a Swiss merchant. Latterly, Mr. Canning was the guest of Colonel Bolton.

He had been about a year and half elected for the fourth time, when having accepted the appointment of Governor-General, he went to Liverpool for the purpose of taking leave of his constituents. On his way down, intelligence overtook him on the road that Lord Castlereagh (now Marquis of Londonderry—but one prefers the more familiar name) had terminated his life at North Cray, in Kent, with his own hand. Connected with this piece of news was a rumour, which gained fresh ground every where, that Mr. Canning was universally looked upon as his successor. But Mr. Canning was slow to yield to the flattering suggestions of popular opinion, and pursued his journey to Liverpool, without pausing even to examine the unexpected contingency which had arisen.

On the 23rd of August he dined with the Canning Club. On the morning of the 30th he received an address from his constituents, unanimously approved and sanctioned by *all* the mercantile associations; and on the evening of that day, a grand Festival, to which 500 gentlemen sat down, was given to him in the great room of the Lyceum. On that occasion he delivered a speech of extraordinary power, in which he reviewed the two great questions of Emancipation and Reform, developing the part he had taken upon each; and ended by declaring that he was entirely ignorant of the arrangements likely to grow out of the recent vacancy, and that in the event of being consulted on the matter, his determination should be guided, not by a calculation of interests, but by a balance and comparison of duties.

It was not until the 8th of September that Lord Liverpool requested to see Mr. Canning. An interview took place on the 11th, when the Foreign Office was offered to him by the Premier, and accepted after a struggle. The delay which occurred before this arrangement was carried out may be attributed mainly to Lord Eldon, whose ancient animosity had received no mitigation from time or events. There were other members of the Cabinet who were no less desirous to promote Mr. Canning's departure for India; but Lord Liverpool was firm: he felt that he could not conduct the business of the country without Mr. Canning's aid; and he stated the necessity to the King. His Majesty surrendered his own scruples. His necessities could not do less. In fact if they had not admitted Mr. Canning the Ministry must have been broken up—the most urgent argument of all.

Mr. Canning accepted the Foreign Secretaryship from an overruling sense of duty. Nothing else could have tempted him to give up a magnificent income and all but unlimited power, for a position from which little glory could be extracted, and in which he was to be associated with colleagues, many of whom were opposed to him on principle, and some from personal feeling. There was only one point on which the members of the Cabinet cordially agreed—Reform. On everything else they differed: and it is curious that for all this difference, on Catholic Emancipation, on Commerce, on Education, they were unanimous on Pitt—so different was Pitt from himself. It was all Pitt: one portion was the Pitt of Thatched House celebrity—another the Pitt of the Revolution; one was the Pitt ready to resign for Ireland—another the Pitt ready to suspend the Habeas Corpus. The most remarkable Pittite of them all was Lord Eldon, who used to boast that he had never been absent from a single dinner of the Pitt Club, and who celebrated the defeat of the Catholic Bill in 1825 at one of its most uproarious festivals.

But the great stumbling block in the way of Mr. Canning's foreign policy was the Duke of Wellington. That able soldier was an intrepid admirer of Lord Castlereagh. He found him in office when he came home from the wars. Lord Castlereagh was the minister to greet him on his return, to move votes of thanks to the army, to eulogize the conqueror of Napoleon, to acknowledge official toasts at city dinners, and to utter all the fine ceremonial things that made the Duke's head more giddy than cannon balls. His grace admired his lordship prodigiously, had an implicit veneration for the Holy Alliance, and thought, of course, that Mr. Canning's "system" was an interference of a very impertinent kind with the established impunities of the world.

The duke was one of the last persons that saw Lord Castlereagh alive. He detected the approach of insanity, and Lord Castlereagh himself seemed to be conscious of it. The sensibilities of the public were revolted at the manner of his death ; but few thinking people were much surprised ; and the multitude exulted. Lord Eldon tells us that when the corpse was taken out of the hearse at the door of Westminster Abbey, the people cheered for joy that he was no more.*

That which was really distressing and painful in Lord Castlereagh's history was, not its ghastly issue, but the dreadful efforts which it must have cost him to sustain a position of responsibility, for which his faculties were totally inadequate. That long strain, and the hopeless play upon the surface to keep up appearances, wore him out in the long run. His mind was never very clear or vigorous. He believed in ghosts. He told Sir Walter Scott once that he had actually seen a ghost. Like most other men who have earned the unpleasant distinction of being very much disliked in public, Lord Castlereagh was said to have been agreeable and amiable in private. It is a poor compensation—so let it go. His manners were simple and conciliatory, with an occasional snatch of pleasantry which rendered him a favourite in the foreign office. Between him and Mr. Canning there were certain points of resemblance ; limited chiefly to that fluency and ease of gentlemanly breeding, which was common to both. In all other things, they were conspicuously dissimilar. Castlereagh had purposes below his agreeable manners—Canning had none. Castlereagh always preferred talking over mooted questions with foreign ministers to the more formal course of interchanging notes : it saved him trouble : it enabled him to glean and surmise confidential opinions which would never be entrusted to paper: and it enabled him also to escape responsibility.

* " Life of Lord Eldon," ii. 465.

Canning preferred writing ; it was more clear, honourable and satisfactory ; besides, it fell in with his literary tastes, of which Castlereagh had none. Literature was out of his lordship's way—a sort of disturbing influence; his nature was worldly. Wilberforce says that he was cold-blooded, and compares him to a fish; and repeats the simile so often that one is in some sort compelled to think it must have been apt and exact.

XIII.

FOREIGN POLICY. SPAIN. SPANISH AMERICA. OREGON. GREECE. PORTUGAL.

Mr. Canning's acceptance of the seals of the Foreign Office led to some changes in the administration. Amongst the rest, Mr. Huskisson was appointed President of the Board of Trade, and Treasurer of the Navy. He demurred at first, without a seat in the Cabinet; but the practical inconvenience of extending its numbers rendered his admission at that moment impossible.* A vacancy, however, was made for him at the end of a few months. Mr. Vansittart was removed at the same time from the department of Finance, which he had held by some miraculous means for eleven years, and drafted into the House of Lords with the title of Baron Bexley. He was succeeded in his office by Mr. Robinson, the present Earl of Ripon. The accession of these gentlemen brought fresh strength to the government; and Mr. Huskisson gave a new direction to the commercial policy of the country. Mr. Canning's personal influence was further improved by the appointment of Lord Francis Conyngham in the Foreign Office, which won the king's heart at once.†

* " Speeches of Huskisson." † " Life of Lord Eldon."

When Mr. Canning entered upon the duties of his office, he found himself surrounded by obstacles of a kind which he had no right to anticipate, arising chiefly from the implied engagements in which his predecessor had involved Great Britain with foreign powers. Whatever may have been the artful obscurity under which Mr. Pitt may have studied to veil the object of the war with France, there is no doubt that the whole of Europe accepted Mr. Canning's definition of it; that administration after administration adopted it; and that from the dawn of the Directory to the last hour of the Empire, it was understood that the object we had in view was "the deliverance of Europe." Yet at the close of the war, when the time came to fulfil that object, Lord Castlereagh at the Congress of Vienna sacrificed every one of the smaller and weaker states which had hitherto been protected by England, leaving the world to conclude that we had only made a pretence of defending the independence of nations in order the better in the end to secure impunity to despots. Genoa was made over to Sardinia; Venice to Austria; half of Saxony to Prussia: and Poland was again partitioned. This was the way Lord Castlereagh vindicated the principle of "deliverance" at the Congress of Vienna. To prosecute a war for the avowed purpose of preventing France from interfering with the separate rights of other countries, and then, having succeeded in the war, to annihilate those rights ourselves, was folly as well as perfidy. All the advantages which were gained in 1808 by Mr. Canning's recognition of Spain, and all the glories of the Peninsula, also resulting from his policy, were thrown away at Vienna. We began the crusade in name of the liberties of Europe, and ended it with the Holy Alliance.

In most cases it is nothing but cowardice which makes men act despotically, when they have power to act generously. But Lord Castlereagh must be acquitted of that. It was not through cowardice he committed himself to the Holy Alliance. He was duped; blinded by vanity and exaltation. At one time he actually praised the principles of that alliance, as being essentially Christian and liberal. There is no doubt he thought so. He was cheated into a belief that the potentates who assembled at that congress, were sincerely actuated by anxiety for the happiness and freedom of their subjects. His position in Vienna dazzled and misled him; and when he found out that the compact he had been recommending so strenuously to the admiration of Parliament, was a conspiracy of crowned heads against human rights, the horrors of his situation may be easily conceived.

The first business which presented itself to Mr. Canning, was to devise a system by which the Holy Alliance could be gradually dissolved, and England rescued from the consequences of her undefined relations with its members. The adjourned congress was on the point of assembling at Verona; and as it was necessary to send a representative in place of Lord Castlereagh, who seems to have been terrified at the prospect that lay before him, the Duke of Wellington was selected, and despatched without loss of time. Mr. Canning would have preferred leaving England unrepresented at that meeting, in order to disconnect her still more emphatically from all responsibility arising out of its proceedings; but as that could not be done without risking worse consequences, he was careful in his instructions to the duke to mark by the firmness and explicitness of his views, the course which it was his determination to adopt.

Even if Lord Castlereagh had been animated by the most earnest desire to release England from the net-work of the Holy Alliance, he could not have accomplished it so effectually as Mr. Canning. His intercourse at conferences with monarchs and their ministers, had to a certain extent hampered him. He never could have felt himself so perfectly unshackled as if he had discharged the functions of his office through the ordinary channels of communication. His range of action was abridged by personal considerations. The diplomatic conversation which he cultivated so much, in preference to diplomatic correspondence, left behind a variety of indefinite impressions which had the practical effect of curtailing his independence. Mr. Canning, on the other hand, was free and unfettered. He had nothing to qualify or recall. There could be no implied obligations, no tacit inferences to embarrass his decision upon any question which might come before him. Whatever course he might think fit to take, was at least clear and unobstructed. The natural consequence of this free position subsequently developed itself in the liberation of England from the attractive influences of the allied powers. Mr. Canning was not two years in office, when England moved once more in her own orbit.

But his progress was beset with conflicting difficulties. A notion had got abroad that England was favourable to the principles of the Holy Alliance. This notion was encouraged by Lord Castlereagh's indiscretions, and sedulously propagated, for their own purposes, by the diplomatists of the continent. The war we had been waging against the revolutionary spirit, gave a strong colouring of probability to this suspicion. Having set ourselves so vigorously against revolution in France, it was not inconsistent at first sight to suppose that we should unite with the powers of the continent in resisting future revolutions. There was a powerful party, too, which held to this doctrine, and looked to the Holy Alliance as a bulwark against popular encroachments. There was another party —the Masses, the Millions—who clamoured to be let loose from the Alliance, and who would be satisfied with no proof of our redemption from its trammels, short of open and armed resistance. Mr. Canning had to counteract these opposite feelings and prejudices; and to move onward to his object, without suffering his policy to be embarrassed by either of the extremes. The very first blow he struck in the Congress of Verona, announced to the world the attitude which England was about to take, and her total denial of the right of the Alliance to interfere with the internal affairs of any independent nation.*

It appeared that France had collected a large army in the south, and not having legitimate occupation for it, proposed to employ it in the invasion of Spain. This monstrous project was submitted to Congress; and ardently approved of by Russia. It was now that England spoke out for the first time in this cabal of despots. Having learned from the Duke of Wellington that such a proposition was likely to be made, and that the allies would probably agree to it, Mr. Canning immediately instructed his grace, that "If a declaration of any such determination should be made at Verona, *come what might*, he should refuse the King's consent to become a party to it, *even though the dissolution of the Alliance should be*

---

* "The Alliance," says Mr. Stapleton, "had arrived at such a pitch of confidence that the ministers of the four courts called *in a body* on Mr. Canning to remonstrate with him against the appointment of Sir William à Court as the king's minister to Madrid, on account of the countenance that his presence would give to the Constitutional Government."—" Political Life of the Rt. Hon. G. Canning," i. 146.

the consequence of the refusal." The proposition was made in due form, and, after some interchanges of notes and discussions, agreed to by the allies, the British Plenipotentiary, as he was instructed, refused all participation in these proceedings, and withdrew from the Congress. This was the first step that was taken to show the Alliance that England would not become a party to any act of unjust aggression or unjustifiable interference.

A long correspondence ensued between Mr. Canning and M. de Chateaubriand. Mr. Canning's despatches on this subject are models of diplomacy. M. de Chateaubriand was secretly for war, but affected the most moderate and reasonable dispositions. The French king's speech on opening the Chambers revealed the real intentions of the government, which Mr. Canning had penetrated from the beginning. The speech was, in fact, a declaration of war against Spain, qualified by the slightest imaginable hypothesis. But happily for all interests there was no possibility of disguising the purpose of this war, which was plainly and avowedly to force upon the people of Spain such a constitution as the king (a Bourbon), in the exercise of his absolute authority, should think fit to give them. This principle, it will be seen, makes constitutional rights flow from the king; inverting that fundamental doctrine of English freedom which recognises in the people alone the source of all political power. Against this principle Mr. Canning entered a dignified protest. If the speech, he said, were to be construed, that "the free institutions of the Spanish people could only be legitimately held from the spontaneous gift of the sovereign, first restored to absolute power, and then divesting himself of such portion of that power as he might think proper to part with, it was a principle to which the Spanish nation could not be expected to submit, nor could any British statesman uphold or defend it. *It was, indeed, a principle which struck at the root of the British constitution."* Thus nobly did Mr. Canning vindicate those doctrines of constitutional liberty, which he lived to see established under his own auspices in the remote colonies of that wretched kingdom, on whose behalf he was thus pleading in vain. But although he could not avert from Spain the calamity of a French invasion, he made it clear to all the world that England objected to that proceeding; and that she was no longer even to be suspected of favouring the designs of the Holy Alliance.

The French army made the passage of the Bidassoa. From that moment Mr. Canning interfered no further. He at once disclosed the system which he had already matured and resolved upon. Having first protested against the *principle* of the invasion, he determined to maintain the neutrality of England in the war that followed. By this course he achieved the end he had in view, of severing England from the Holy Alliance, without embroiling her in any consequent responsibilities.

This neutrality—ominous and motionless—had a strange effect upon a people who had been so accustomed at the slightest provocation to fly to arms. But it must be remembered that Europe of 1823 was in a different condition from Europe during the war. The Balance of Power was no longer an intelligible thing to be fought for. It was shadowy and speculative, and represented nothing but dead forms which no art of gunpowder could make live. France had lost her conquests—her central fire was turned into ashes. The little states that used to make the small weights in the huge Balance were all soldered into the large ones: other states had been dismembered; some had been blotted out; others enlarged; none held their original length and breadth: the map was a new map; and although France did march an army across the Pyrenees, and although there was a chance of her marching into Portugal also, and disturbing still farther the palpitations of the Balance—it was not a question nor a time for war. The war policy was over—the necessity was over—there was no contingent benefit to be derived from a war, equivalent to the certain mischief. England had strained her strength, as Canning described it, to the utmost, "and her means were at that precise stage of recovery which made it most desirable that the progress of recovery should not be interrupted." In addition to all this it might be urged, that the beginning a new war, with all its fearful liabilities, is quite a different matter from fighting out one that has already begun.

There were not wanting persons who, with the best intentions, had not sagacity enough to discern the wisdom of Mr. Canning's gradual renunciation of the Holy Alliance. They could not detect on the horizon the first blush of this dawn of liberal principles. They insisted that the sun should rush to his meridian height at once. Neutrality was denounced as timidity; and a distinct motion was brought forward in the Commons condemning the government for want of boldness in its negotiations. The speeches were disorderly and clamourous. Mr. Canning spoke on the third night, and completely turned the tide. He declared his immediate object at Verona was to prevent a war with Spain growing out of "an assumed jurisdiction of the Congress; and the keeping within bounds that *areopagitical* spirit which was beyond the sphere of the original conception and understood principles of the Alliance." This startling declaration fairly lifted the house off its legs. The enthusiasm it produced cannot be very distinctly conveyed in any common form of words. Every body voted for the government, except a few members who were obliged to remain in the body of the house, because the lobby was too crowded to hold them!

The result of the invasion abundantly justified the neutrality. "By a strange course of events," said Mr. Canning, " the whole situation and business of the French in Spain has become changed. They went into the country to defend the fanatical party against the constitutionalists; and now they are actually interfering for the constitutional party with the fanatics." During the progress of these events, several motions were made against the policy of government; but before the debate closed, each motion was regularly converted into a panegyric. Even Hobhouse congratulated the country on the foreign policy of ministers, and said that if the same language had been held at Troppau and Laybach which he believed to have been held at Verona, England would then be in a different situation. He might have gone still farther and said, that if Mr. Canning had been in office a few months earlier, England would never have had a representative at the Congress of Vienna. Canning always protested against the system of holding Congresses for the government of the world.

Mr. Canning's " system" of foreign policy, as described in his own language, resolved itself into this principle of action, that "England should hold the balance, not only between contending nations, but between conflicting principles; that in order to prevent things from going to extremities, she should keep a distinct middle-ground, *staying the plague both ways.*" But as, when he came into office in 1822, the Anti-Liberal influence preponderated, it was necessary for the purpose of preserving the equilibrium, to favour the Liberal scale.* It was not his design to give a triumph to either, but to adjust the balance between both.

The development of this principle, as it applied to nations, was illustrated in the strict but watchful neutrality observed between France and Spain; and, as it applied to principles, in the recognition of the independence of the Spanish-American colonies. The latter act may be regarded as the most important for which Mr. Canning was officially responsible, as that which exerted the widest and most distinct influence over the policy of other countries, and which most clearly and emphatically revealed the *tendency* of his own. It showed that England would recognise institutions raised up by the people, as well as those which were created by kings. It gave the death-blow to the Holy Alliance.

Mr. Canning's conduct in this crisis discovered a magnanimity of spirit worthy of the statesman who enjoys the glory of having called the South American republics into existence; an honour which unquestionably belongs to him. The measure had been strenuously opposed by Lord Castlereagh, and retarded, even as it was, for a quarter of a year by Lord Eldon, who retarded every thing; and had it not been for the energy displayed by Mr. Canning, and the effect produced by the unexpected declaration of his opinions, Mexico, Columbia, and Buenos Ayres might have struggled through a season of ricketty independence, but must have fallen back again into a worse servitude than before. At the first outbreak of the colonies, numbers of young persons volunteered from this country to fight

* "Political Life," i. 474.

on their behalf; but Mr. Canning brought in a bill to prohibit their interference, which he declared would be a direct violation of our treaties with Spain. He consoled them, however, for the disappointment by assuring them that the colonies, if left to themselves, must inevitably become free in the natural course of things. He next opened a confidential communication with Mr. Rush, the American minister, to ascertain whether he was authorised to enter into any convention with England respecting the colonies. But Rush had no powers. He then at once addressed himself to the French minister, and took so bold and decisive a tone, that France, who was suspected of intending to indemnify herself for the war by territorial acquisition in South America, abandoned her design, and left Mr. Canning free to take his own course. He immediately appointed consuls, and the republics from that moment were secure. But he had incredible difficulties to contend against in these negotiations —calumny, deceit, and harassing resistance in a thousand petty shapes. Before he carried the recognition of the independence of Spanish-America to its final triumph, he was twice on the point of resigning his office.

A question was discussed during Mr. Rush's residence in this country, which as it is not yet adjusted, carries with it a surviving interest, greater than its historical importance is likely to sustain. This question concerned the right of territory in that dismal and inhospitable district of country, lying between the Rocky Mountains and the Pacific Ocean, called the Oregon. Both England and America claimed a right of settlement and sovereignty in Oregon, and successive negotiations seemed to have no other result than that of demonstrating the hopelessness of arriving at a point of common agreement. The great error on our part was committed in 1818, when the British plenipotentiaries (Mr. Robinson and Mr. Goulburn), for the sake of a temporary evasion of the difficulties, agreed to throw the country open to both claimants for ten years—leaving the question of boundary for future settlement. But what could be settled at the end of ten years, could have been more easily settled then, before the question had become embarrassed by new liens established in the interval by emigrants on both sides. It is impossible to comprehend the policy of postponing the settlement until the difficulties shall have become increased by the acquisition of local possessions, of which one or the other, or both, to some extent, must be deprived in the long run; adding a practical grievance to be adjusted in addition to the general right. Thus perplexed, the question of the Oregon descended to Mr. Canning.

Mr. Rush, who had instructions to re-open this discussion, waited upon Mr. Canning, and found him ill in bed with the gout. But they nevertheless proceeded to the investigation of the claim. The map of America was spread out upon the bed, and Mr. Rush traced the boundary demanded by America, which ran along the 51° of latitude. Mr. Canning expressed his surprise at the extent of the American claim; and when the negotiations were again renewed, the American minister reduced his demand to the 49°; to which Mr. Canning refused to accede. Further attempts were made to bring about a pacific settlement of this disputed boundary; and Mr. Canning, from an anxious desire to avoid hostilities, proposed a middle course, which was rejected by America. Mr. Canning never omitted an opportunity in public or private of testifying his amicable disposition towards the United States. The weight of his influence tended materially to restrain the temper of the English people, which was such, throughout these and other similarly hopeless negotiations, that Lord Castlereagh told Mr. Rush that war could be produced by holding up a finger.

Having failed in obtaining our acquiescence in her demand up to the 49° of north latitude, America has lately set up a claim to the whole country. She claims upon two grounds:—One by right of discovery, the other by right of treaty with Spain. Her claim by right of discovery, dates in 1792 ;—her claim by right of treaty, dates in 1819, when Spain made over all her own possessions in that unmapped country to the United States. Without descending into details, it is clear that these two rights cannot co-exist. America cannot claim through Spain in 1819, that which, she says, she acquired by right of discovery in 1792. Spain could not confer upon America, that which America herself already possessed. There is another reason why Spain could not bestow Oregon upon America—namely, that it did not belong to her. "Such a union of titles," says Mr. Rush, "imparting validity [perhaps he means *in*-validity] to each other, does not often exist," —an observation which might be safely carried a little further, by saying that such an union never existed before.

The same principles which Mr. Canning had already applied to the case of Spain were brought to bear upon all parts of the world, in which either our interests or our sympathies were engaged, and they were uniformly crowned by equally gratifying results: loosening everywhere the gripe of despotism, enlarging the rights of the people, and establishing liberal institutions within the limits which he considered to be essential to their permanence. In this way he obtained the amelioration of the Turkish rule in Greece, without hurting the just dignity of the Porte, who protested very properly against foreign interference in her domestic affairs.

So long as it was possible to conduct this enlightened policy noiselessly, and without any specific exposition of the system upon which it was based, Mr. Canning was content to abide by the results of his exertions; every day becoming more and more visible in the growing prosperity of England, and the rapidly-declining influence of the Holy Alliance. But an occasion at last arose, which drew him into a more decided manifestation of his views. In violation of an existing treaty, and urged onward by apostolical fury, Spain had made a perfidious attempt to overthrow the new constitution of Portugal. She dreaded the close neighbourhood of free institutions; and, sustained by the sinister influence of France, she resolved to make a powerful effort to annihilate them. Intelligence of the imminent peril of our ancient ally reached ministers on the night of the 8th of December, 1826; on the 11th (Sunday intervening) a message from the King was communicated to Parliament; and on the 12th, a discussion ensued, which as long as a trace of English eloquence shall remain amongst the records of the world, will never be forgotten.

Mr. Canning was now at the height of his power, wielding an influence more extended and complete than any foreign minister in this country had ever enjoyed before. The subject to which he addressed himself in this instance, was one that invoked the grandest attributes of his genius, and derived a peculiar felicity from being developed by a British minister ; and, above all, by that minister who had liberated the new world, and crushed the tyrannies of the old. It was not surprising then, that, bringing to it all the vigour and enthusiasm of his intellect, and that vital beauty of style which was the pervading charm of his great orations, he should have transcended on this occasion all his past efforts, and delivered a speech which not merely carried away the admiration of his hearers, but literally inflamed them into frenzy. The fabulous spells of Orpheus, who made the woods dance reels and sarabands, never achieved so wonderful a piece of sorcery as this speech of Mr. Canning's achieved over the passions, the judgment, the prejudices, and the stolid unbelief of the House of Commons.

After giving a luminous detail of the long-existing connexion between Portugal and England, and the obligations by which we were bound to assist our old ally, Mr. Canning proceeded to state the case. It would be impossible to describe the effect produced by the following little sentence:

"The precise information, on which alone we could act, arrived only on Friday last. On Saturday the decision of the government was taken—on Sunday we obtained the sanction of his Majesty—on Monday we came down to Parliament—and at this very hour, while I have now the honour of addressing this House —BRITISH TROOPS ARE ON THEIR WAY TO PORTUGAL!"

The House fairly vibrated with emotion at this unexpected statement. It was the concentration in a single instant of the national enthusiasm of a whole age. At every sentence he was interrupted with huzzas! Then, when he spoke of the Portuguese constitution :

" With respect to the character of that constitution, I do not think it right, at present, to offer any opinion; privately I have my own opinion. But, as an English minister, all I have to say is, may God prosper the attempt made by Portugal to obtain constitutional liberty, and may that nation be as fit to receive and cherish it, as, on other occasions, she is capable of discharging her duties amongst the nations of Europe."

Luckily there is always an obstructionist in the House of Commons—a Mr. Hume—to start up with an objection by way of rider to the very climax of unanimity : this useful functionary discharged his office on this memorable occasion with the happiest effect, for he succeeded in calling up Mr. Canning a second time, when he delivered a speech of loftier eloquence, and even more sustained energy than that with which he introduced the address. With reference to the French occupation of Spain, he admitted that it was to be lamented, but he denied that it was worth a war, and asserted that its effects had been infinitely exaggerated. As to Spain herself, she was no longer what she had been:

"Is the Spain of the present day, the Spain of which the statesmen of the times of William and Anne were so much afraid ? Is it indeed the nation whose puissance was expected to shake England from her sphere ? No, sir, it was quite another Spain—it was the Spain, within the limits of whose empire the sun never set—it was Spain *with the Indies* that excited the jealousies and alarmed the imaginations of our ancestors."

Admitted that the entrance of the French into Spain disturbed the balance of power. Ought we to have gone to war to restore it ? Was there no other way to adjust this balance of power, which fluctuated eternally with the growth and decay of nations ?

" Was there no other mode of resistance, than by a direct attack upon France—or by a war to be undertaken on the soil of Spain ? What, if the possession of Spain might be rendered harmless in other hands—harmless as regarded us—and valueless to the possessors ? Might not compensation for disparagement be obtained, and the policy of our ancestors vindicated, by means better adapted to the present time? If France occupied Spain, was it necessary, in order to avoid the consequences of that occupation, that we should blockade Cadiz? No. I looked another way—I sought materials of compensation in another hemisphere. Contemplating Spain such as our ancestors had known her, I resolved that if France had Spain it should not be Spain *with the Indies*. I CALLED THE NEW WORLD INTO EXISTENCE TO REDRESS THE BALANCE OF THE OLD."

This speech as has been said of the eloquence of Chatham, " was an era in the Senate." The effect was tremendous. " It was an epoch in a man's life," says a member of the Commons, " to have heard him. I shall never forget the deep, moral earnestness of his tone, and the blaze of glory that seemed to light up his features when he spoke of the Portuguese Charter." The same writer furnishes the following details.

" He was equally grand when, in his reply, he said: 'I do not believe that *there* is that Spain of which our ancestors were so justly jealous, that Spain upon whose territories it was proudly boasted the sun never set!' But when, in the style and manner of Chatham, he said, ' I looked to Spain in the Indies ; I called a *new* world into existence, to redress the balance of the old,' the effect was actually terrific. It was as if every man in the house had been electrified. Tierney, who before that was shifting in his seat, and taking off his hat and putting it on again, and taking large and frequent pinches of snuff, and turning from side to side, till he, I suppose, wore his breeches through, seemed petrified, and sat fixed, and staring with his mouth open for half a minute! Mr. Canning seemed actually to have increased in stature, his attitude was so majestic. I remarked his flourishes were made with his left arm; the effect was new, and beautiful ; his chest heaved and expanded, his nostril dilated, a noble pride slightly curled his lip ; and age and sickness were dissolved and forgotten in the ardour of youthful genius; all the while a serenity sat on his brow, that pointed to deeds of glory. It reminded me, and came up to what I have heard, of the effects of Athenian eloquence."*

* " Diary of an M.P."

Mr. Canning had now reached the pinnacle of his fame. His ambition had accomplished nearly its highest aims—his genius had overwhelmed all opposition. How little did England anticipate, at this proud moment, that she was so soon to lose her accomplished and patriotic statesman!

XIV.

COMMERCIAL POLICY. PARLIAMENTARY REFORM. CATHOLIC EMANCIPATION. TEST ACT.

Mr. Canning's commercial policy was indentical with that of Mr. Huskisson. His general principle was this —that commerce flourished best when wholly unfettered by restrictions. But, as modern nations had grown up under various systems, and were never secure from fluctuation, he maintained that it was necessary to observe a discriminating judgment in the application of this principle. The wise course was always to keep it in sight, and to work towards it, as the final aim of legislation. He held the doctrine of protection, in the abstract, to be unsound as well as unjust. Bounties, monopolies, and all special exemptions in favour of particular classes or particular interests, were consequently the objects against which his commercial system was cautiously but continuously directed.

The Reciprocity Act, brought in by Mr. Robinson in 1823, was an indication of that system. By this act the King in council was authorised to place the ships of foreign states, importing articles into Great Britain or her colonies on the same footing of duties as British ships, provided such foreign states extended a like equality to British ships trading with their ports. It will be seen at a glance that the *principle* of extinguishing restrictions was thus fully declared, while its practical application was carefully regulated by a scale of safe equivalents.

The powers granted by this act, were sufficiently expansive to meet every contingency. If the King in council had the power of relinquishing the duties on foreign ships and cargoes, where the principle of reciprocity was mutually conceded, he had also a retaliatory power of imposing increased duties where that principle was evaded or resisted. Mr. Canning was not slow to avail himself of this power, as an indirect means of compelling other countries to admit a more reasonable spirit into their tariffs. A curious instance occurred with reference to Holland, in 1826. M. Falck, the Dutch minister, having made a one-sided proposition for the admission of English ships, by which a considerable advantage would have accrued to Holland, a long and tedious negotiation ensued. It was dragged on, month after month, without arriving one step nearer to a consummation, the Dutch still holding out for their own interests. At last Mr. Canning's patience was exhausted. Sir Charles Bagot, our ambassador at the Hague, was one day attending at court, when a despatch in cypher was hastily put into his hand. It was very short, and evidently very urgent; but unfortunately Sir Charles, not expecting such a communication, had not the key of the cypher with him. An interval of intense anxiety followed, until he obtained the key; when to his infinite astonishment he decyphered the following despatch from the Secretary of State for Foreign Affairs:

" In matters of commerce, the fault of the Dutch
  Is giving too little and asking too much ;

> With equal advantage the French are content,
> So we'll clap on Dutch bottoms a twenty per cent.
> Twenty per cent.,
> Twenty per cent.,
> Nous frapperons Falck with twenty per cent.
> GEORGE CANNING."

The minister kept his word. While this singular despatch was on its way to the Hague, an order in council was issued to put into effect the intention it announced.

The three great domestic questions in Mr. Canning's time, and which every year acquired increased urgency and importance were Parliamentary Reform, Catholic Emancipation, and the Test Act. They have all been disposed of since, and very little interest attaches to them now except that of the vague wonder with which we look back upon such strange monuments of an unwise antiquity. And twenty years ago was a barbarous age touching such questions in England.

In 1827, Mr. Canning made use of the following declaration:

"There are two questions to which I wish to reply. I have been asked what I intend to do with the question of Parliamentary Reform, when it is brought forward? What do I intend to do with it? Why, oppose it, as I have invariably done during the whole of my parliamentary career. What do I intend to do with the Test Act? Oppose it."

These were the incomprehensible points of Mr. Canning's political creed. It seems that he took them up from the beginning, as articles of faith, and could never consent to submit them to the test of reason.

He held that reform meant revolution. So did Mr. Pitt—when it suited his purposes. But it is remarkable that neither of them perceived that their own measure of Catholic Emancipation had been resisted all along by their own party upon precisely the same ground. Mr.

Canning was constantly told that Emancipation meant nothing more nor less than the destruction of Church and State; and he over and over again showed the fallacy of the assertion. Yet he could not detect the same fallacy when it was applied to the question of Parliamentary Reform.

It is surprising, too, that the barefaced corruption of the old system did not strike him as something inconsistent with the spirit and obligations of the Constitution. In 1792, the borough of Gatton was publicly advertised for sale, not for a single parliament, but the fee simple itself, with the power of nominating two representatives for ever, described by the auctioneer as "an elegant contingency." In 1801, Fox described Old Sarum as consisting of an old encampment and two or three cottages; another borough sustained its privileges upon the stump of a tree, which was duly represented in the English Parliament by two very respectable members. The franchise was equally rotten. These facts were notorious; but Mr. Canning resisted all attempts to remedy the monstrous evils they disclosed, because he believed that every advance towards the independence of the Commons would be, in effect, an advance towards a preponderating democracy, under the influence of which the Crown and the peerage would be ultimately overwhelmed. "The reformers mean democracy," he exclaimed, in his celebrated speech at Liverpool on this subject, in 1818; "they mean democracy, and nothing else; and give them but a House of Commons constructed on their own principles, the peerage and the throne may exist for a day, but may be swept from the face of the earth by the first angry vote of such a House of Commons." His whole theory is enclosed in these few words; making no account whatever of that principle of elasticity by which our constitution is always enabled to adapt itself to the requisitions of social progress.

At an early period of his career, Mr. Canning agreed with Pitt in treating reform, not as a question shut out for ever from consideration by an immutable necessity, but as a question which might be entertained under certain circumstances. It was then argued, that, however justifiable it might be to demand a reform in Parliament in times of tranquillity, the case was altered in times of disturbance. This method of treating reform, although apparently more friendly, was in reality more hostile than the other, which at least had the merit of throwing the whole question open to discussion. By this more ingenious device, the constitutional right was set aside on the very threshold. If the demand for reform might be set up at one time, and not at another, what became of the constitutional right of petition, with which the people are supposed to be invested at all times? Is it a privilege which depends on the complexion of the sky? Is it to be exercised only in fine weather? Must a man never utter his opinions when it rains or thunders? Is this essential element of popular liberty dependent on the weather-glass? Mr. Canning appears to have been ashamed of the hypocrisy of this way of dealing with reform, and to have adopted, latterly, the bolder course of opposing it *in limine*. To that mode of argument—which placed the question fairly on its merits—we are largely indebted for the rapid strides it afterwards made; and thus, even on this last fortress of ancient Toryism, we find his happy genius promoting the conquests of the people over the prejudices of party.

Over the final accomplishment of Catholic Emancipation—so long contested, and so pertinaciously resisted—

he exercised a direct and important influence. The question itself presents one of the most extraordinary chapters in our history. Its progress may be tracked, by its disturbing power, through the successive administrations of thirty-five years. It divided all the cabinets, in spite of the strenuous efforts that were made to keep it out—and finally broke them up. The members of the government were divided upon it, before the coalition between Pitt and the Duke of Portland; the coalition increased the dissentions. Lord Fitzwilliam was sent to Ireland, to reflect, in the government of that country, the checks and balances of the English Cabinet. Then came the Union, with its implied promise of Emancipation, which the minister could not keep. The King was flickering in various stages of insanity; one day ill, another well, in his general capacity—such as it was: but never well enough to see the justice or policy of Emancipation. In this dilemma, and upon this question, Pitt was forced to resign. The next administration was formed in the forlorn hope of being able to stand between the insanity of the King and the common sense of the country. It failed, as a matter of course—this terrible nightmare hovering over its head, and paralysing its energies. In 1804, Pitt returned. He tried to evade the difficulty by a subterfuge, and finally escaped from it by death. The Grey and Grenville administration was annihilated by the same Catholic Question in eighteen months; and Perceval was shut up from 1807 to 1812, between the King's insanity and the Catholic Claims. His government resisted them all throughout; but we have Sir Robert Peel's authority for the assertion, that it did not resist them upon permanent grounds or upon principle. Even at that time, Emancipation had so far vanquished its opponents, that they could no longer construct a cabinet upon the avowed principle of hostility to it; and then came Lord Liverpool's administration, when it was made an open question. Even in this shape, it was a terrible obstruction to the government; the system of neutral opinions and open voting having been found, from experience, to be most unfortunate and unfavourable to the administration of the affairs of the country. But in whatever shape it came, open or closed, this Catholic Question hung, like the Old Man of the Sea, upon the neck of the Tory party, through all its phases, for nearly half a century, and broke it at last.*

From disclosures which have been subsequently made, it is now known that the sturdiest antagonists of the Catholic Claims had been giving way from time to time within the Cabinet itself. Lord Liverpool had become convinced that the period was approaching when the Catholic Claims could no longer be resisted; and it is said, that, although he felt it would have been inconsistent in him to give them his support as Premier, he had resolved at least to mitigate the opposition to them in the Lords; that it was his intention to retire from office, leaving Canning as his successor, and, when the Claims should have been disposed of, to accept some less laborious

* Yet even when Emancipation was on the eve of being carried, such was the steadfastness of the old faith, that the extreme Tory party had not the least suspicion that such a thing was possible. Wilberforce tells us that he called on Southey in May, 1828, and found him anticipating civil war. He said that the Roman Catholic priests would, undoubtedly, excite their flocks to insurrection. Wilberforce concurred, but thought the House would concede, as they had done in 1782. To which Southey replied, that the Administration of 1782 was weak; "but *now*— the Duke of Wellington," said he, stretching out his arm stiffly and pulling up his sleeve—" ha !—the duke IS a great man!"—" Life of Wilberforce," v. 300. It is very remarkable that the opposite opinion was held by some of the Liberal party. Sydney Smith predicted that the No Popery leaders would desert their followers, when it suited their purposes.—" Works of the Rev. S. Smith," ii. 418.

appointment under the administration of his friend.*
His illness arrested all these plans.

Sir Robert Peel made a similar confession in 1829. He said, that when he found himself in a minority of twenty-one on the Catholic Question, in 1825, he felt his position as home minister untenable. He thought it was no longer advisable that he should remain charged with the administration of Irish affairs, when he was thus defeated on an Irish question; that he went to Lord Liverpool, told him *that the time was come when something respecting the Catholics, in his opinion, ought to be done;* and begged to be relieved from his office. But Lord Liverpool threatened in that case to retire also; so Sir Robert consented to remain, and " try another experiment on the feelings of the country." In 1826, there was a new House of Commons, which increased the majority in favour of the Catholics in the following year to twenty-three. The " experiment," therefore was making fearful advances towards a crisis, one way or the other. In 1828, the fruit ripened into the affirmation of a resolution favourable to the principle of adjustment; and Sir Robert's sense of expediency was wound up to its height. He saw clearly that the question had got a-head of the bigotry and intolerance, and even of the influence, in doors and out of doors, of the party with which he had been connected all his life, and whose exclusive doctrines he had pledged himself over and over again to maintain to the death. He saw that whoever was minister, Emancipation must be carried, by somebody, in spite of King, Lords, and Commons; and, therefore, in the critical moment, when office lay in one scale, and the civil and religious freedom of some seven millions of the King's liege sub-

* " Speeches of Mr. Huskisson," i. 128.

jects lay in the other, he resolved to carry it himself. He immediately went to the Duke, and intimated to his grace that he was not only prepared and anxious to retire from office, but that, seeing the current of public opinion setting in, in favour of the Catholic Claims, he should no longer feel justified in opposing them, in whatever situation he might find himself. " To this," he continued, " I afterwards added, that to this GREAT OBJECT *I was ready to make a sacrifice of consistency and friendship.*" This was too significant to be misunderstood. The secretary was secure either way; in office, to float with the aforesaid current of public opinion, which he found setting in with such extraordinary force and rapidity, or, out of office, to embarrass and destroy, by the help of his new ally, public opinion, any administration that might attempt the government on the principle of resistance to the Catholic Claims.

There is a very excellent maxim of the good old Tory school, which insists upon the prudence of taking the ball at the hop ; but never in the experience of an English cabinet was there such a hop of the ball as this, and never was a hop taken with such timely dexterity.

But, the most curious part of the secretary's case was his sudden discovery of the overwhelming importance of an object which, in the face of the most convincing proofs to the contrary, adduced by himself in another part of this same speech, for a widely different purpose, he had all along resisted, as utterly incompatible with the safety of existing institutions. Catholic Emancipation had it seems become a great object in 1828—so great that he was ready to keep office, even at the total sacrifice of his consistency and his friends, in order to be enabled to carry it. Yet upon his own showing—(and his statement of the ministerial and parliamentary history of the question is so full and explicit that it hardly needs any addition)—this very question had been disorganising every cabinet for the previous five-and-thirty years ; distracting their councils ; rendering effective co-operation for the public good nearly impossible ; and frequently forcing them either to capitulate for place by a compromise of differences under a veil of neutrality so thin that the whole world could see hypocrisy, selfishness, and insincerity behind it—or to abandon office from inability to keep out the tide that was flooding them in their seats; and yet with all these accumulating evidences of the irresistible nature of these claims before him, and of the pernicious consequences of continuing to resist them, Sir Robert Peel never saw the imperative necessity of conceding them until he conceded them himself in 1829. He could not even see it (notwithstanding the revolution his mind had undergone in 1825), when Mr. Canning came into power in 1827, on which occasion we find him vindicating his refusal to take office under Mr. Canning on this sole ground—*that it was impossible for him to acquiesce in any proposition for granting further concessions to the Catholics.* His words were these:

"The grounds on which I retired from office are simply these; I have taken, from the first moment of my public life, an active and decided part on a great and vital question—that of the extension of political privileges to the Roman Catholics. * * *My opposition is founded on principle.* I think that the continuance of those bars which prevent the acquisition of political power by the Catholics, is necessary for the maintenance of the constitution and the interests of the Established Church."

This was in 1827. What became of the "maintenance of the constitution," and the "interests of the Established Church," in 1829?

From this rapid outline of the progress of the Catholic Question, it will be seen that, notwithstanding all the impediments thrown up against it by kings, chancellors, and cabinets, it continued gradually to make way from the expiration of the regency restrictions, when Mr. Canning, released from all personal obligations to the King, first devoted himself to its advocacy, down to the very last hour when he bequeathed to his successors the glory of carrying it. The sacrifices he made for the sake of this question were great. Office was the least of them. He sacrificed for it all prospect of representing in Parliament that university in which he had been educated, the crowning object of all the dreams of his youthful ambition. Every thing was against him on this question: his own party, the King, the Duke of York, the premier, the chancellor, the House of Lords; and, for many years the House of Commons, and even popular prejudices in England. He persevered against them all. He brought his influence and his eloquence to bear upon all these masses of resistance. He kept aloof from all personal intercourse with Catholic delegates, that he might stand clear of suspicion, and that the purity and independence of his motives should be above impeachment. He bore down these antagonist forces one by one—weakened their powers of hostility, and effectually succeeded in winning over the most influential and indispensable opinions. What actual steps he took in the Cabinet cannot be known, but they may be readily surmised. It was quite evident that, under his influence, the tone of the Cabinet became slowly liberalised ; and that he had secured the right to propound the Catholic Question for discussion amongst his colleagues, and to communicate with his Majesty upon it, whenever he saw fit. To his judicious and unwearied labours in this cause, must be mainly attributed its early settlement. He prepared the way for it; he overcame the greatest obstacle of all, the reluctance of George IV. If he had not done wonders with the servile bigotry of that monarch, the Duke of Wellington and Sir Robert Peel would have been powerless in his hands in 1829.

It is singular that, earnestly engaged as he was in this struggle for the rights of conscience on behalf of the Catholics, Mr. Canning should have entertained so strong an opinion on the subject of the Test Act. He would have relinquished any conviction rather than that. It was the one invincible resolution of his life, never to yield up the Test Act.* Upon this question his determination was as fixed, as it must always remain inexplicable.

* "Is there no satisfactory reason," demands the late Lord Rossmore, "why a mind like that of Mr. Canning should depart from his own general principles in the case of the dissenters alone ? May he not have reasoned thus ? If I concede the wishes of the dissenters separately may I not weaken the common cause, the dissenters not having much sympathy with the claims of the Catholics? But if I carry Emancipation I secure the repeal of the Test and Corporation Acts; for if the former succeeds the latter follows."—" Letter on Catholic Emancipation," i., 1828.

How Mr. Canning might have ultimately acted on this question, it would be a bold assumption to predicate; but it is quite certain that his opinions were as strong against the repeal of the Test Act as against Parliamentary Reform. Of that fact there is no doubt whatever.

XV.

THE CROWN OF THE STATESMAN'S AMBITION.   THE GRAVE.

IN 1824, Mr. Canning visited Dublin, and was received with enthusiasm by all classes of the people. Some of the newspapers speculated upon the object of his visit, which they supposed to be connected with political affairs; but the marriage of his only daughter, in the following year, to the Marquis of Clanricarde, set curiosity at rest.

In 1826, he paid a visit to Paris. The King treated him with unusual marks of distinction; court etiquette was especially relaxed in his favour; and he had the honour of dining at the royal table, which, at that time was considered an extraordinary stretch of condescension to confer on an untitled gentleman.

He had now held the office of Foreign Secretary nearly five years; and during that time had been the principal labourer. Lord Liverpool's utility seemed to consist principally in the torpid weight of his character. Mr. Canning, as leader of the House of Commons, discharged, in effect, the most responsible duties of the government. These constant exertions made visible inroads on his health; and his situation was otherwise rendered irksome by the known political hostility of the

Duke of York, on account of his opinions on the Catholic Question. The Duke had gone so far as to address his Majesty on the necessity of securing uniformity of sentiment in the Cabinet against the Catholic Claims; an interference with the royal discretion, which, coming from the Heir Presumptive, might have led to serious inconvenience, so far as Mr. Canning was concerned, had not the illness and death of his Royal Highness, which followed soon afterwards, removed the necessity of any discussion on the subject. The Duke died in January, 1827. Mr. Canning, whose state of health was already precarious, caught a cold at the funeral of his Royal Highness, which laid the foundation of his mortal illness.

Early in the following month, while Mr. Canning was at Brighton, endeavouring to shake off his malady, he received the painful intelligence that Lord Liverpool had been seized with apoplexy, followed by total insensibility. Mr. Peel happened to be in Brighton at the time, and it was agreed, upon an interview with his Majesty, that no step should be taken in the matter until some time should have been allowed to elapse. This was from a sense of delicacy to his lordship; for no reasonable expectations were entertained of his recovery. All that could be hoped for was, that he might be restored to sufficient consciousness of his condition to send in his resignation.

In the meanwhile the Corn Bill and Catholic Emancipation were coming on in both Houses of Parliament, the absence of Lord Liverpool deprived the one of an influential supporter, and relieved the other from an adverse vote. But it was of little consequence; for neither of these measures had the slightest chance of success. Mr. Canning struggled on against illness until the close of March, still performing his arduous duties in the Commons, and endeavouring to avert the inconveniences arising from the state of the administration; the most dangerous of which was the opportunity it gave for speculation and cabal on the part of those who were inimical to liberal principles. At length all personal delicacy concerning Lord Liverpool was at an end. There was no hope of his lordship's restoration: Parliament and the country were getting restless, and it was absolutely necessary that something should be done.

In Lord Liverpool, now lost to the public service for ever, Mr. Canning had to mourn the deprivation of a steadfast and honourable personal friend;—the Mr. Jenkinson of Christ Church, whom he remembered so well in his brown coat and the buttons with the initials of the great orators; the Lord Hawkesbury of the young days of parliamentary strife and experimental diplomacy, who used to make such gallant prophecies about the war in France, and whose empty seriousness used to give such offence to George III.; and, finally, that Lord Liverpool who, by mere respectability of character, kept together for fifteen years a cabinet composed of the most incongruous materials that had probably ever been assembled. The secret of Lord Liverpool's success in retaining so long a lease of power lay in the fact that he did not possess a single quality calculated to provoke the jealousy or excite the insubordination of his colleagues. His control was purely nominal. Slow, upright, practical—he never intefered with others, and was suffered to go on in his track without check or interruption. Nobody feared him, nobody disliked him, nobody doubted his probity. His good qualities were all of a negative kind—the safest for a minister who seeks strength in combination. And this was Lord Liverpool's pre-eminent merit. He had not a particle of genius; but he possessed precisely the cast of understanding by which he was enabled to surround himself with able men, and, in spite of specific differences, to preserve a sort of loose harmony amongst them, amply sufficient for all the purposes of an effective government.

On the 27th of March Mr. Canning had a long interview with the King on the subject of a new administration. His Majesty desired to have Mr. Canning's opinion upon the practicability of placing a peer holding Lord Liverpool's views on the Catholic Question, at the head of the government. Mr. Canning replied that in such a case he should feel it his duty to retire from a situation in which he could no longer render any efficient service; and that, in fact, he could not accept of any other position than that which should confer on him the powers of the First Minister of the crown.* This assertion of his personal claims appears to have thrown the negotiations once more into embarrassment; and another delay intervened before any further step was taken. Mr. Canning looked upon the office of Prime Minister of England as his "inheritance." He was the last survivor of the great race of statesmen who had been contemporaneous with Pitt and Fox. As second minister also in the late administration, he had a right upon being thus consulted, to vindicate in his own person the principle of direct succession.

Public opinion was strongly in favour of his appointment. It was manifest that the intelligent of all parties looked to him as the only man fit to direct the councils of the government. The Tory aristocracy began to be alarmed —that aristocracy whose pride of place he had so often had occasion to rebuke. There was not a moment to be

* "Political Life," iii. 315.

lost in laying before his Majesty an imperious remonstrance and protest. These noble persons had an undoubted right in their capacity of privy councillors to offer their advice to the King; but in this instance it assumed a shape of menace and dictation. A certain noble duke—whose name is not withheld from prudential motives, but simply because it might renew discussions which could now be productive of no useful result—waited upon his Majesty on the 31st of March, four days after Mr. Canning's interview, and explicitly informed his Majesty that he, and eight other peers (great borough-mongers), whom he was then and there authorised to represent, would at once withdraw their support from the government, if his Majesty placed Mr. Canning at its head. The threat was at best ill-considered, and showed that passion had overcome the proverbial craft of Toryism on this occasion. His Majesty's sense of the conditional allegiance of the Duke and his pocket peers, was shown in the course which he adopted immediately after his grace retired from the royal closet—his grace congratulating himself no doubt all the way home on the impression his energetic conduct had produced on the mind of the King. On the 12th of April, Mr. C. Wynn rose in the House of Commons, and made the following announcement:—"I move for a new writ for the borough of Newport (Isle of Wight), the Right Honourable George Canning having accepted the office of First Commissioner of the Treasury." The announcement was received with deafening cheers, which, again and again renewed, testified unequivocally the feelings with which Mr. Canning's appointment was regarded by the popular branch of the legislature. Whatever opinion the House of Lords might entertain on the subject, it was evident that he had the King and the Commons with him, at all events.

It was only now, however, that Mr. Canning's practical difficulties commenced. Hitherto the malice of his own party—for he had nothing to dread from his opponents,—had exhausted itself in petty obstructions and supercilious calumnies, by which they tried to whisper away his character and his influence, and failed conspicuously. But they still had it in their power to throw obstacles in the way of the formation of the new Cabinet. To this point, therefore, they assiduously addressed themselves, with a community of sentiment which looked very like premeditation, although we are compelled, for honour's sake, to take their word that there was no concert in their proceedings.

Mr. Canning's first aim was to secure the services of all the members of Lord Liverpool's government, and he immediately invited them to join the administration which he had been commanded to construct. His reception amongst them—amongst the very persons with whom he had been for some years past intimately associated in office,—was significant. Their unanimity was wonderful! Lord Eldon was very old, and had long wished to resign, and thought this a favourable moment to carry out his purpose. Lord Westmoreland could not say what he would do, until he knew what everybody else would do, and then he would do nothing. Mr. Peel could not join any administration with a person at the head of it who was known to be favourable to Catholic Emancipation. The Duke of Wellington had the same scruples. Lord Bathurst fluttered a little, and then resigned. And Lord Melville, for whom Mr. Canning had done so much in the old times, went with the rest of the pack. There remained firm only four members of Lord Liverpool's government; and in addition to this wholesale desertion, there were four members of the King's household, and nine members of the government, who also seceded. In short, the whole of the Anti-Catholic party refused point-blank to serve under Mr Canning—a circumstance which might have been borne with a calmer endurance, had it not been accompanied by demonstrations of personal ill-will, which chafed the proud spirit it could not subdue.

It was supposed (or hoped) that this almost total defection of the old cabinet would paralyse Mr. Canning, and compel him to abandon the task he had undertaken. This was a mistake. All the great vacancies were rapidly filled up. Having failed with the Anti-Catholic party in the attempt to form a ministry on the principles of Lord Liverpool's government, he had recourse at once to the Whigs and to his personal friends. On the 27th of April, every office in the government was filled up. The Duke of Clarence, heir presumptive to the throne, took the head of the Admiralty, on the very day following Lord Melville's resignation. Lord Anglesey succeeded to the Duke of Wellington's seat at the Ordnance; Lord Lyndhurst was made Chancellor; Lord Dudley and Mr. Sturges Bourne were appointed to the Foreign and Home Departments; Mr. Robinson was called to the Upper House; and Mr. Canning, retaining the valuable services of Mr. Huskisson in his former office, united in his own person the offices of Chancellor of the Exchequer, and First Lord of the Treasury, for the purpose of giving full effect to the budget, which it was his intention to bring in himself. The last great political appointment sanctioned by Mr. Canning, or under his immediate auspices, was that of Lord William Bentinck to the government of India.* He might have bestowed this important office in a more influential quarter, had he been disposed to buy up the vote of a powerful opponent. For there were persons capable of making proposals for so lucrative a place, stating at the same time, that upon the answer depended their determination as to whether they should support or oppose the government. Such proposals, it is needless to say, received a direct and summary negative.

Of all the seceders, Mr. Canning considered Mr. Peel the only one who was justified by his position, or governed by sincere motives. Mr. Peel's manner was very cordial to him on this occasion, and Mr. Canning, who had never before given him credit for heartiness of feeling, easily suffered his *amour propre* to be flattered into the persuasion that Mr. Peel's retirement was dictated by the most upright principles. Perhaps it was. But as Mr. Canning was not aware that, only two years before, Mr. Peel had privately announced to Lord Liverpool, his conversion to the necessity of Emancipation; and as he could not be aware that, only two years afterwards, Mr. Peel actually carried Emancipation himself—it may be affirmed, that Mr. Canning was not sufficiently enlightened upon facts, to decide finally on the purity of Mr. Peel's conduct towards him. Posterity will put all these strange particulars together, and draw its own deductions.

The Duke of Wellington retired from the Cabinet, and in order to mark his retirement more energetically, threw up the command of the army also, because he could not conscientiously join an administration, presided over by a minister who differed from the King on the subject of

* "Political Life," iii. 345.

Emancipation. Yet immediately after Mr. Canning's death he resumed the command of the army under Lord Goderich, who had differed from the King all his life on the subject of Emancipation. The letters to the King, to Lord Eldon, and Lord Goderich, in which his Grace endeavoured to explain away this proceeding, only make the matter worse, and reduce it at once to a personal question. It was supposed that the Duke looked to the office of Prime Minister himself; and during these negotiations, the proposition to place his Grace at the head of the government was more than once made to Mr. Canning. But his Grace declared that he had no such desire ; and it is not for anybody, let circumstances suggest what they may, to contravene what the Duke says was passing in his own mind. But how is the Duke's conduct on broad principles in 1829 to be reconciled with his inflexible resistance in 1827 ? What became of the King's conscience, or the Duke's, then ?*

The explanations which ensued in both Houses of Parliament partook of this same character, and were full of false professions and sinister inconsistencies. Mr. Peel got great credit for the frankness of his speech, in which he denied that he had acted in concert with the rest of the retiring ministers ; but people still thought, nevertheless, that it was a remarkable coincidence that four out of five resignations should have been sent in within three hours. A few hundred years hence, when these debates come to be read by an antiquarian posterity, the same thought will

* The Duke's correspondence with Mr. Canning was very plausible. He tried to make it appear that Mr. Canning's temper had placed matters in a wrong light ; but that he was himself too calm and elevated to be moved by the passions of the lower world. " I am not in the habit," he says, " of deciding upon such matters hastily or in anger ; and the proof of this is, that I never had a quarrel with a man in my life." A few months afterwards he fought a duel with Lord Winchelsea.

probably strike the mind of the curious explorer of our records.

The *tone* of the opposition throughout the irregular and intemperate discussions which took place at different times on the ministerial changes, plainly betrayed the *animus* which lay at the bottom. Mr. Canning was literally baited in both Houses. The attacks which were made upon him are unparalleled in our parliamentary history for personality;— their coarseness, malignity, and venom are all of a personal character. It was not against a system of policy they were directed—nor against special opinions or doctrines; but, against Mr. Canning himself. His eminence, his popularity, his talents, made him the prey of envy and detraction; and this was the ground of hostility upon which he was hunted to the death, when official difficulties were thickening round him, and his health was giving way under mental anxiety and physical sufferings. They chose their moment well, and used it remorselessly.

To all the assaults in the Commons, Mr. Canning made instant response. In the Lords, his new Whig allies rendered full and ample justice to his character. There was only one speech left unanswered—that of Lord Grey. His lordship in the latter part of his career, exhibited some symptoms of a disposition to recede slightly from the popular doctrines of his youth, and his conduct on this occasion may be referred to as a prominent illustration of the fact. While the other leaders of the Whig party went over to Mr. Canning, and assisted him in the formation of the only efficient government mainly based on Liberal principles which had been called into existence for upwards of twenty years, Lord Grey held aloof. Nor was he satisfied with separating himself from his friends; he opened at once a violent attack upon Mr. Canning. It is possible that Lord Grey was moved to this by a private sense of resentment on behalf of his " order," which could not brook the ascendency of the commoner. But whatever may have been the purpose that animated him, it is certain that his speech, elaborate and luminous, bore all the characterictics of intense personal animosity. His lordship addressed himself particularly to Mr. Canning's foreign policy, charged him with having compromised the honour of the country, and asserted that he had claimed exclusive credit for acts which did not belong to him, and in which he only shared the glory with others. The whole speech was disingenuous, angry, and full of mistakes. Mr. Canning might have answered it triumphantly. But he never did. It seems that he thought of replying to it in the House Commons; a proceeding which is generally avoided, except in extreme cases. But he was not in a state of health to justify such an exertion; and he was induced to postpone his vindication until the time should arrive, which he thought was not very distant, when he could reply to Lord Grey *in person.** That time never came!

About the middle of May, Lord Lansdowne, Lord Carlisle, and Mr. Tierney, were introduced into the Cabinet. Thus, notwithstanding the unprecedented opposition, public and private, by which he had been systematically impeded, Mr. Canning was now at

* Mr. Stapleton has supplied an able and satisfactory answer to Lord Grey's criticisms on Mr. Canning's foreign policy. He traces each objection succinctly, plucks out the fallacy that lies concealed in it, and shows in every instance some strange errors in the mere facts of his lordship's statement. Upon the main principle at issue—the peace maintained by Mr. Canning, or the maritime war recommended by Lord Grey—the country has long since decided against his lordship. See " Political Life," iii. 401—25.

the head of the strongest government that had existed in England since the days of Pitt.

Early in June he brought forward the Budget; and subsequently some resolutions founded on the Corn Bill. The last time he ever spoke in Parliament was on the 29th of June, when he briefly answered an unimportant question. On the 2nd of July Parliament was prorogued.

The exertions he had latterly been compelled to make, operating upon a peculiarly sensitive constitution, speedily began to display their terrible effects. The excitement of the session was over; and there was leisure now for the fatal struggle between disease and the powers of life. On the 10th Mr. Canning dined with the Chancellor at Wimbledon, and, incautiously sitting under a tree in the open air, while he was yet warm with exercise, caught a cold which ended in rheumatism. Mr. Huskisson, whose health was also suffering, and who had been recommended to try the air of the continent, called on Mr. Canning to take leave, and found him in bed, looking very ill. Struck by the change in his looks, he observed that he, Mr. Canning, was the person who most stood in need of change and relaxation. Mr. Canning smiled, and replied cheerfully, " Oh ! it is only the reflection of the yellow linings of the curtains !" He never saw him again—that faithful life-long friend.

On the 20th, Mr. Canning removed to the Duke of Devonshire's villa, which his grace had lent to him for change of air : the same villa and the same room to which Fox, under circumstances painfully similar, and at the same age, had also removed—to die.

His disease—still increasing—fluctuated from day to day; and he was occasionally able to attend to public business. On the 25th he dined with the Marquis of

Clanricarde, but complained of debility, and returned early to Chiswick. On the 30th he paid his last visit to the King at Windsor: his Majesty saw that he was very ill, and desired Sir William Knighton to call upon him. It was too late. Mr. Canning received some friends at dinner on the following day; retired early; and never rose again. He suffered excruciating pain, which rent his frame so violently, as to deprive him at intervals of all mental consciousness. On the Sunday before his death, he requested his daughter to read prayers: his own unvarying custom, whenever he was prevented from attending church. At length his strength fell, his agonies diminished in proportion, and on the 8th of August, a little before four o'clock in the morning, he expired in the fifty-seventh year of his age.

His funeral took place at Westminster Abbey, where he was buried at the foot of Mr. Pitt's tomb, on the 16th of August. It was attended by the members of the Royal Family, the Cabinet Ministers, the Foreign Ambassadors, and a number of political and personal friends.

The morning after his funeral the King conferred a peerage on his widow. Other no less gratifying marks of public estimation were showered upon his memory, abroad and at home—statues, medals, and monuments. But the most grateful of all was the profound and universal sorrow of the people. All jealousies and animosities were extinguished in the common grief; and Faction herself wept upon his grave.

THE END.

C. WHITING, BEAUFORT HOUSE, STRAND.

FEBRUARY, 1846.

WORKS

PUBLISHED BY

CHAPMAN AND HALL,

186, STRAND.

JUST PUBLISHED.

In two volumes, octavo, cloth, price £1 12s

NARRATIVE OF THE EXPEDITION TO BORNEO

IN 1843-4,

OF H.M.S. DIDO, FOR THE SUPPRESSION OF PIRACY.

With Extracts from the Journal of JAMES BROOKE, Esq., of Sarawak, now Agent for the British Government in Borneo.

BY CAPT. THE HON. HENRY KEPPEL, R.N.

With numerous Maps and Illustrations in tinted Lithography.

In one volume, octavo, cloth,

LETTERS ON THE CONDITION OF THE PEOPLE OF IRELAND.

BY THOMAS CAMPBELL FOSTER, Esq.,

BARRISTER-AT-LAW,

"The Times Commissioner."

Reprinted from "THE TIMES," with copious Notes and Additions.

In one volume, post octavo, price 12s., extra cloth,

NOTES OF A JOURNEY FROM

CORNHILL TO GRAND CAIRO.

BY MICHAEL ANGELO TITMARSH.

With a Coloured Frontispiece, and numerous Illustrations from Designs by the Author.

In one volume, post octavo, price 12s., extra cloth,

RECREATIONS IN SHOOTING;

WITH

Notices of the Game of the British Islands,

INCLUDING FULL DIRECTIONS TO THE YOUNG SPORTSMAN FOR THE MANAGE-
MENT OF GUNS AND DOGS.

BY "CRAVEN."

With Seventy Illustrations of Game and Sporting Dogs, from Original Drawings by William Harvey; engraved in the first style of the art by F. W. Branston.

In two volumes, post octavo, price 24s., cloth gilt,

STORIES FROM THE ITALIAN POETS,

Being a Summary in Prose of the Commedia of Dante, and the most celebrated Narratives of Pulci, Boiardo, Ariosto, and Tasso, with Comments throughout, occasional Passages versified,

And Critical Notices of the Lives and Genius of the Authors.

By LEIGH HUNT.

"Leigh Hunt shows, we think, to greater advantage in these 'Stories of the Italian Poets,' than he ever did before. Years have mellowed his genius and refined his taste, without diminishing his buoyant spirit or his wide sympathies with humanity."—*Spectator.*

"It is not merely a book of the best Italian poetry, made readable and appreciable in the sweetest English prose, but it is, as far as it goes, a valuable insight into Italian history, given in that form in which history is most attractive—by perfect pieces of biography."—*Morning Herald.*

Second edition, octavo, price 12s., cloth gilt,

THE CHILD OF THE ISLANDS,

A Poem,

By THE HON. MRS. NORTON.

"There can be no question that the performance bears throughout the stamp of extraordinary ability—the sense of easy power very rarely deserts us. But we pause on the burst of genius; and they are many."—*Quarterly Review.*

"We find in almost every page some bold burst, graceful allusion, or delicate touch—some trait of external nature, or glimpse into the recesses of the heart—that irresistibly indicates the creating power of genius."—*Edinburgh Review.*

In one volume, post octavo, price 14s., cloth gilt,

A TOUR THROUGH THE VALLEY OF THE MEUSE;

WITH THE

Legends of the Walloon Country and the Ardennes.

By DUDLEY COSTELLO.

WITH AN ORNAMENTAL FRONTISPIECE AND NUMEROUS WOODCUTS.

"This tastefully-illustrated volume will find its way not only into the hands of tourists who may propose to travel over the same ground as the author (in which case it will be found an excellent hand-book or guide), but into the study and library, where arm-chair travellers, for lack of means, or health, or time, are forced to visit foreign lands mentally. Mr. Costello opens up, too, comparatively new ground, and shows us that the Valley of the Meuse contains treasures of nature, art, romance, and tradition, which have hitherto been overlooked, or nearly so."—*John Bull.*

NEW BOOKS FOR THE YOUNG.

In small 4to, price 4s. 6d, cloth,	*In small 4to, price 4s. 6d., cloth,*
WONDERFUL STORIES FOR CHILDREN. FROM THE DANISH OF ANDERSEN. By MARY HOWITT.	**HUNTERS AND FISHERS;** OR, SKETCHES OF PRIMITIVE RACES IN LANDS BEYOND THE SEA. By MRS. PERCY SINNETT.
In small 4to, price 4s. 6d., cloth, **A STORY ABOUT A CHRISTMAS** IN THE **SEVENTEENTH CENTURY.** By MRS. PERCY SINNETT.	*In small 4to,* **THE HORSE AND HIS RIDER.** *(IN THE PRESS.)*

Each embellished with Four coloured Engravings.

In Imperial 4to, elegantly bound in red morocco, gilt edges, 2l. 2s., or in Atlas 4to, with proof impressions of the plates on India paper, price 3l. 3s.

FINDEN'S BEAUTIES OF THE POET MOORE;

BEING

A SERIES OF PORTRAITS

Of the Principal Female Characters in his Works,

From Paintings by eminent Artists, made expressly for the Work. Engraved in the highest style of Art, by, or under the immediate superintendence of

MR. EDWARD FINDEN.

WITH DESCRIPTIVE LETTER-PRESS.

In one volume 4to, bound in cloth and gilt, price 32s.

THE ARCHÆOLOGICAL ALBUM;

Or, Museum of National Antiquities.

EDITED BY THOMAS WRIGHT, M.A., F.S.A.

With a beautiful illuminated Frontispiece and Title-page, in Chromolithography, Twenty-six Etchings on Steel (four of which are coloured) of remarkable Buildings and Antiquities, and upwards of One Hundred and Seventeen Engravings on Wood, all drawn by F. W. FAIRHOLT, F.S.A.

In one large folio volume, price 2l. 12s. 6d., cloth,

A SERIES OF DIAGRAMS,

ILLUSTRATIVE OF

The Principles of Mechanical Philosophy and their Application

Drawn on Stone by Henry Chapman, and printed in colours by C. F. Cheffins,

WITH DESCRIPTIVE LETTER-PRESS.

Under the superintendence of the Society for the Diffusion of Useful Knowledge.

In one vol., cloth, gilt edges, price 5s.

ST. PATRICK'S EVE;

Or, Three Eras in the Life of an Irish Peasant.

BY CHARLES LEVER.

WITH FOUR ETCHINGS AND NUMEROUS WOODCUTS, BY "PHIZ."

In one volume, small octavo, in Ornamental Boards, price 5s.

LIFE IN DALECARLIA.

THE PARSONAGE OF MORA.

BY FREDRIKA BREMER.

TRANSLATED BY WILLIAM HOWITT.

In one volume, cloth, price 5s.

CHESS FOR BEGINNERS,

In a Series of Progressive Lessons:

Showing the most approved Methods of beginning and ending the Game, together with various Situations and Checkmates.

BY WILLIAM LEWIS.

THIRD EDITION.

With 24 Diagrams printed in Colours.

In three volumes, post octavo, cloth,

ZOE: THE HISTORY OF TWO LIVES;

A NOVEL.

BY GERALDINE E. JEWSBURY.

In large 8vo, price 4s. 6d. each, handsomely bound in cloth and gilt,

VOLUMES ONE AND TWO OF

THE EDINBURGH TALES,

CONDUCTED BY

MRS. JOHNSTONE.

CONTENTS OF VOL. 1.

The Experiences of Richard Taylor, Esq.	By Mrs. Johnstone
The Three Christmas Dinners	"
Mary Anne's Hair : a London Love Story	"
Governor Fox	"
Little Fanny Bethel	"
Frankland the Barrister	"
The Sabbath Night's Supper	"
The Cousins	Mrs. Fraser
The Renounced Treasure (*From the Swedish*)	William Howitt
The Maid of Honour	Mrs. Gore
The Rangers of Connaught	Edw. Quillinan
The Elves (*From the German of Tieck*)	By Thomas Carlyle
West Country Exclusives	Mrs. Johnstone
The Freshwater Fisherman	Miss Mitford
Story of Martha Guinnis and Her Son	Mrs. Crowe
The Deformed	M. Fraser Tytler
The White Fawn : an American Story	Col. Johnson
Johnny Darbyshire, a Primitive Quaker	William Howitt
Story of Farquharson of Inverey	Sir T. D. Lauder

CONTENTS OF VOL. II.

The Author's Daughter	Mary Howitt
The Balsam-Seller of Thurotzer	Mrs. Gore
The Golden-Pot *From the German of*	Hoffmann
The Days of Old	John Mills
Country Town Life	Miss Mitford
Marion Wilson	By the late Robert Nicoll
Violet Hamilton; or, the Talented Family	Mrs. Johnstone
Christmas Amusements	Miss Mitford

These Stories, printed in the usual way of Modern Novels, would fill EIGHTEEN VOLUMES post 8vo.

The EDINBURGH TALES are publishing in WEEKLY NUMBERS, of sixteen pages large 8vo, double columns, in a clear type, price *Three Halfpence;* and in MONTHLY PARTS, each containing four numbers, stitched, with a wrapper, price *Sevenpence.*

OPINIONS OF THE PRESS.

" We must give a word of hearty and unreserved praise to the *Edinburgh Tales,* a weekly issue of stories and novelettes, conducted by Mrs. Johnstone. It is amazingly cheap, but that is its least merit. The tales are delightfully told : naturally, cheerfully, with great refinement of feeling, and a skilful variety of manner. The character of ' Richard Taylor' has touches Charles Lamb might have given ; and the prudent heart of Miss Edgeworth would rejoice in ' Young Mrs. Roberts' Three Christmas Dinners.' "—*Examiner.*

" Why, this is a more exquisite song than the other !' sixty-four 8vo double-columned pages for sevenpence ; containing tales, original or selected, and strung together by means of a frame-work which will give place even to the selected stories, and unity and character to those which are original."—*Spectator.*

BY CHAPMAN AND HALL.

CHAPMAN AND HALL'S MONTHLY SERIES.

A COLLECTION OF ORIGINAL WORKS OF

FICTION AND BIOGRAPHY.

This series of Books will consist exclusively of new and original works, chiefly of the class of Novels and Romances; and the price of each work will be less than one-half the sum charged for an equal amount of matter in the ordinary system of publication.

The NOVELS will be published in FOUR MONTHLY PARTS, price *Three Shillings* each; and although containing the amount usually included in THREE VOLUMES, will be completed in TWO, and sold for *Fourteen Shillings* in cloth. The BIOGRAPHIES will never exceed Two Parts, or One Volume.

"The commencement of a new, and, as it seems to us, very spirited attempt to reduce the price of this class of literature."—*Examiner.*

"If the 'Monthly Series,' continues as well as it has begun, the old three-volume system is at an end. The world will no longer be willing to pay thirty shillings for rubbish, when, for fourteen, it can enjoy the best inventions of the best writers."—*Athenæum.*

VOLUMES ALREADY PUBLISHED.

In one volume, Post Octavo, cloth, 7s.,

THE FALCON FAMILY;

Or, Young Ireland,

A COMIC NOVEL.

"In this book, if we mistake not, we have the promise of a new writer of satirical fiction, not unworthy to take his place with the writer of 'Crotchet Castle' and 'Headlong Hall.'"—*Examiner.*
"A vein of genuine comedy runs lavishly through every page, and equally exhibits itself whether in the conception of character and incident, or in the construction of the sparkling dialogue which floats down before the imagination of the reader."—*Morning Chronicle.*

In one volume, Post Octavo, cloth, 7s.,

THE LIFE OF MOZART,

INCLUDING HIS CORRESPONDENCE.

By EDWARD HOLMES,

AUTHOR OF "A RAMBLE AMONG THE MUSICIANS OF GERMANY," &c.

"A clear, complete, and judicious view of Mozart's Life. * * * * We can safely recommend this volume."—*Blackwood.*

"In every respect a most admirable piece of Biography."—*New Monthly Mag.*

"We cannot conceive a more fascinating story of genius. * * * * To a style which would alone have sufficed to the production of an interesting and striking narrative, Mr. Holmes unites a depth of knowledge and musical appreciation very rare and remarkable."—*Examiner.*

"An acceptable addition to our stores of Biography. More rich and complete in the assemblage of its materials than any previous publication on the subject."—*Athenæum.*

CHAPMAN & HALL'S MONTHLY SERIES, continued.

In one volume, post 8vo, cloth, 7s.

LONG ENGAGEMENTS.

A TALE OF THE AFFGHAN REBELLION.

In two volumes, post 8vo, cloth, 14s.

THE WHITEBOY;

A STORY OF IRELAND IN 1822.

By MRS. S. C. HALL.

"Indisputably Mrs. Hall's best novel. * * * 'The Whiteboy' is an excellent contribution to Messrs. Chapman and Hall's Monthly Series.'"—*Athenæum.*

"This forms the second novel of 'Chapman and Hall's Monthly Series,' a publication set on foot for the laudable purpose of breaking up the system of three volume novels; a system which carries absurdity upon the face of it, and which practically has led to the production of piles of trash. Mrs. Hall's style is easy, graceful, and effective. The Death of Abel Richards, the middle-man, in which the Banshee or Death-herald is introduced, is described with thrilling effect."—*John Bull.*

"The design of the work is exceedingly well worked out, while the story is full of vivid descriptions, life-like sketches of character, dashes of genuine Irish humour, with occasionally scenes exhibiting the strong passions and affections of the Irish people, drawn with exceeding energy and power."—*Atlas.*

In two volumes, post 8vo, cloth, 14s.

MOUNT SOREL;

Or, THE HEIRESS OF THE DE VERES.

A Novel,

BY THE AUTHOR OF THE "TWO OLD MEN'S TALES."

"A tale of singular beauty. * * * The commencement of a new, and, as it seems to us, very spirited attempt to reduce the price of this class of literature."—*Examiner.*

"'Mount Sorel' is its author's best invention. * * * We have rarely read a book exciting so strong an interest, in which the mean, the criminal, and the vulgar had so small a share; and for this, as a crowning charm and an excellence too rare, alas! in these days, does it give us pleasure, to commend and recommend 'Mount Sorel.' * * * If the 'Monthly Series,' opened by 'Mount Sorel,' continues as well as it has begun, the old three-volume system is at an end. The world will no longer be willing to pay thirty shillings for rubbish, when, for fourteen, it can enjoy the best inventions of the best writers."—*Athenæum.*

IN PREPARATION,

THE LIFE OF GEORGE CANNING,

By ROBERT BELL,

AUTHOR OF THE "LIVES OF THE POETS," &c.

THE LIFE OF TALLEYRAND.

By W. M. THACKERAY.

BY CHAPMAN AND HALL.

Publishing every alternate Month,

THE BARONIAL HALLS,

PICTURESQUE EDIFICES,

AND

ANCIENT CHURCHES OF ENGLAND,

FROM

Drawings made expressly for the Work,

BY

J. D. HARDING, G. CATTERMOLE, S. PROUT, J. HOLLAND, F. MULLER, &c.

Executed in Lithotint by and under the superintendence of Mr. HARDING.

WITH DESCRIPTIVE LETTER-PRESS BY S. C. HALL, F.S.A.

Each Part contains Three Plates, and Twelve Pages of Letter-press, interspersed with Woodcuts.

PRICE—Prints, Imperial Quarto, 5s.; Proofs, Colombier Quarto, 7s. 6d.; India Paper, Imperial Folio, 12s.

THE FIRST VOLUME,

COMPRISING THE FIRST EIGHT PARTS, IS COMPLETED.

PRICE—Prints, Imperial Quarto, half-bound, £2 5s.; Proofs, Colombier Quarto, half-bound, £3 7s. 6d.

Contents:

Shottesbrooke Church	Berkshire	Penshurst, the Courtyard	Kent
Sawston Hall	Cambridgeshire	Turton Tower	Lancashire
Brereton Hall	Cheshire	Kirby Hall	Northampton
Moreton Hall	"	Blickling	Norfolk
Naworth	Cumberland	The Great Chamber, Montacute	Somersetshire
Naworth long Gallery	"	Ingestrie	Staffordshire
Hinchinbrook House	Huntingdon	Helmingham Hall	Suffolk
Charlton House	Kent	Hengrave Hall	"
Cobham Hall	"	West Stow Hall	"
Cobham Church, Interior	"	Arundel Church	Sussex
Hever Castle	"	Boxgrove Church	"
Penshurst, from the Park	"	Warwick Castle	Warwickshire

PART IX.

Ham House .... Surrey
St. Osyth's .... Essex
Knole, Retainers' Gallery .... Kent

PART X.

Beauchamp Chapel .... Warwickshire
The Oak House .... Staffordshire
Bramshill .... Hampshire

PART XI.

Speke Hall, Exterior .... Lancashire
Speke Hall, Interior .... "
Caverswall Castle........... Staffordshire

PART XII.

Hall in the Wood .... Lancashire
Charlecote .... Warwickshire
Charlecote Great Hall ...... "

PART XIII.

Hardwicke Hall .... Derbyshire
Loseley House .... Surrey
Throwley Hall .... Staffordshire

PART XIV.

Crewe Hall .... Cheshire
Aston Hall .... Warwickshire
Smithell's Hall .... Lancashire

WORKS PUBLISHED

AUTHORIZED TRANSLATIONS OF M. EUGENE SUE'S WORKS,

Embellished with several hundred beautiful Illustrations on wood, drawn expressly for these editions by the first Artists in Paris, and executed by the most eminent English Engravers,

UNDER THE SUPERINTENDENCE OF MR. CHARLES HEATH.

In one volume 8vo, price 12s., cloth gilt,

PAULA MONTI; OR, THE HOTEL LAMBERT.

WITH

TWENTY BEAUTIFUL ILLUSTRATIONS, DRAWN BY JULES DAVID.

In three volumes, imperial 8vo, handsomely bound in cloth, gilt, price 2l. 14s.,

THE MYSTERIES OF PARIS,

ADAPTED TO THE ENGLISH READER.

ILLUSTRATED WITH UPWARDS OF SEVEN HUNDRED ENGRAVINGS

OF ALL

The Characters, Scenes, Costumes, and Localities,

Described in this extraordinary work.

In three volumes, 8vo, price 23s., cloth,

THE WANDERING JEW.

In one volume, uniform with the work, price 15s.,

A SERIES OF 104 BEAUTIFUL

ILLUSTRATIONS TO THE WANDERING JEW.

In three volumes, 8vo, handsomely bound in cloth, gilt, price 1l. 16s.,

THE WANDERING JEW,

WITH THE ABOVE

ONE HUNDRED AND FOUR BEAUTIFUL ILLUSTRATIONS.

These Works may still be had in Numbers, Parts, and Volumes; and Subscribers are recommended to complete their sets without delay.

BY CHAPMAN AND HALL. 9

NEW ILLUSTRATED WORK BY FINDEN.

Publishing on the first of every Month,

FINDEN'S BEAUTIES OF MOORE;

BEING

SERIES OF PORTRAITS

OF THE

Principal Female Characters of that popular Poet.

From Paintings by eminent Artists, made expressly for the Work. Engraved in the highest style of Art,

BY, OR UNDER THE IMMEDIATE SUPERINTENDENCE OF

MR. EDWARD FINDEN.

WITH DESCRIPTIVE LETTER-PRESS.

Each Number contains Four Plates, with Illustrative Letter-press from the pen of a distinguished Female Writer.

PRINTS. Imperial Quarto............................ *Five Shillings.*
PROOFS, on *India paper*, Atlas Quarto................ *Eight Shillings.*
PROOFS, ditto, Colombier Folio, of which a few only will be printed, without Letter-press .. } *Twelve Shillings.*

"The beginning of a charming publication. The portfolio redolent of beauty; and every single picture so bewitching that it deserves a frame, and the whole series to adorn a gallery. A portrait of Moore, after Lawrence, is set in a border of exquisite grace; English and appropriate, and without a borrowed touch from the German school. It is of the utmost elegance. Then follow the subjects: "Black and Blue Eyes," W. Frith—the former, according to the song, wounding without caring for the consequences, but the latter better pleased to heal the wounds they have inflicted—is delightfully embodied in two lovely girls, with expression suited to the words. "St. Jerome's Love," H. O'Neil, is a single female form of touching pathos; and "Young Kitty," J. Wright, with her face reflected from a mirror, a pleasing fancy. The last, "Laughing Eyes," another by W. Frith, is perfectly delicious; and the whole are engraved, the first by W. Edwards and the rest by E. Finden, in a style of great excellence. They are quite poetical—transparent, with tender yet effective shadows; and the accessaries, whether we refer to costume or the framework around, at the same time finely correct and profusely rich. A neat and interesting letter-press exposition accompanies each picture. The work is one of the fairest promise; and in these days of admiration for the really superior productions of art must be a very popular public favourite."
—*Literary Gazette.*

In imperial quarto, price Three Guineas; Proofs on India Paper, Four Guineas,

THE PRINCIPLES AND PRACTICE OF ART.

TREATING OF

BEAUTY OF FORM, IMITATION, COMPOSITION, LIGHT AND SHADE, EFFECT AND COLOUR.

BY J. D. HARDING,

AUTHOR OF "ELEMENTARY ART."

With numerous Illustrations, drawn and engraved by the Author.

In one volume 8vo, price 8s. 6d. in cloth gilt, or in morocco gilt, 14s.

SYRIA AND THE HOLY LAND

POPULARLY DESCRIBED;

Their Scenery and their People, Incidents of Travel, &c. From the best and most recent authorities.

By WALTER KEATING KELLY,

WITH ONE HUNDRED AND EIGHTY WOODCUT ILLUSTRATIONS.

"Never was information more amusingly conveyed—never were the results of voluminous works of travel more spiritedly condensed. The execution is truly admirable. The moral, social, physical, political, and geographical features of the East are well brought out, and the reader is at home with the Turk, the Arab, the Jew, the Druse, and the Maronite."—*Westminster Review.*

In one volume, 8vo, price 9s. in cloth gilt, or in morocco gilt, 15s.,

EGYPT AND NUBIA

POPULARLY DESCRIBED;

Their Scenery and National Characteristics, Incidents of Wayfaring and Sojourn, Personal and Historical Sketches, Anecdotes, &c. &c.

By J. A. ST. JOHN,

Author of "Egypt and Mohammed Ali," "Manners and Customs of Ancient Greece," &c.

ILLUSTRATED WITH

ONE HUNDRED AND TWENTY-FIVE WOOD ENGRAVINGS.

In one volume, cloth, gilt edges, price 6s.

SKETCHES OF YOUNG LADIES, YOUNG GENTLEMEN, AND YOUNG COUPLES.

WITH EIGHTEEN ILLUSTRATIONS,

By "PHIZ."

Second Edition with Additions, in small 8vo, price 5s. cloth, gilt,

SONGS AND BALLADS.
By SAMUEL LOVER.

*⁂ This Edition contains the Songs sung in Mr. LOVER's "IRISH EVENINGS."

Second Edition.—In two volumes, post 8vo, price 14s.,

THE IRISH SKETCH-BOOK.

By MR. M. A TITMARSH.

With numerous Engravings on Wood, from the Author's designs.

"One of the most valuable books of travelling Sketches that has been published for many a day; and excepting 'Inglis,' it presents the best idea of Ireland and the Irish that we have met with. Not that it contains any elaborate disquisitions on politics, religion, anarchy, or distress, or any deep proposals for their remedy; but the reader has set before him as graphic a picture of Irish manners, character, and modes of living, as if he himself had made the tour of Mr. Titmarsh. Taken as a whole, the book is capital."—*Spectator.*

BY CHAPMAN AND HALL. 11

The Foreign Library.

A SERIES OF TRANSLATIONS OF
POPULAR AND INTERESTING FOREIGN WORKS,

Published as soon as possible after their appearance on the Continent.

"The project of a FOREIGN LIBRARY we thought, in the first instance, very highly of, and are particularly glad to observe its confirmed success. The books have been well chosen, and, without an exception, well translated."—*Examiner.*

VOLUMES COMPLETED.

THE AUTOBIOGRAPHY OF HEINRICH ZCHOKKE.
Price 5s.

"One of the best autobiographies ever published."—*Chambers' Journal.*

"This exceedingly interesting piece of autobiography forms the thirty-third part or volume of that valuable series of works published under the general title of the Foreign Library. It will be read with intense interest; with all the interest of a work of fiction. It is a beautiful picture of a good man's life, of a good man's struggles, of a benefactor of the human race."—*John Bull.*

"Autobiographies are generally pleasant reading, and this one of Heinrich Zschokke fully bears out the rule. It is one of the very best of the many excellent foreign works which the 'Foreign Library' has made accessible to English readers. It presents us with a vivid picture of the mind and life of a man worthy to be known—one who has striven with success, by speculation and by action, to improve the condition of his fellow man."—*Morning Chronicle,* July 22, 1845.

RUSSIA. BY J. G. KOHL.
Comprising St. Petersburgh—Moscow—Karkhoff—Riga—Odessa—The German Provinces on the Baltic—The Steppes—The Crimea—and the interior of the Country. With a Map, price 11s. cloth.

AUSTRIA. BY J. G. KOHL.
Comprising Vienna—Prague—Hungary—Bohemia—The Danube—Galicia—Styria—Moravia—Bukovino, and the Military Frontier. Price 11s. cloth.

"Mr. Kohl's volumes upon Russia and Austria deserve the rank which has, by universal consent, been awarded to them. They are the very best books about the two countries which have yet appeared, containing a greater quantity of solid information, digested into the pleasantest possible form than all the tours and journals extant."—*Fraser's Magazine.*

IRELAND, SCOTLAND, AND ENGLAND. BY J. G. KOHL
Price 11s. cloth.

"Mr. Kohl's work on Ireland is beyond all comparison the most succinct and faithful that we have yet seen, and exhibits the lamentable condition of that country in a light in which none but a foreigner, or at least a sagacious traveller, could paint it. His testimony is doubly valuable from the weight of experience and authority which his name carries with it."—*Times.*

LIFE IN MEXICO. BY MADAME CALDERON DE LA BARCA.
Price 11s. cloth.

"Madame Calderon's book has all the natural liveliness and tact, and readiness of remark, which are sure to distinguish the first production of a clever woman. * * * A more genuine book, in air, as well as in reality, it would be difficult to find."—*Edinburgh Review.*

The Foreign Library, *continued.*

TALES FROM THE GERMAN.
Comprising Specimens from the most celebrated Authors. By J. OXENFORD and C. A. FEILING. Price 11s. cloth.

> "Mr. Oxenford is one of the best German scholars we have. Mr. Feiling, with whom he has before been associated in foreign literature, is a German known for his proficiency in the studies of his native language. The combination was the most fitting conceivable for a work of this kind. Selection and translation are alike characteristic and spirited."—*Examiner.*

CELEBRATED CRIMES. BY ALEXANDER DUMAS.
Containing The Borgias—The Countess of St. Geran—Joan of Naples—Nisida—The Marchioness of Brinvilliers—The Cenci—The Marchioness de Ganges—Karl Ludwig Sand—Vaninka—Urban Grandier. Price 10s. cloth.

> "Dumas' book is very striking. The Tragedy of Truth—the serious side of what is called the Romance of Real Life—had never such startling illustration as this remarkable book affords. Its capital constructive art is only a less admirable feature than its perfect and close fidelity of detail. What a story is that of the Marchioness de Ganges!"—*Examiner.*

HISTORY OF THE EIGHTEENTH CENTURY,
And of the Nineteenth till the Overthrow of the French Empire, Literary and Political. By F. C. SCHLOSSER. Six Volumes. Price £3 : 7s. cloth.

> "Schlosser is as an historian second to none of his contemporaries. We possess in England no writer between whom and himself it would not be mere irony to institute any comparison. We must look to countries where literature is thought its own reward for his competitor. Ranke among German, and Thierry among French historians, may enter the lists with him. In the depth and variety of his attainments, and the range and compass of his view, he is superior to them, and, among modern writers, quite unrivalled. In vigour of expression, sagacity of judgment, and complete command of his materials (which are like the spear of Achilles, what its owner alone can wield), he is fully equal—and it is a praise of which any historian might be proud—to those great writers."—*Westminster Review.*

HISTORY OF GERMANY.
From the earliest period to the present time. By F. KOHLRAUSCH. Price 14s. cloth.

HISTORY OF TEN YEARS: 1830–1840.
FRANCE DURING THE THREE DAYS, AND UNDER LOUIS-PHILIPPE. By LOUIS BLANC. In Two Volumes. Price £1 : 6s.

> "This is a remarkable work. The ten years 1830—1840, were troubled, stirring, and important times to every European nation—to none so much as France. * * 'L'Histoire de Dix Ans' is one of those works so often libelled by being called as interesting as a novel. It is a narrative of events, real, striking, absorbing—the subjects of immense interest to all readers—the style unusually excellent."—*Foreign Quarterly Review.*

HISTORY OF FRANCE. BY M. MICHELET.
Translated by WALTER K. KELLY. Volume the First, price 13s. cloth. (*to be completed in Two Volumes*).

IN THE PRESS.

KING OF SAXONY'S JOURNEY IN ENGLAND IN 1844.
By Dr. CARUS, His Majesty's Physician.

BY CHAPMAN AND HALL.   13

UNDER THE SUPERINTENDENCE OF THE SOCIETY FOR THE
DIFFUSION OF USEFUL KNOWLEDGE.

A SERIES OF MAPS,

Ancient and Modern,

COMPLETE, WITH THE INDEX, IN THE FOLLOWING BINDINGS:—

	IN ONE VOLUME.		IN TWO VOLUMES.	
	Plain.	Coloured.	Plain.	Coloured.
	£ s. d.	£ s. d.	£ s. d.	£ s. d.
HALF MOROCCO, plain, sprinkled edges	6 17 0	9 14 0	7 12 0	10 5 0
———— ditto, gilt edges	7 0 0	9 17 0	7 17 0	10 10 0
———— gilt back and edges	7 2 0	9 19 0	8 0 0	10 13 0
HALF RUSSIA, plain, sprinkled edges	6 18 0	9 15 0	7 14 0	10 7 0
———— ditto, gilt edges	7 1 0	9 18 0	7 19 0	10 12 0
———— gilt back and edges	7 3 0	10 0 0	8 2 0	10 15 0

☞ *Any Numbers of the Series may at present be obtained, and Subscribers are recommended to complete their Sets without delay.*

BINDING THE MAPS.

SPECIMEN COPIES, in various styles of Binding, may be seen at the PUBLISHERS; and Subscribers may have their Copies bound in the best and strongest manner, with *India-rubber backs*, by sending them through their respective Booksellers, or direct to 186, Strand.

	IN ONE VOLUME.		IN TWO VOLUMES.	
	£	s. d.	£	s. d.
HALF MOROCCO, plain, sprinkled edges	0	18 0	1	12 0
———— ditto, gilt edges	1	1 0	1	17 0
———— gilt back and edges	1	3 0	2	0 0
HALF RUSSIA, plain, sprinkled edges	0	19 0	1	14 0
———— ditto, gilt edges	1	2 0	1	19 0
———— gilt back and edges	1	4 0	2	2 0

Strongly half-bound morocco, with India-rubber backs, price, plain, 2l. 2s. coloured, 2l. 16s.

A FAMILY ATLAS,

CONTAINING FIFTY-FOUR MAPS: WITH AN INDEX OF PLACES.

Strongly-bound in cloth, with India-rubber backs.

A SCHOOL ATLAS,

MODERN.—Comprising Twenty-one Maps, with Index of Places. Price, plain, 17s. 6d.; coloured, 23s.

ANCIENT.—Eighteen Maps. Plain, 12s.; coloured, 16s. 6d.

ANCIENT AND MODERN.

Strongly half-bound in One Volume. Price, plain, 1l. 7s.; coloured, 1l. 17s.

AN INDEX, of more than 25,000 Places, by Rev. JAMES MICKLEBURGH, A.M., the size of the Atlas. Price 5s.

NEW MAP OF LONDON, ENLARGED, and with all the Recent Improvements. In a Leather Case, price 3s. 6d., or on a Sheet, 1s. 6d. coloured.

POCKET COUNTY MAPS,

NEW EDITIONS, WITH ALL

THE RAILWAY STATIONS CORRECTLY LAID DOWN.

ENGRAVED BY SIDNEY HALL. PRINTED ON CHAPMAN'S PATENT PAPER-CLOTH.

On a Sheet, price 6d., or in a Case, price 9d. and 1s. each.

Bedfordshire	Dorsetshire	Isle of Wight	Monmouthshire	Staffordshire
Berkshire	Durham	Isles of Man,	Norfolk	Suffolk
Buckinghamshire	England	Jersey, and	Northamptonshire	Surrey
Cambridgeshire	Essex	Guernsey	Northumberland	Sussex
Cheshire	Gloucestershire	Kent	Nottinghamshire	Warwickshire
Cornwall	Hampshire	Lancashire	Oxfordshire	Westmoreland
Cumberland	Herefordshire	Leicestershire	Rutlandshire	Wiltshire
Derbyshire	Hertfordshire	Lincolnshire	Shropshire	Worcestershire
Devonshire	Huntingdonshire	Middlesex	Somersetshire	

On a Sheet, price 1s., or in a Case, price 1s. 6d. each, double the size of the above,

YORKSHIRE, IRELAND, SCOTLAND, AND WALES.

Bound in roan, with a tuck, price 16s.,

A POCKET TRAVELLING ATLAS,

OF THE ENGLISH COUNTIES,

With all the Coach and Rail Roads accurately laid down and Coloured.

ENGRAVED BY SIDNEY HALL.

NEW EDITION, COMPRISING ALL RAILWAYS SANCTIONED TO THE CLOSE OF LAST SESSION.

"The best Atlas we have seen for neatness, portability, and clear engraving. The Maps are quarto size, but fold in the middle, so that the whole, when closed, forms a moderately thick octavo volume, stitched in a Spanish morocco cover, exactly the size, without being too bulky for the pocket of a great coat."—WESTMINSTER REVIEW.

Small octavo, price 7s. cloth, or bound in morocco, 10s. 6d.

HOURS OF MEDITATION
AND
Devotional Reflection;

Upon various subjects connected with the religious, moral, and social duties of life.

TRANSLATED FROM THE GERMAN OF

H. ZSCHOKKE.

MULLEN'S POEMS.

In a handsome volume, uniform with ROGERS' "*Italy," price 12s. boards,*

POEMS:

THE PILGRIM OF BEAUTY;
THE COTTAGER'S SABBATH;
SONGS, AND MINOR POEMS.

BY SAMUEL MULLEN.

With Twenty-three Vignette Illustrations, Engraved in line by W. R. SMITH, from Drawings by H. WARREN.

In one volume, post 8vo, price 10s. 6d. cloth,

THE BOOK OF SYMBOLS.

A Series of SEVENTY-FIVE SHORT ESSAYS, on as many different subjects, in connexion with Morals, Religion and Philosophy; each Essay illustrating an ancient Symbol, or Moral Precept.

"The Essays are sensible and judicious * * * We recommend the Book to our readers, as the production of a learned and thinking mind."—JOHN BULL.

In foolscap 8vo, price 2s. cloth, Second Edition, corrected and enlarged,

NURSERY GOVERNMENT;
OR

HINTS addressed to Mothers and Nurserymaids, on the Management of Young Children.

BY MRS. BARWELL.

BY CHAPMAN AND HALL.

WORKS OF THOMAS CARLYLE.

In two volumes, thick octavo, price 36s. cloth,
OLIVER CROMWELL'S LETTERS & SPEECHES.
With Elucidations and Connecting Narrative.
With a Portrait of Cromwell, copied by permission from an Original Miniature by Cooper, in the possession of the Rev. Archdeacon Berners.
A new Edition in the press.

In one vol., small 8vo, with a Portrait, price 8s. 6d., cloth,
THE LIFE OF SCHILLER.
A NEW EDITION.

In one vol., post 8vo, price 10s. 6d., cloth,
PAST AND PRESENT.
SECOND EDITION.

In one vol., small 8vo, price 9s., cloth,
LECTURES ON HEROES AND HERO WORSHIP.
SECOND EDITION.

In three vols., small 8vo, 1l. 5s., cloth,
THE FRENCH REVOLUTION: A History.
SECOND EDITION.

In one vol., crown 8vo, price 5s., cloth,
CHARTISM.
"It never smokes but there is fire."
OLD PROVERB.
SECOND EDITION.

In five vols., small 8vo, 1l. 15s., cloth,
CRITICAL AND MISCELLANEOUS ESSAYS.
SECOND EDITION.

In three vols. small 8vo, price 18s. cloth,
TRANSLATION OF GOETHE'S WILHELM MEISTER.
CONTAINING
Meister's Apprenticeship and Meister's Travels.
SECOND EDITION, REVISED.

WORKS OF CHARLES DICKENS.

In one volume, 8vo, price 1l. 1s., cloth,
THE PICKWICK PAPERS.
With Forty-three Illustrations by "PHIZ."

In one volume, 8vo, price 1l. 1s., cloth,
NICHOLAS NICKLEBY.
With Forty Illustrations by "PHIZ."

In one volume, 8vo, price 1l. 1s., cloth,
SKETCHES BY "BOZ."
A NEW EDITION.
With Forty Illustrations by GEO. CRUIKSHANK.

In one vol., 8vo, price 1l. 1s., cloth,
MARTIN CHUZZLEWIT.
With Forty Illustrations by "PHIZ."

In one volume, price 13s., cloth,
THE OLD CURIOSITY SHOP.
WITH
Seventy-five Illustrations by G. CATTERMOLE and H. K. BROWNE.

In one volume, price 13s., cloth,
BARNABY RUDGE.
A Tale of the Riots of 'Eighty.
WITH
Seventy-eight Illustrations by G. CATTERMOLE and H. K. BROWNE.

In two vols., post 8vo, price 1l. 1s. cloth,
AMERICAN NOTES,
For General Circulation.
FOURTH EDITION.

NEW WORK BY THE AUTHOR OF
"HARRY LORREQUER," "CHARLES O'MALLEY," &c.

On the First of January was published, Part I., price 1s.,
(To be continued Monthly,)

THE KNIGHT OF GWYNNE,
A TALE OF THE TIME OF THE UNION.
By CHARLES LEVER,
WITH ILLUSTRATIONS BY "PHIZ."

"THE KNIGHT OF GWYNNE.—Such is the title of a new tale, with the first number of which the dashing author of 'Harry Lorrequer' commences the year. The narrative takes date at the time of that union between Great Britain and Ireland, which Daniel O'Connell pretends to be so anxious to repeal; and the very first page introduces us to no less important a personage than the Lord Castlereagh of the day. 'The Knight of Gwynne' bids fair to rival in popularity the best of Mr. Lever's former works—and that is no faint praise."—CHESTER COURANT.

In one volume, price 7s. 6d. in cloth,
WITH TWELVE STEEL ENGRAVINGS OF DINNER COURSES, FOR VARIOUS SEASONS, AND DIRECTIONS FOR CARVING,

THE PRACTICAL COOK:
English and Foreign;

Containing a great variety of Old Receipts improved and remodelled, and many ORIGINAL RECEIPTS in

| ENGLISH | GERMAN | SPANISH | DUTCH |
| FRENCH | RUSSIAN | POLISH | AMERICAN |

SWISS, AND INDIAN COOKERY.

With copious Directions for the choice of all Provisions—the laying out Table—giving small and large Dinners—and the Management of a Cellar.

By JOSEPH BREGION,
Formerly Cook to H. E. Prince Rausmosski; to H. H. the Prince Nicholas Esterhazy; to the Marquis of Ailesbury; the Russian Ambassador at Paris, &c. &c.

AND ANNE MILLER,
Cook in several English Families of distinction.

"This is an excellent and truly "Practical Cook." * * Every body can understand it and get benefit by it."—FRAZER'S MAGAZINE.

"This is a most formidable rival to all previous existing cookery-books. While Kitchener and Rundell are quite equalled, Ude and the 'Cuisinier Royal' are simplified and economised. We are further introduced to the curiosities of Russian and American cookery, while a host of receipts which every one was anxious for, from the repertory of Indian and German kitchens, are also to be met with. The "Practical Cook" appears really to be the richest compendium of good things, and the best guide to the art of cooking them, that is now to be met with.—*New Monthly Mag.*

"A priceless volume for the epicure."—JOHN BULL.

"The style throughout is careful and methodical, and the receipts given with such clearness, that 'she who bastes may read.'"—MORNING CHRONICLE.

"To all persons who wish to excel in cooking, the present volume must prove highly useful, as, in addition to all the most approved English receipts, it contains copious directions for the preparation of all kinds of continental and Indian delicacies. It will likewise be of great service to all young housekeepers, who have yet to learn the proper arrangements of a dinner-table, as it contains not only a 'bill' of fare for every month in the year, but is illustrated by very neat engravings, showing the proper method of placing the dishes on the table, and the order in which the courses and dessert are to appear. Indeed, the work will prove a complete guide to all who wish to place a dinner properly on the table, from the plain family joint to the three courses and a dessert. The name and position of Bregion are a guarantee for superiority of skill and excellence of taste."—BRITANNIA.

Printed in Great Britain
by Amazon